Law Is a Moral Practice

SCOTT HERSHOVITZ

HARVARD UNIVERSITY PRESS

Cambridge, Massachusetts

London, England

2023

First printing

Library of Congress Cataloging-in-Publication Data

Names: Hershovitz, Scott, author.

Title: Law is a moral practice / Scott Hershovitz.

Description: Cambridge, Massachusetts ; London, England :
Harvard University Press, 2023. | Includes bibliographical references and index.

Identifiers: LCCN 2023005794 | ISBN 9780674258556 (cloth)

Subjects: LCSH: Law and ethics. | Law—Moral and ethical aspects. |
Law—Interpretation and construction.

Classification: LCC K247.6 .H47 2023 | DDC 340/.112—dc23/eng/20230509

LC record available at https://lccn.loc.gov/2023005794

Contents

Law Is a Moral Practice

Introduction

That Is Not a Rule

———•◆•———

"I don't want blueberries."

"I know, but you have to taste them. That's the rule in our house—you have to try the food on your plate."

I've had that conversation seven or eight million times, because I have two children and limited parenting skills. With our older son, Rex, the conversation would wrap up rather quickly. Mentioning the rule would settle the matter; he would do as directed, though sometimes I'd have to make airplane noises to make it happen. Hank, however, is another story. He's the youngest, and he's a picky eater. He comes by it honestly. I was also a picky eater, and I suspect that if my mother could have programmed Hank, she would have seized the opportunity to take revenge. But there was no need; genetics did her dirty work.

Hank is not impressed by the rule, and his resistance has grown more sophisticated over time. When he was three, he would simply declare his desires. "I don't want apples," he'd say, in an increasingly insistent tone of voice, which all too often I made the mistake of matching. I am not in-timidating, but at the dinner table, I'm Darth Vader: "Hank, I am your father. Eat your peas or meet your destiny." Of course, we'd never punish Hank for failing to eat peas. But we would insist that he stay at the table until he took a taste. And we would not offer him any other food until he did. It took a while, but eventually Hank came to understand that his desires did not trump the rule: he had to try what was on his plate, whether or not he wanted it.

But that didn't end Hank's resistance. Just after he turned four, he hit on a new strategy. He gave me a reason for refusing to comply.

"I want yogurt."

"Did you try a tomato?"

"No."

"Hank, you know you can't ask for more food until you've tried all the food on your plate."

"But I don't need to try a tomato. I already know that I don't like them."

That was true. He did know that he didn't like tomatoes, since we'd had several showdowns over them already. If he tried one, he would wince, so that I'd know that tomatoes are, in fact, disgusting, at least to his tiny taste buds. There was no chance of any other outcome, and we both knew that. So why go to the trouble?

I ask myself that a lot. One reason is that the evidence suggests that the more you try something, the more likely you are to like it. We are also concerned that, if we let Hank choose what to eat on his own, he would subsist on a diet of yogurt, cheese, and chocolate, with a bit of bread on the side. (It could be worse, I know, but we think it important that he eat a plant or two.) So we have reasons to insist that Hank try tomatoes, even if he knows he doesn't like them. But, if we are honest, a large part of the answer has little to do with food. Hank has to learn that, sometimes, you have to do things you don't want to do. He has to learn that, sometimes, you have to defer to others. And he has to learn what is worth fighting for and what one should simply swallow. (A tomato, for instance.) Perhaps most important, he has to learn that you don't always get to look behind rules; rigidity is part of the point, since it helps us to avoid endless litigation over just what, on this occasion, Hank must eat before he gets yogurt. So even though I was impressed that Hank discerned a purpose for the rule and realized that it wasn't applicable in this case, I nevertheless insisted that he try a tomato.

We did some version of that dance for weeks on end, and from time to time, still do. But after a couple months, Hank hit on yet another strategy.

"I want yogurt."

"Did you have a carrot?"

"I don't want a carrot."

"Remember, Hank, the rule in our house is that you have to try everything on your plate."

"THAT IS NOT A RULE. THAT IS NOT A RULE IN OUR HOUSE."

"Yes, it is, Hank."

"NO, IT IS NOT. THAT IS NOT A RULE."

We went round on this a few times. I said that it was a rule. Hank said that it wasn't. But it was clear that was a losing game—or, at least, not a winning one. So I simply informed him that he wasn't getting yogurt until he tasted a carrot. He stared me down for a while, then grudgingly raised a carrot to his mouth, took the tiniest bite possible, and said, "I tried the carrot." Realizing I had been defeated, I declared victory and retrieved the yogurt.

As a parent, I was frustrated, and more with myself than Hank.[1] As a philosopher, I was amused. Hank had unwittingly raised a central question in jurisprudence. I said there was a rule in our house that requires Hank to try everything on his plate. Hank denied it. Who was right? I was, I think. But then, I would. And Hank thought that he was right too. To know who was right, we'd need to know something other than what Hank and I thought. And, no, adding his mother, Julie, to the mix would not help. She's on my side. But she could be wrong too, and sure enough, that was Hank's view. It didn't matter what we said, or how many times we said it, Hank simply would not accept that there was a rule in our house that required him to try everything on his plate.[2]

Was there such a rule? I'm pretty sure there was. Indeed, I'm pretty sure there still is. But why? What makes it the case that a rule in our house requires that Hank try the food on his plate? Is it just that I said so? Or that my wife did? Or that we agreed? Hank said the opposite. Why doesn't what he said count? Why, for that matter, does what any of us say count? How is it that we can make rules? Questions like these have absorbed philosophers of law for decades, even though few of them have met Hank.

• • •

Why do I think there's a rule in our house that requires Hank to try everything on his plate? Because I said so. But, of course, Hank said the opposite, so that's not an adequate answer. Perhaps what I say counts because I back it up with force. I insist that Hank stay at the table until he's tried everything on his plate; if he tried to leave, I'd restrain him, or return him. But that won't work either, for at least two reasons. First, Hank punishes me almost as effectively as I punish him. He drags things out, says that he's taken a bite when he hasn't, wails, and tries to wear down my resolve. Sometimes, he succeeds. More often, I do. But it hardly seems like the question whether Hank is required, by rule, to try the things on his plate depends on who wins this tug-of-war. The question whether the rule is enforced depends on that; the question whether it's in force doesn't. Second, and more important, I restrain Hank because he is required to try everything on his plate. The rule is the justification for the restraint, so it must exist independently of its enforcement.[3]

So why does what I say count? Perhaps there is a rule that says that what I say counts. I have never made such a rule, and it is difficult to see how I could. If what I say doesn't count, I can't make it count by saying it does. So what I say has to count independent of what I have to say about it, if it is to count at all. Happily, there are reasons to think that what I say does count. I am, after all, Hank's parent, and parents, we might suppose, have the right to set the rules of their house, at least within limits. They do not have this right because they say they do. Rather, they have this right because it is necessary for them to discharge their responsibilities. Among other things, I have an obligation to keep Hank healthy and raise him such that, in the not-so-distant future, he will be capable of fending for himself. Rules, we might think, are an indispensable aid to that, so the right to set rules travels with the responsibilities parents owe to their children.

There's a lot more to say about parental authority. The fact that many children have two parents complicates the picture, as does the fact that, as children grow up, they can take on ever more responsibility for themselves. But I think the picture presented roughly right. That is, I think that Hank is required to try everything on his plate because I set that rule. And I think that I have the right to set that rule, not because of anything that I said or did, but simply because morality assigns me that right, as an adjunct to the responsibilities it assigns me to care for my children. In contrast, what Hank says does not count, because he is a

child, and morality does not grant him the power to reject the rules that
I set—at least, not yet.

• • •

What does all this have to do with law? Well, when lawyers go to court,
they often argue about the rules. They are not, of course, arguing about
the rules of our house. Rather, they are arguing about the rules of law,
and the rights and obligations that people have in virtue of them.
Sometimes, these disputes are similar to the one that Hank and I had:
someone has said there is a rule, and the question is whether their say-
so counts. On several occasions, the Federal Communications Commission (FCC) attempted to establish a rule barring internet service
providers from treating traffic on their networks differently depending
on its source. (This is the net-neutrality rule.) Some of the companies
that would have been subject to the rule sued, arguing that the FCC
did not have the authority to impose it. And twice, courts agreed.[4]
Eventually, the FCC adjusted the rule, and a court upheld its authority
to impose the new version.[5]

The details of those disputes were more complicated than the conflict I had with Hank. They turned on the text of statutes, which establish the FCC and grant it authority to issue rules. Everyone in those
disputes took it for granted that what the statutes said mattered. But
sometimes that is in dispute. Congress may attempt to establish a rule, but
those subject to it may protest that it lacks the authority to do so. For
instance, in the Affordable Care Act, Congress mandated that people
maintain health insurance or face a fine for their failure to do so. Some
people who would have been subject to the mandate said that Congress
lacked the authority to impose it. The question turned on whether, in
attempting to impose the mandate, Congress was acting within the
powers granted to it by the Constitution. The Supreme Court said that
the mandate was not a proper exercise of Congress's power under the
Commerce Clause, as the government had urged. But it nevertheless
held that Congress had the authority to impose the mandate as part of its
power to levy taxes, since the fines could be construed as a kind of tax.[6]

Why did it matter what the Constitution said? Again, everyone
involved took it for granted that it did, though they disagreed about just

what the Constitution authorized Congress to do. But why? Does the Constitution matter because courts say it does? Or because the people who drafted the Constitution thought it did? These answers suffer from the same sort of problems that my saying that what I say matters does. The courts, after all, are creatures of the Constitution. And the Framers could hardly confer authority on themselves by claiming it. If the Constitution matters, it must matter for reasons independent of the fact that its creators or creatures say it matters.

Is there a moral argument that could establish the authority of the Constitution, in the way that a moral argument establishes the authority of the rules that Julie and I adopt for our house? That strikes many people as a more dubious proposition. The men—and they were all men—who drafted the Constitution had many talents. But many of them were also slaveholders, and the document they produced not only countenanced slavery, it was written to preserve it. If the Constitution has authority, it does not rest on the superlative character of the rules themselves or the people who made them. Both were—and in the case of the rules, still are—seriously defective.

Are there any other arguments that could establish the authority of the Constitution? Many people would like to claim democratic authority for it, including those who drafted it. That aspiration is on display in the preamble:

> We the People of the United States, in Order to form a more perfect Union, establish Justice, ensure domestic Tranquility, provide for the common defence, promote the general Welfare, and secure the Blessings of Liberty to ourselves and our Posterity, do ordain and establish this Constitution for the United States of America.[7]

But the Constitution was not drafted by the People; it was drafted by people who appointed themselves to the task. There was a public ratification process, but the People were not a party to that either. Only white men with property participated. If the People had actually played a part in the adoption of the Constitution, then it might be plausible to say that it once had democratic authority. But we would still have to contend with the fact that the People now are rather different from the People then, and not just demographically. We face different challenges, so it's not clear why decisions made long ago should govern the way we live today.

All that said, I think there is a moral argument for thinking that the Constitution matters—for thinking that we should care what it says, even though we have little reason to defer to the people who drafted it or the process by which it became ours. We disagree about how we ought to live, and we need ways of resolving that disagreement so that we can live together. The rules set out in the Constitution are the best way that we have of resolving that conflict. They are not, to be sure, the best we can imagine, and we ought to patch them up as best we can. But while we work on that, we have reasons to respect the Constitution. The alternative is not just conflict, but chaos, since many of the challenges of living together are, at least in part, coordination problems. The Constitution's authority rests on the fact that many of us are willing to defer to it. It also rests on the fact that, as things stand now, we have no prospect of agreeing on anything better, even though it is easy to imagine better constitutions.

This argument does not just tell us that the Constitution matters; it also tells us something about how it matters—and what else matters with it. If the authority of the Constitution rested on the personal authority of the people who drafted it, then we might have reason to defer to their views about how its rules should be applied. But the argument I have given suggests that we should care more about settled understandings, even if they depart from the views of those who drafted the document. For instance, the text of the First Amendment suggests that its guarantee of free speech is good only against Congress ("Congress shall make no law . . . abridging the freedom of speech"). But it has long been understood to restrict judges and executive branch officials too.[8] The argument also suggests that we should defer to the litany of traditions that are constitutional—in that they constitute the processes by which we resolve our disagreements about how to live—even though they are not reflected in the text of the Constitution. For instance, the Dormant Commerce Clause restricts states' ability to interfere with interstate commerce. It is not actually a clause in the Constitution, since the text says nothing about state power to interfere with interstate commerce.[9] But tradition gives us a reason to apply Dormant Commerce Clause doctrine nonetheless.

There's lots more to say about all this, and constitutional lawyers have said lots of it. I won't delve any deeper here. I simply want to say that the question why and how the Constitution matters—or why and how a statute matters—or why and how a court decision matters—is the same sort of question as why and how what I say matters when I set rules for our house. To know why and how what I say matters, we need a moral argument. And to know why and how what the Constitution, Congress, or the courts say matters, we need a moral argument too.

• • •

Some will resist what I just said. They might think the moral argument I offered mistaken. They might deny that the Constitution has authority or insist that its authority rests on its ratification or the moral character of the men who drafted it. The constitutional law literature is chock-full of people who take these views, and many others besides. There is, however, another way of resisting what I just said. Instead of engaging on the question whether the Constitution has moral authority, some will want to deny that the question has any relevance at all when we attempt to ascertain what the Constitution requires.

These folks might tell us that the rules of law are the rules that are applied, which we can identify without engaging in moral argument. If courts apply the Dormant Commerce Clause, then it's a rule of law, whether or not we can identify any reason to comply with it. This is like saying that the rules of the house are the rules that I enforce, and it has just the same problem. Courts take the Dormant Commerce Clause to justify the decisions they make in its name. It couldn't play that role if the Dormant Commerce Clause was just whatever courts happened to do in its name.

There is, however, another way to resist the view that we need to engage in moral argument to figure out what the Constitution requires. Some think that there is a rule that establishes which rules are rules of law and which are not. But they deny that this rule is a moral rule. H. L. A. Hart made a view like this famous. He argued that every legal system has a rule of recognition, which identifies other rules in the system.[10] But the rule of recognition is not a moral rule. Rather, it's a rule that's constituted by a shared social practice.[11] Judges apply the rule of recognition when they decide cases, and their applying it—and demanding that others do so—gives it a kind of existence that is independent of the moral merits of the rule. This view is more sophisticated than the last because it allows rules to justify the decisions that courts make in their name. If the rule of recognition picks out the Dormant Commerce Clause as a rule of law, then it exists independently of its enforcement, and enforcement can be justified by reference to the rule—at least, up to a point. If the rule of recognition is not justified, then enforcement might not be either. The only justification that is guaranteed is justification relative to the rule of recognition.

There are lots of problems with this view. Here, I will mention just one, and once again, Hank can help. Why is there a rule in our house that requires Hank to try everything on his plate? Hart might say that my wife and I share a rule of recognition. We agree, perhaps, that the rules of the house are whatever we say they are.[12] Relative to that rule of recognition, there is a rule that requires Hank to try everything on his plate. But Hank isn't denying *that*. He knows that both Julie and I think—and act as if—there is such a rule. But he does not think that sufficient to make it the case that there is a rule that requires him to do so. When Hank and I argue over whether he is required to try things on his plate, we are not debating whether he is required according to the rules that I recognize. Rather, we are debating whether he is required to do so, sans qualification. In other words, Hank and I are having a debate about his actual rights and responsibilities, not the rights and responsibilities that I take him to have.[13]

$$\bullet \quad \bullet \quad \bullet$$

What happens in court? Do lawyers argue over the rights and responsibilities that litigants have relative to a rule of recognition? Or do they argue about the rights and responsibilities that the litigants have, sans qualification?

Hart's claim—that lawyers in court argue over rights and responsibilities relative to a rule of recognition—has been highly influential. But it's just one instance of a broader idea: that law is something other than morality. Different philosophers offer different takes on what law is, how it comes to be, and how it works. Hart says that law is a system of rules, picked out by a rule of recognition. Scott Shapiro offers a competing view; he says that law is a set of plans, made pursuant to a master plan for planning. Those are different ideas, but they share something in common. They construe law as a self-contained normative system, separate from morality. We won't take sides in the conflict between Hart, Shapiro, or anyone else who has a similar theory of law. But we should restate our question about what happens in court, so that it's less tied to Hart's particular variant of the separate-systems view. With that in mind, we'll ask: Do lawyers in court contest the rights and obligations that litigants have according to a self-contained normative system, separate from morality? Or do they argue about rights and obligations of the ordinary moral sort?

Here's an argument for the separate-systems view. In many places, the law is morally pernicious. In antebellum America, for instance, legal institutions recognized a right on the part of some to enslave others. That right couldn't possibly be a moral one. (Slavery is morally abhorrent.) And that suggests that legal rights are *not* rights of the ordinary moral sort. They belong, it seems, to a separate normative system, whose content may or may not match up with morality. This is by far the dominant view among philosophers of law. And I suspect it would be a common view among practicing lawyers and laypeople too, if they considered the question. The law is often morally objectionable, and sometimes worse than that. The best way to make sense of its shortfalls, it seems, is to suppose that the law is something other than morality—a separate system of rights and obligations, which we create through our legal practices.

That's an intuitive picture. And I feel tugged toward it, sometimes. But I think it's mistaken. There's a better way to understand law and its relationship to morality. Indeed, my aim in this book is to persuade you that, when lawyers go to court, they contest the moral rights and responsibilities of the parties, such that every legal argument is, in a way, a moral argument. Indeed, the central idea in this book is that law is a moral practice—a practice that aims at creating, extinguishing, enforcing, articulating, arranging, and rearranging our moral rights and responsibilities— and that court is a place we go to resolve conflict about them. This book is an invitation to try that view out, to see how it works, to see where it leads—and to see (among other things) what it has to say about morally objectionable laws, like the ones that underwrote slavery. (Here's a hint:

the fact that legal institutions recognize a right doesn't ensure that it exists. Legal institutions can be mistaken, just as individuals can. The fact that I believe you have a right doesn't guarantee that you do, even if I treat you like you have that right.)

I'm not the first person to hold a view like this. Ronald Dworkin did, both early in his career and late, though in the middle he may have gone on a misadventure.[14] Mark Greenberg, Steven Schaus, Nicos Stavropoulos, and Jeremy Waldron have also defended versions of the view that I will develop, and my work is deeply influenced by theirs.[15] In a different way, it bears the mark of the many who would—and will—disagree with it: Hart and Shapiro, to be sure, but also Jules Coleman, John Gardner, and Joseph Raz, among others. The ideas in this book also reflect the influence of philosophers who write about adjacent issues, especially, but not only, Seana Shiffrin and Judith Jarvis Thomson.

Debates in jurisprudence are difficult. The arguments are intricate because the issues are hard. My plan in this book is to cut past some of the clutter, so as to provide a concise account of the idea that law is a moral practice. That means that, for the most part, I won't engage these philosophers or the many others who have made important contributions to the debate. Or at least, I won't do that in the main text. (Hart and Dworkin will get more of a hearing than the others, but even they won't get much.) There's more in the notes. And at the back of the book, you'll find an appendix with frequently asked questions (FAQs). There, I'll say more about the relationship between the view on offer here and prominent alternatives.

But my aim is not to prove any particular theory of law wrong. I won't offer you an inescapable argument that Hart, Shapiro, or anyone else is mistaken about what law is. I think there are good arguments against the dominant views in jurisprudence. Indeed, I've developed some of them myself. And I'll share some criticisms along the way, but only when necessary to move the ideas in this book forward. I see little reason to litigate old disputes. Instead, I want to explore a view that's underexplored and mostly misunderstood. I want to show the appeal of the idea that law is a moral practice.

To see that appeal, we'll have to correct two misimpressions about morality, which are rarely made explicit but lurk in the background of lots of bad jurisprudence. First, many people imagine that morality is insulated from our activities—that we don't control what it requires— that it's independent of us. There's truth in that. We don't have complete control over morality. (For example, there's nothing we could do to make slavery morally permissible.) But there's lots we can do to shape morality's demands. And many legal practices, I'll argue, aim to do just that.

Related, but different: many people believe that morality requires whatever it ought to require—that morality is, by its own lights, perfect— that there's no space from within morality to critique the demands it makes on us. And they take that to be a reason to reject the idea that legal rights are moral rights. The law, after all, is clearly subject to moral critique. We often lack legal rights that we ought to have. Or have legal rights that we shouldn't. But it turns out, that's true of morality too. Often, we lack moral rights that we ought to have. Or have moral rights we shouldn't. Once you appreciate that fact, it's much easier to make sense of the idea that legal rights are moral rights.

I'll say more about all this later. (And I'll identify further mistakes about morality that undermine our efforts to understand law.) For now, I just want to make clear that this book is as much about morality as it is about law. I hope to persuade you that morality is more complex than is commonly supposed—and that it contains within it lots that we do under the banner of law. Indeed, at points I will invite you to consider legal cases from a purely moral perspective—to ask what the right answer would be if the judge wanted to do nothing other than make the decision that would be morally justified. And I'll show you that answering that question typically requires us to trace the same path that legal reasoning takes, to the point that we ought to doubt that there is any gap between the two.

If you're already inclined to think that law is a moral practice, that's terrific. I hope the chapters that follow will deepen your appreciation of the idea and solidify your sense that it's true. If you're on the fence (or so new to these issues that you have no views at all), even better. I hope to persuade you that law is a moral practice. But if you're inclined in the other direction—if you're already mounting your defense of the idea that law and morality are separate normative systems—then I've got a favor to ask. Suspend your disbelief, and immerse yourself in the idea that law is a moral practice. I hope that you'll come to see the appeal of the view. But even if I don't persuade you that it's true, I hope to show that many of the reasons people resist the view simply aren't sufficient. For instance, the manifest immorality of many laws and legal systems doesn't at all undercut the idea that law is a moral practice. By the end of the book, I hope you'll ask: Are there any reasons to suppose that law and morality are separate normative systems? What does that view allow us to appreciate about law that we can't see if we suppose it's a moral practice? I'm open-minded, but I don't think there's an answer to those questions. And by the end of the book, I hope you won't either.

• • •

Why should we care whether law is a moral practice? Why should we care whether the rights lawyers assert in court are moral rights? It is hard to overstate the importance of law in our lives. As the Due Process Clause reminds us, law deprives people of life, liberty, and property. Indeed, there's nearly no aspect of our lives that law does not touch. It determines who lives and dies, who is rich and poor, who can marry whom—and much, much more. To see ourselves clearly, we need to see law clearly.

We have another reason to care: we disagree about law. Often we disagree about what the law should be; that is part of what we contest through our politics. But we also disagree about what the law is; that is part of what we contest in court. Since law plays such a central role in our lives, we should aim to understand those disagreements. Are they, as I will contend, moral disagreements? Or do they have a different character? Seeing that they are moral disagreements, I will suggest, helps us to understand why they run so deep. And it helps us to understand the role that law plays in managing moral conflict.

Finally, there is a long tradition of distancing law from morality, and not just among philosophers. Lawyers are apt to say that they traffic in law, not morality, and to insist that the two are importantly different. I think that's a mistake, and I want to encourage lawyers to see what they do differently. At the end of this book, I'll argue that well-trained lawyers have a kind of moral expertise. But I think that lawyers could exercise better moral judgment than they do, and if they came to see the legal enterprise as a moral enterprise, they might just be better stewards of it.

• • •

Let me sketch the plan for the book, so that you have a sense of where we are headed. We will return to the questions that Hank raised—What makes something a rule of the house? Or a rule of law?—but we're going to set rules aside for a moment, as I think jurisprudence has suffered from its obsession with them. In Chapter 1, I'm going to develop the idea that law is a moral practice—a practice that aims at creating, extinguishing, enforcing, articulating, arranging, and rearranging our rights and responsibilities. I'll also argue that litigation poses moral questions, and I'll try to isolate the moral questions that we contest in court from the ones that we don't. In Chapter 2, I'll further illustrate the idea that litigation poses moral questions, asking just what is in dispute when lawyers contest the proper interpretation of a statute in court. I'll argue that those disputes are best seen as conflicts about the moral significance of acts of legislation.

In Chapter 3, we will return to rules. We will take up the idea that the law is a set of norms, like the rules of our house. I will argue that this picture—which has shaped our thinking about law for several decades— is misleading. Rules, and other sorts of norms, play an important part in legal practice. But it's not helpful to imagine that our legal practices generate a single set of norms—called *the law*—that holds the answer to all legal questions. Moreover, I will suggest that once we see that there are many sets of norms we might call law, we can also see that many traditional views in jurisprudence say something that is true of one of those sets. The trouble comes from pushing the other sets offstage.

In Chapter 4, we will confront the central worry that people have about linking law and morality. Laws can be arbitrary, stupid, or just plain evil. We will see that this fact—which is undeniable—is not a barrier to thinking that law is a moral practice. Indeed, seeing that law is a moral practice will allow us to think in a more sophisticated way about the moral significance of bad legal practices. In Chapter 5, we will take up an ancient question: whether people are obligated to obey the law. I will argue that recent conversation about this question misses the mark, because it misunderstands the moral difference that legal practices make.

In Chapter 6, we'll explore the rule of law. I'll argue that it rests on a shared moral outlook—an outlook that is (at least where I live) rapidly in retreat. Finally, in Chapter 7, we will consider what the lessons we've learned about law can teach us about lawyers. I'll argue that lawyers have moral expertise, at least in a limited domain. But we'll also explore the reasons people find lawyers repugnant. And I'll suggest that lawyers might be less repugnant if we did a better job teaching them that they are part of a moral practice.

• • •

One last note before we get started: I haven't yet used any of the labels that pervade philosophical discussions about law: positivism, natural law, realism, and the like. I will have a lot to say about them later on, but they are part of the clutter that I want to cut past. The positions these labels name presuppose particular ways of thinking about the problems in jurisprudence—ways that can be counterproductive. Worse yet, they prompt people to dig in and cheer for a team.

I'm not trying to hide anything. If you know a bit about jurisprudence, then you can already tell that my view is apt to be called antipositivist. But I've borrowed ideas from positivists, not just their critics, and I have little interest in attaching labels to the view that results. I think it is a view everyone can and should endorse, since it is supple enough to accommodate the observations that have historically driven people toward one or another of the labels above. But whether you are steeped in the old debates or not, let's turn the page—literally—and get a fresh start thinking about law.

CHAPTER ONE

A Moral Practice

Why Law?

Let's start at the start, with one of the most basic questions we could ask about law: What is the point of it? Why have legal practices at all? Of course, any practice as pervasive as law will serve many purposes, and lots of those will be peculiar to particular times and places. But if we think about law in a general way, two purposes stand out as significant, and neither is parochial. First, we have law because we want people to act differently than they would without it. This works in a variety of ways. People are amenable to instruction, and the law can provide instruction. People are amenable to incentives, and the law can provide incentives. The law can also help people act in ways they could not act absent law. Sometimes, it does this by coordinating their conduct, so as to make collective action possible. At other times, it does this by creating new action types; for instance, you can't pay taxes or devise property absent law. All this should feel familiar, as the possibility of influencing the ways that others will act is perhaps the primary reason that people participate in legal practices.

But there is another prominent reason for participating in legal practices: sometimes, we want to rearrange our moral relationships. We want, for instance, to impose obligations that people would not have absent law. Think about taxes for a moment. There are lots of practical reasons for imposing them. We might want to raise revenue or discourage a disfavored activity. But if we plan to collect a tax—and to punish people who fail to pay it—then we should make sure that they are obligated to pay the tax. Otherwise, we won't be justified in demanding that they pay, let alone in punishing them for failing to do so.[1] That gives us reason to structure our legal practices such that they generate genuine obligations.

In this sort of case, rearranging our moral relationships is an adjunct to inducing people to behave the way we want them to behave: if we did not want people to pay a tax, we would not have a reason to obligate them to do so. Sometimes, we have a further reason to impose an obligation: if people are motivated to discharge their obligations, then imposing one might be a way of getting them to do what we want them to do. That won't work if people are indifferent to their obligations or unaware of them. But many people want to do what they are obligated to do and seek information about it.

In other cases, we want to rearrange our moral relationships for reasons that have little to do with how we want people to act. This will be true whenever we think it intrinsically important that we stand in certain moral relationships. For instance, many people argue that we ought to be mutually accountable to one another, at least with respect to certain classes of wrongs. The institutions of private law—torts, contracts, and restitution—are ways of rendering us accountable to one another. They grant us the power to haul each other into court, where we can demand compensation and have the court back up the claim.[2] Of course, we have further ambitions for these institutions; we hope that tort, for example, will reduce the incidence of accidents. But those reasons are distinct from our aspiration to live in a community in which we are answerable to one another with respect to wrongdoing, and that aspiration is, on its own, a reason to have an institution like tort.

The question how legal practices affect what people do is a perennial subject of study among social scientists. The question how legal practices affect our moral relationships has been much discussed by philosophers, but often in a ham-handed way. It is not hard, however, to find deep and detailed discussions of the moral significance of our legal practices; indeed, more are written every day. The people who produce them are called lawyers. And exploring the moral significance of legal practices is the lion's share of what they do, at least whenever they advance arguments about law.

I suspect that claim will sound odd, especially to lawyers, who may not recognize their work in that description of it. As I said already, lawyers are accustomed to distinguishing law from morality. I think that's a mistake. Law is a moral practice. There are, to be sure, differences between the arguments that lawyers make and the arguments that we deploy as part of everyday moral discourse. That's part of the reason that lawyers must go to law school to learn how to do the job. Later on, we will think about what is distinctive about law. But to start, I want to explore the link between law and morality, since so much about law snaps into focus if we see it as a moral practice.

Promises

What do I mean when I say that law is a moral practice? I certainly do not mean that all laws are moral. With little effort, we could list dozens that are downright evil. I also do not mean that law is inherently good or that legal practices necessarily have moral merit. There may be some truth in those propositions, though it would take some work to locate it. When I say that law is a moral practice, however, I mean something altogether different, and the claim I will advance does not rest on the supposition that law is good simply in virtue of the fact that it is law. When I say that law is a moral practice, I mean just this: legal practices are tools for adjusting our moral relationships, and they are typically employed for the purpose of doing so.

To get clear about the claim, it might help to have other moral practices in view. To start, let's think about promises. What is the point of promising? Once again, two answers stand out. We make promises because we want people (ourselves included) to act differently than we would without them. This works in a variety of ways. To name just two: a promise can induce reliance from the recipient; it might also stiffen the resolve of the person who promised. But affecting how people will act is not the only reason that we promise. Promises also rearrange our moral relationships. When all goes well, promises generate obligations. Before you promised to meet me for lunch, you had no obligation to do so. After you promised, you did, and that has consequences. If you plan to miss the lunch—even for a good reason—you should let me know and try to reschedule. If you miss the lunch without telling me in advance, you should apologize and make it up to me. And it almost goes without saying that absent a good reason to miss the lunch, you should turn up when you said you would.[3]

A promise makes a moral difference, and that is part of the point of it. After all, you can tell someone what you intend to do without promising to do it:

"I'm going to the party."

"Are you sure?"

"Well, that's the plan, but don't hold me to it."

That last bit ("don't hold me to it") is there to make clear that no promise is being proffered. If the conversation went a bit differently— "Are you sure?" "Yes, you can count on it."—then there would be rights and responsibilities where there were none before. And we often have reasons to create rights and responsibilities. They invite robust reliance, because a breach will count as a wrong and generate a further right to a remedy. They also bind us together, since a wrong tends to rupture a relationship.

Promising, then, is a moral practice, in that part of the point of the practice is to rearrange our moral relationships. But not every promise is moral. Some are corrupt. A mob boss might promise one of his thugs a reward if he knocks off a member of a rival family. This is a promise that ought not be made, and it is embedded in a practice that people ought not participate in. That does not, however, preclude the possibility that the promise is intended to rearrange the moral relationships of the people party to it. A mob boss can give his word, just like the rest of us, and in so doing, he can intend to take on an obligation to do as he says he will. Whether his giving his word actually generates the obligation he intends is a further question. In this case, I am doubtful, though the mobster and thug would surely disagree. But consider a slightly different case: alongside the reward, the mobster promises to see to it that the thug's family is provided for in the event that the hit goes sour and the thug is killed or arrested. That is another promise that ought not be made, as it is offered as an inducement to murder. But it is, I think, a promise that ought to be kept.[4] The mobster would wrong the thug if he let his family slip into poverty while he served time. Or at least that is how it seems to me. Whether I am right depends on the morality of promising, and this is not a book about that. But questions like these will crop up again, since law is like promising, in that it is a moral practice, even though many instances of it are immoral.

The Rules of the House

We'll take up law in a moment, but it might help to think through another moral practice. After all, there are lots of them: among other things, we swear oaths, issue orders, and make rules. All those activities are aimed, at least in part, at rearranging our moral relationships—at shifting our rights and responsibilities—so they are moral practices in the relevant sense. But one of them—making rules—shares a lot in common with law. Indeed, H. L. A. Hart argued that law is a system of rules.[5] In Chapter 3, we'll see why that's a misleading way to look at law. But there's no question that our moral lives include lots of activities that look a bit like legislation. We make rules for our workplaces, teams, clubs, and, as we saw in the Introduction, our families.

I already told you about one rule in our house—the rule that requires Hank to try everything on his plate. But we have lots of rules—rules about television, video games, and bedtime. Our children take particular interest in the rules about who may play with what. Many of the toys in our house are held in common, available to anyone who wants to play with them, first come, first served. But some of the toys in our house are Rex's, and some are Hank's. Ownership depends on how the toy was acquired; a gift given to Rex, for example, remains his, at least until he outgrows it. The rule in our house, however, is that our kids may play with each other's toys. No advance permission is required, though if a toy is in some way special, a child may reserve it to himself by putting the other one on notice. Then, permission is required to play with it.

This is just a small glimpse into the complicated property regime we instituted in our house. Why did we make these rules? Without doubt, we wanted to influence how our children would act. We hoped that clear rules would minimize conflict and that the particular rules we adopted would make the kids less possessive. But we also wanted to rearrange the boys' moral relationships, by giving them rights and obligations they would not have absent the rules. To some extent, that was instrumental to the aim of getting them to play together nicely. But there were further reasons for structuring their relationship as we did. By granting the boys rights to exclude, we helped support their special attachments to prized possessions. And by giving them rights to use each other's things, we minimized the opportunity for them to refuse out of spite, which is a major motivation for miniature people.

Adopting these rules had another happy consequence, which we did not anticipate. It introduced the boys to the realm of rights and obligations. They learned to press claims and defend themselves against accusations of wrongdoing. They learned that, when someone asserts their right, we yield, at least absent good reason to override it. But they also learned that it can be wrong to stand on your rights—that sometimes, for instance, it's mean to prevent someone from using something that's yours, even if you have the right to do so. In other words, the property rules in our house introduced the boys to the building blocks of morality.

Rights and Wrongs

But wait: What is morality? The word is used in many ways, and I do not think much turns on the way in which it is used, so long as we are clear about it. As I use the term here, morality is the part of practical reason that concerns what we owe each other; that is, it's the part that deals with rights and wrongs.[6] To be sure, there are other ways to construe morality, and on a different occasion I might sign up to different conception of it. On some renderings, morality is intimately connected with assessments of our character. A moral failing might mark one a bad person—or at least, a person who has acted badly, in a way that makes them blameworthy. This way of thinking about morality is both broader and narrower than the one

I plan to employ. It's broader because it encompasses failings that might not register as wrongs to others, like laziness or extravagance. And it's narrower since, as we'll see in a moment, you can wrong someone in a way that does not reflect poorly on your character.

That rendering of morality is different yet again from one that's entrenched in popular culture. Many people associate morality with the set of sins that have, over the years, bothered many religious authorities: lust, gluttony, greed, and so on. On this picture, morality cares a great deal about our sexual practices, even when they don't harm (or even involve) other people. But it might not care at all how a community funds health care or whether it provides public schools. Those issues, some might say, pose political questions, not moral ones. As I'll use the term, however, the question how health care should be funded is paradigmatically moral, as it is (in part) a question of what we owe each other.

In emphasizing what we owe each other, some will say that I'm leaving out lots of morality. To be sure, morality is concerned with rights and wrongs. But it also tells us what we ought to do, even when no rights or wrongs are involved. For instance, morality might tell me that I ought to give money to charity, even though no one has a right that I make a donation. Or it might tell me that I shouldn't spend large sums of money on art or champagne, though no one stands to be wronged by my doing so. I think there's something to this; morality cares about what we ought to do, not just what we're obligated to do. Nevertheless, I shall keep the focus on rights and wrongs, since they're central to the way that law works.[7] Morality might condemn pointless extravagance, but if the law wants to limit it, it assigns obligations (to pay taxes, perhaps), creates offenses, and so on. So even if morality is best construed as encompassing more than what we owe each other, it's that bit that's important for thinking about law.

I should also add: morality concerns what we genuinely owe each other, not what we believe we owe each other. Sometimes, we talk about the morality of particular communities. They could be real, like the ancient Israelites or modern-day bond traders. Or they might be fictional, like the Jedi of *Star Wars* lore. When we talk about the morality of these communities, we're calling attention to beliefs that these communities had about what their members owed each other.[8] We're trying to capture a social fact, not a moral one. Sometimes, we make this distinction clear by talking about a community's *mores,* rather than its morality. But we don't always swap words, so I want to make my meaning clear. Morality, as I'm using the term, concerns what we genuinely owe each other, not our beliefs about it.[9]

Why use *morality* to refer to our genuine rights and obligations? There's a long tradition in legal philosophy of using the word in roughly that way. Some philosophers who use the word that way want to distinguish law from morality. They deny that legal obligations are genuine obligations, insisting instead that they are obligations "according to law." Other philosophers reject that distinction. They say that legal obligations are moral obligations and by that mean to mark them as genuine.[10] That is where my sympathies lie, and I'll make my case in a moment. But I want to underscore that nothing turns on the way I'm using the word *morality*. What matters is what we owe each other.[11] *Morality* is simply the shorthand I'll use to talk about that.

Now that you know what I mean by *morality,* let me say a bit more about it. We are all subject to the demands of morality because we are all subject to the demands of reason. Morality does, to be sure, afford us some freedom to choose what obligations we will have. That is, as we just saw, part of the point of promising. It is also part of the point of law. But even though we have some control over what obligations we have, we cannot opt out of morality entirely, in the way that we might opt out of a game. If there are sufficient reasons to hold that a person has a right against us, then that person has that right whether we wish her to or not.

That last point must be made with some care, so that we can distinguish the cases in which there are reasons to think that someone has a right from the cases in which there are reasons to think that she ought to have a right, even though she doesn't yet. Suppose that John has a bike that he's outgrown. We might think that his friend Jane ought to have the right to use it, and we might think so because it strikes us that John ought to give the bike to Jane. Jane, however, will not have that right unless and until John gives it to her. As things stand now, she has to ask his permission to use the bike; it is, after all, still John's. This case shows that we might not have all the rights that we ought to have. But we do have whatever rights reason suggests that we do, since rights just are grounded in the reasons for recognizing them.

Some doubt that, so defined, there is such a thing as morality. Or at least some profess doubt. Nearly no one, however, lives it. I have met people who act as if they do not owe anything to others. But I have never met anyone who acted as if no one owed anything to her. It could be that we are all mistaken to carry on as if we owe things to one another, but I will not worry about that possibility here. When I say that law is a moral practice, I mean that we employ legal practices in an effort to adjust who owes what to whom. If no one owes anyone anything because no one could owe anyone anything, then that ambition would be misguided. But I shall assume it is sound, since I think we can and do owe each other an awful lot, and I am far from alone in that.

Before we go on, I should say a few words about rights and wrongs. We use the words *right* and *wrong* in lots of ways. Sometimes, talk about what's right or wrong conveys an assessment, relative to some relevant standard. I might tell Rex that he set the table wrong or that he put the fork in the right place. In each case, I'm comparing what he did to a criterion for success. But when we talk about rights and wrongs, we are up to something different. Rights are relationships. If I have a right that you pay me $100 next Friday, then you and I have a relationship in respect of that payment. You owe it to me. That is, you are obligated to pay me $100 on the date it's due. There are many aspects to this relationship.[12] I can release you from the obligation, at least in the standard case. (Most rights are alienable, but some are not.) If you know in advance that you won't be able to make the payment, you should tell me and seek a release. If you fail to discharge your obligation without having obtained a release, you've committed a wrong, and there are consequences to that. You should apologize and seek to set things right as best you can. It is hard to say in advance what would count as setting things right. Sometimes, compensation helps. Other times, substitute performance is in order. But sometimes, nothing will help, except perhaps expressing remorse.

When someone holds a right against you, you ought to discharge your corresponding obligation, unless you have a good reason not to do so. What counts as good reason will vary with the obligation, so it is difficult to say anything in general, but some cases are clear enough.[13] If you need the money you owe me to pay for your child's urgent medical treatment, then you ought not pay me. Some philosophers would say your obligation in that case is only prima facie or pro tanto since it is outweighed by your responsibilities to your child. I don't think those phrases are necessary; in fact, I think they are misleading.[14] They are introduced to preserve the idea that full-fledged obligations are absolute, such that your conduct is defective simply on account of your failure to discharge them. But that is not an idea we should preserve. Sometimes, the right thing to do is to wrong someone. If your child needs medical treatment urgently, then you should breach your obligation to me. You won't be acting wrongly, even though you will wrong me.[15] But it is important that we see your failure to pay me as a breach of your obligation, since that breach explains your further responsibilities—to explain, apologize, and make it up to me when you can.

I raise this now because I want you to have the right thing in mind when I talk about rights and wrongs. The ideas just introduced will be important later on, when we think about the circumstances in which we should (or shouldn't) do what law demands. But for now, I simply want to clarify what I mean by morality. Morality is the domain of rights and wrongs; rights are relationships; and wrongs are breaches of rights.[16]

Practices

I keep mentioning practices: moral practices, legal practices, promising practices, and so on. What's a practice? Some philosophers use the word in a theory-laden way, such that talk about a practice implies that an activity is constituted by rules in, say, the way that chess is.[17] Castling, capturing a pawn, and putting an opponent in checkmate are activities that are possible only because there are rules that constitute the game of chess. That sets those activities apart from taking a walk or tossing a ball, which are activities we can engage in even absent any rules for doing so. Sometimes, our pursuit of those activities is constrained by rules. My father-in-law lives in an assisted living facility. He's permitted to take a walk in the adjacent park only when accompanied. The rule limits his chances to take walks. But no rule is necessary to constitute the possibility that he might.

In mature legal systems, lots of legal activities seem chess-like. There are rules, for instance, that specify what counts as an act of legislation from Congress. But as we've just observed, legislation is a close cousin of other activities, like making rules for a household. And as we learned in the Introduction, my ability to do so does not rest on some further rule that creates the possibility. I can make rules because morality attaches moral significance to some of my pronouncements. There are good reasons for the law to specify who can legislate and how. But we shouldn't presume that all legal activities, everywhere and always, are carried out pursuant to rules that create the possibility of those activities. Indeed, it's hard to see how that could be so. The rules by which Congress legislates are found in the Constitution. But the Constitution itself was not created according to any rules for doing so. That suggests that at least one legal activity (adopting a constitution) is not a move in a game constituted by rules. And we shouldn't assume that any legal activities are best seen that way. In Chapter 3, I'll question the idea that law is a set of rules.

Partly for that reason, I'm not using the word "practice" in a theory-laden way. The dictionary definition is more modest: a repeated action.[18] "Her practice was to cut her nails in faculty meetings" does not signal that she was empowered by a rule to do so. (Quite the opposite, I can assure you.) It's simply something that she did with some regularity. That said, some repeated actions hang together; they form rough sets that make up significant parts of our lives. The practice of medicine, for instance, involves lots of actions that aim at the promotion or preservation of health, the treatment of disease, and so on. When I talk about practices, I mean to pick out activities that hang together in that way.

What makes a practice moral? Or legal? As I said before, our moral practices are tools we use to adjust our moral relationships. They are activities (like forgiving, excusing, waiving, claiming, and consenting) that we employ for that purpose. And I'm inclined to say something isomorphic about law. A legal practice is a tool we use to adjust our legal relationships. It's an activity (like legislating, regulating, adjudicating, charging, sentencing, and suing) that we employ for that purpose. My claim in this book is that legal practices are moral practices; the corollary is that legal relationships are moral relationships. But nothing in the argument that follows depends on a particular way of sorting practices (or relationships) into and out of the category "legal." As I'll explain in a bit, I think there are many ways we might draw the boundaries of that category, depending on what we want to emphasize. For now, it's sufficient to work with a rough sense of which activities in the world constitute the legal bits of our lives. They are the ones studied in law school.

Authority, Law, and Morality

Enough with the windup. Here's the pitch: just about everyone thinks that law is a moral practice in the sense just explained. Most philosophers of law sign on to some version of the thought that our legal practices aim at adjusting who owes what to whom—not just legally, but morally.[19] Joseph Raz, for instance, says that law claims authority over its subjects, and by authority, he means, among other things, the power to confer rights and impose obligations.[20] Of course, Raz does not mean that everyone who participates in legal practices sees themselves as having that authority, or even that everyone who participates sees the legal system as having that authority. Some may be alienated from it. Rather, what he means is that legal officials generally present themselves as having authority. They make claims about what others are genuinely obligated to do as a result of legal practices, and the practices are presented as ways of generating those obligations.[21]

Moreover, Raz says, the authority that legal officials claim is moral. They assert the power to interfere in people's lives, often in intrusive ways. They put people in prison and make them pay taxes. They may not have the authority they claim. But if they have it, that's because moral principles confer it on them. As Raz explains, the relevant principles are moral because they "allow, perhaps even require, some people to interfere in important ways in the lives of others. Valid principles that have such content are moral principles, or nothing is."[22]

Of course, some legal officials claim the power to adjust our rights and responsibilities insincerely. And it's possible that there's a legal system somewhere in which every single official is insincere. They all act as if they intend for their practices to generate obligations, but they're really

just in it for the tax revenue, which they take happily, even though they
know they're not entitled to it. Is the point of their practice to make a
moral difference? No, probably not. But notice how they trade on the
purposes people normally have when participating in legal practices. They
do not present themselves as the extortionists they are. Rather, they dress
up their activities in legal language, so that they can maintain the fiction
that people are obligated to pay the money that they take. In any event,
we ought not worry about deviant cases like this. There is no doubt that
promising is a moral practice, even though some people promise insincerely. And I suspect that most legal officials, in most places, intend for
their activities to adjust people's rights and obligations.

Of course, legal officials don't always achieve what they intend. Sometimes, they are confused about the impact their practices have on people's
rights and obligations. This might be because they do not have the authority to adjust the rights and responsibilities of their supposed subjects.
Or it might be their authority is limited in ways they do not appreciate. Or
it might be because their attempt to adjust their subjects' rights and responsibilities misfires, generating rights and responsibilities that are not quite
what they intended. These sorts of confusion are common, and I shall say a
lot about them later. For now, all I want to say is this: even if legal officials are
often confused about the impact their activities have on people's rights and
obligations, they typically aim to adjust them. And that aim is not confused, since legal practices—like legislation and adjudication—are the
sorts of activities that might, in the right circumstances, rearrange people's
moral relationships. That is what I mean when I say that law is a moral
practice. And I think it clear—and uncontroversial—that it is.

Moral Conflict

Why spend so much time on the claim that law is a moral practice?
Because once we have that thought in place, it is a short step to another:
litigation poses moral questions. Here is a simple story that connects those
two thoughts. Suppose that I am right: we employ legal practices in an
effort to adjust who owes what to whom. Oftentimes, we might expect,
we will agree about how our legal practices have adjusted our moral re-

lationships. We would recognize that we have rights and responsibilities that we would not have absent those practices. And most of the time, we might hope, we would be willing to honor each other's rights by discharging our obligations.

But conflict, we might think, is inevitable. Morality is complicated and often contested. And people are not always willing to do what they are obligated to do. We might negotiate solutions to some conflicts. But if deeper disagreements are common enough to be troublesome, then we might think it helpful to establish institutions to resolve them. These institutions would hear arguments about what rights and obligations people have, gathering facts as necessary to inform their judgment. And once all that was in, they would make decisions about who owed what to whom. If, by and large, people deferred to those decisions, then we would have a way of resolving conflict about our rights and obligations.

We do, of course, have institutions like that. We call them courts, and in well-functioning legal systems, people do defer to them.[23] This simple story is what lies behind the suggestion that I made at the start: litigation poses moral questions, at least whenever the rights and obligations of the parties are contested. Of course, I do not offer the simple story as history; in some legal systems, perhaps, adjudication preceded legislation. Rather, the simple story illustrates a logic at work in our legal practices. Some activities aim to adjust our rights and obligations (for example, legislation, regulation). Other activities aim to resolve conflict about rights and obligations (for example, litigation, arbitration). The line can be blurry; common-law adjudication, for instance, does double duty. We are about to take it up in detail. But as we wade into the weeds, I want you to keep the simple story in mind, for in it lie two messages of this book: Law is a moral practice. And litigation poses moral questions, since court is a place that we go to contest what we owe each other.[24]

What Courts Do

The conversation so far has been rather abstract. Let's make it less so. A plaintiff comes to court. She says that the defendant owes her compensation for an injury he inflicted. The defendant denies it. Who is right? The answer will depend on what transpired between them. It will also depend on what rights the plaintiff has in respect of what transpired. Suppose that they agree on the relevant facts. The defendant was checking his text messages when he lost control of his car, crashed into a pole, and knocked down the power line that served the plaintiff's restaurant. The restaurant closed, and the plaintiff wants compensation for the loss that she suffered.

Does she have a right to it? That is a moral question, since it is a question about who owes what to whom. It is also a legal question, since the answer turns on the details of our legal practices. Why do I say that? For many reasons, which shall emerge shortly. But to start, there's this: the plaintiff does not just claim that the defendant owes her compensation; she also claims that the court should issue an order, holding the defendant liable to pay it. In other words, she is claiming a right of a certain sort: one that is enforceable on demand in court. In fact, she asserts two rights, one nested in the other: she claims a right to have the court enforce her right to compensation.[25] To decide whether the plaintiff has that compound right, we need to know something about courts: what they do and why they do it. Courts, after all, do not stand ready to enforce just any right. John may owe Jane an apology for the abrupt way he treated her at work yesterday. But Jane cannot take John to court and demand the apology that she's owed. If she filed a complaint, it would be dismissed for failure to state a claim on which relief could be granted.

Why can't Jane state a claim against John? There are two ways to answer this question. The most straightforward way is to point out that courts will hear a claim only if the plaintiff has a cause of action, and they restrict the number that they recognize. As it happens, there is no cause of action that allows an employee to hold a coworker responsible for acting rudely. A more roundabout answer would point to the reasons that courts restrict causes of action. To start, there are only so many judges, and they have only so much time. They cannot resolve every conflict, and though we could have more judges than we do, there are costs to that, and at some point, they exceed the benefits. By limiting causes of action, courts can spend their time on cases that are, in some way, significant. But resource constraints are not the only reason to limit causes of action. Courts are not the best place to resolve every dispute. Jane has a justified complaint against John, but litigation would be as likely to exacerbate their conflict as resolve it. There are also cases in which courts cannot offer effective remedies. An apology may be just what Jane needs, but courts are in a poor position to provide it, since a forced apology is not the same sort of thing as a sincere one.

To all that, we might add another cluster of reasons for limiting causes of action. People want to know when they might be held responsible, so that they can take steps to limit their liability or insure against it. That puts pressure on courts to make sure that the set of rights they recognize is stable, at least in the short term. Of course, this value has to be weighed against the gains to be had from recognizing new rights where there are reasons to do so, and sometimes it loses out. Common-law courts do, from time to time, adopt new causes of action. But it is easy to see why they would be reluctant. And they have further reason to be reluctant if they have considered the question in the past and declined to do so. Recognizing a new cause of action always raises concerns about predictability and fairness. But if there is a prior decision on point, an about-face raises concerns about equality and integrity too.

Add all that up, and it is easy to see why the case of the rude colleague is not going anywhere in court. John owes Jane an apology, but Jane does not have a right to enforce that right in court. But what about the power-line plaintiff? Does she have the right she claims? In her case, there is a cause of action that might fit: negligence. The defendant was careless in checking his text messages, and the plaintiff suffered an injury as a result. But though those facts are enough to get us thinking about negligence, they are not yet enough to establish that the plaintiff has a right to hold the defendant liable. And it is doubtful that she does, though we'd need to know more about the accident to be sure. If the defendant damaged some part of her property, then she might have a right to recover, but only to the extent that her losses are a consequence of that damage. But if the telephone pole was at some remove from the plaintiff's property, and she was injured only because she lost access to power, then she almost certainly does not have a right to compensation.

Why does the plaintiff's right to compensation depend on whether she suffered property damage? The most straightforward answer points to the pure economic loss rule, which holds that we do not have a duty

to protect one another from pure economic losses (absent special circumstances, none of which obtain here).[26] That rule is long-standing and
widespread, though there is some disagreement about its rationale. One
reason often given for the rule is that the economic consequences of an
act can spread far and wide.[27] The power line came down, and the restaurant closed. There was a hotel on the block too, which had to cancel
a convention, losing business not just this year but in out years too, as the
outraged organizers took their event elsewhere. Restaurants that did not
lose power still lost revenue due to the canceled convention, as did local
T-shirt printers and their more distant suppliers. Already it seems absurd to
ask our hapless driver to make good all these losses. And we could trace
these consequences further out or inquire into other businesses that lost
power to see what misery might flow from them. Responsibility just
cannot run that far, some courts say, so we insist on damage to person or
property, not just a pocketbook, as a way of containing the consequences
for which we can be called to account.[28]

I do not find that persuasive. The physical consequences of an act can
spread far and wide too, and that does not stop us from holding people
responsible for them. (Imagine a mislabeled medicine that poisons patients
for many years before anyone discovers the mistake.) And if we suppose that
the restaurant was close to the scene of the accident, then responsibility
does not have to run very far for the plaintiff to recover. In my view, the
pure economic loss rule reflects an entrenched feature of morality. Other
people are not required to be vigilant for our economic interests. Indeed,
they are often entitled to act against them.[29] Markets would not be moral
if that were not true.[30] There are limits, of course. If you agree to serve
as my accountant, you will have a responsibility to watch out for my
economic interests, insofar as they are affected by your work. That is
part of the commitment that you make when you take on that role. But,
except in special cases, you need not worry about my business as you go
about your own.[31]

If our power-line plaintiff was the first person in her jurisdiction to
raise the question whether we have a duty to protect each other from
economic losses, a court would have to work through the reasons just
raised. But if, as in most places, the issue has already been mooted, the
moral calculus is different. As we saw with John and Jane, prior decisions

have a weight of their own, and for lots of reasons: stability, fairness, equality, and integrity. In most places, I'd expect, the plaintiff's case would be dismissed as soon as it was established that she did not suffer any damage to her person or property. And that would be the right result, unless the plaintiff could show something special about her case that warranted treating it differently than the ordinary economic loss. Or unless she could show that the standard practice is misguided *and* that the consequences of sticking to it are awful enough to outweigh concerns about stability, fairness, equality, and integrity. It is difficult to imagine she could carry that burden, and that makes it doubtful that she has the right that she asserts.

Mistakes That Make a Difference

Things could have gone the other way. I think that the pure economic loss rule reflects a background feature of morality. I could be wrong about that. But even if I am right, courts could have gotten it wrong. They could have decided that we do, in fact, have a duty to watch out for each other's economic interests, not just in special cases, but generally. In that case, the power-line plaintiff might well have the right that she claims, at least if we suppose that there are no further rules that raise doubts about her right to hold the defendant liable.[32]

That might sound a bit odd, given all that I've said so far. I've suggested that legal claims are moral claims, but now I've acknowledged that our plaintiff might have a right to recover, even though recognition of that right seems to flout morality, rather than reflect it. There is, however, no inconsistency here. As we saw in the previous section, the decisions that courts make matter. Indeed, they can rearrange our moral relationships. Suppose that a court did decide that people in the plaintiff's jurisdiction have a duty to watch out for one another's economic interests. It would not be surprising to find people adjusting their lives in response to that decision. They might be more cautious about other people's economic interests, and they might in turn demand more caution from others. Or they might choose to run risks that they would otherwise have avoided, or insured against, knowing that someone else can be held responsible if the danger comes to pass. Insurance companies, for their part, might shift the sorts of policies that they offer or adjust the way that they are priced. If these sorts of changes cascade through society, there will be reasons—which were not present before the court's decision—to hold that people do have a duty to watch out for each other's economic interests. The mere fact that activity proceeds on that premise bolsters the case for it.

Of course, that story is speculative. There is no guarantee that anyone will notice the court's opinion or adjust their behavior in response to it. Typically, people do, if only because insurance companies take an interest in the outcome of tort suits. But the strength of the reasons I just described will depend on the extent to which society is rearranged in reliance on the decision. If there's little reliance, then arguments of the sort just offered will carry little force. If there's lots, then their weight may well be dispositive. It's no surprise, then, that courts think a lot about reliance when they are invited to revisit a decision that they have made.

But even if not much has happened in response to the court's decision, there are other ways in which it might make a moral difference. As we saw in the previous section, concerns about equality and integrity put pressure on courts to remain consistent in the rights that they recognize. Equality requires that like cases be treated alike. And integrity requires that courts aim to make the law as a whole coherent.[33] The more cases that have been decided under a rule, or the more deeply embedded a decision is in a network of decisions, the more force these reasons have. Once again, these reasons have to be weighed against other concerns, and there is no guarantee that they will carry the day. Sometimes, courts should reverse course. But oftentimes, these reasons carry enough weight to make it the case that subsequent litigants have the rights recognized in a decision that was mistaken at the time it was made.

What Courts Don't Do

There are other ways in which a judicial decision might make a moral difference, but we do not need an exhaustive account here. The point of taking up the power-line plaintiff's case was to help us identify the sorts of moral questions that are posed in litigation, as well as the sorts of considerations relevant to resolving them. A plaintiff in a tort suit asserts a right. The court must decide whether she has it. As I said, that is a moral question, since it is a question about who owes what to whom. It is also a legal question, since the answer depends on the details of our legal practices.

There are many other moral questions we could ask about the incident. For instance, we could ask whether the defendant wronged the plaintiff. In a tort suit, the plaintiff will not have a right to compensation unless the defendant wronged her, so we should expect that to be a live question in the litigation. (But it might not be: the defendant might be immune from suit or the claim might be time-barred, in which case the court would have no need to determine whether the defendant wronged the plaintiff.) If the plaintiff's claim sounded in restitution, however, she might be entitled to recover without showing that the defendant wronged her, since restitution does not rest liability on wrongdoing. The plaintiff's complaint—and the defendant's answer—pose the moral questions that a court must resolve.

There are questions nearby, however, that courts typically don't take up. For instance, courts rarely ask whether a plaintiff ought to have the right she claims. As we saw before, the question whether a person ought to have a right is distinct from the question whether she has it. (Remember John, Jane, and the bike.) A plaintiff might have a right that she ought not to have. Or she might lack a right that she ought to have. By and large, courts are in the business of deciding what rights people have, rather than what rights they ought to have. In common-law courts, those questions sometimes shade into one another, especially when a court confronts a question it has not addressed before. In civil-law systems, the questions are easier to keep separate, since courts do not have the authority to adjust the rights that are recognized in the way that common-law courts do. But even in common-law systems, courts are always operating under the constraints imposed by statutes, regulations, and prior decisions. So there will often be a difference between the rights that a plaintiff ought to have and the rights that she does have.

This is a point I want to underscore. Some think that we must distance law from morality lest we lose our ability to draw a distinction between the law as it is and the law as it ought to be. But that is a mistake. We just

have to get the relation right. I have argued that law is moral practice, in
that it aims to adjust our moral relationships. There is, however, no
guarantee that any legal practice will make those relationships what they
ought to be. Indeed, there is no guarantee that they will affect them at
all. But when our legal practices do rearrange our moral relationships,
we can recognize that we have new rights and responsibilities and nevertheless think it regrettable that we do.

We should linger here just a bit longer. It is tempting to think that
morality is just what it ought to be. If that were true, it would mark a
contrast between law and morality, since law so often falls short of what
it ought to be. But there is no contrast here, because morality can fall
short of what it ought to be too. There may be some fixed moral truths,
which are what they ought to be and could not be otherwise. ("We should
respect one another's humanity" seems like a promising candidate.) But
most of morality is not like that. Morality is sensitive to social facts, so if
they are not what they ought to be, we are apt to have rights and responsibilities that we ought not to have. John asked Jane to take on an arduous
task. She said yes, and now people are relying on her to get it done. As a
result, Jane has an obligation to do as she said she would. But Jane shouldn't
have said yes; the task will get in the way of other commitments. And John
shouldn't have asked; he's asked too much of Jane already. Jane should
not have the obligation she does. It may be that she should back out or
that John should substitute someone else in her place. But if Jane is far
enough along with the work, it might not make sense to shift the responsibility to someone else. She might just be stuck in a morally regrettable
moral situation.

Our legal practices create lots of those. For the most part, courts are
not in the business of commenting on them—their job is to figure out
what rights litigants have, not what rights they ought to have. But judges
are in a good position to notice when the law is not what it ought to
be, and sometimes they invite the legislature (or a higher court) to fix it.
Justice Ginsburg did this, to great effect, in her dissent in *Ledbetter v.
Goodyear Tire & Rubber Company*.[34] Lily Ledbetter discovered that Goodyear had been paying her less than men who were doing the same job, so
she filed suit, demanding back pay for the discrepancy. The Court held
that Ledbetter's claim was time-barred.[35] Title VII requires a plaintiff to

file a claim within 180 days of a discriminatory act.[36] Ledbetter proved that Goodyear paid her less because of her sex.[37] But the decisions to pay Ledbetter less had piled up over a long period of time, and all of them were more than 180 days past when she filed her claim.[38] So even though she had been wronged, Ledbetter had no right to recover, at least according to the majority.

Justice Ginsburg thought the majority's decision mistaken. In her view, Ledbetter's claim was not time-barred, because the relevant discriminatory act was paying Ledbetter less than her male colleagues, not deciding to pay her less.[39] And Ledbetter was paid less every time she received a paycheck. Ginsburg had compelling reasons for reading the statute as she did. Title VII permits a court to award up to two years of back pay—counting back from the time a claim is filed—which suggests that Congress did not intend to insulate decisions from review once they were 180 days old.[40] For that reason, among others, Ginsburg would have held that Ledbetter had the right that she claimed.

But Ginsburg lost—five justices sided with Goodyear. And since the Court has the last say on what a statute means, no one in Ledbetter's position could claim back pay going forward. In her dissent, Ginsburg explained why that was regrettable. Pay is often set in secret, so it can take years for an employee to discover that she's paid less than her colleagues, if she ever does. The majority's rule would ensure that lots of discriminatory pay decisions would go unchallenged, even if they continued to have consequences when they came to light.[41] In closing, Ginsburg recalled that Congress had responded to one of the Court's earlier Title VII decisions by correcting its "cramped interpretation" of the statute, and she invited it to do so again.[42] "[T]he ball," she said, "is in Congress' court."[43]

Congress accepted the invitation, adopting the Lily Ledbetter Fair Pay Act,[44] which was the first piece of legislation that President Obama signed.[45] The Act made clear that an employee suffers discrimination every time she is paid less on account of her sex, even if the decision that led to the discrepancy was made in the distant past.[46] In Ginsburg's view, this was a restoration of a right that employees had before *Ledbetter*. In the majority's view, the statute created a new right, which no one had before. I think Ginsburg had the better of the argument, but it does not matter much here. I simply want to highlight the difference between asking what rights a plaintiff ought to have and asking what rights she has. Courts are in the business of asking the latter question, but as Ginsburg's dissent illustrates, judges can and do comment on the former, at least from time to time.

Morality, in Court and Out

Does Goodyear owe Ledbetter back pay? I mean right now—today. Ledbetter is still alive, and so far as I know, Goodyear has never compensated her for the discrepancy in her pay.[47] It is tempting to say no. After all, Ledbetter lost her suit. But it is important to remember why Ledbetter lost. The Court concluded that her claim was time-barred. The Court did not say whether, absent the time bar, Ledbetter could have claimed compensation under Title VII. It also did not say whether Goodyear might owe Ledbetter compensation on some other ground, not presented in court.

I think that Goodyear does owe Ledbetter compensation. After all, Goodyear discriminated against her; it paid her less than her male counterparts, and for no good reason. That's a wrong, and Goodyear should right it, as best it can. The fact that time ran out on Ledbetter's Title VII claim does not mean that Goodyear does not owe Ledbetter compensation. It simply means that Ledbetter cannot claim compensation in court.

I have said that the questions posed in court are moral questions as well as legal ones. The question whether Ledbetter had a right that the Court enforce her right to compensation is a moral question, since it is a question about who owes what to whom. And it is a legal question, since the answer depends on the details of our legal practices. But there are other moral questions we can ask, and one of them is whether Ledbetter has a right to compensation, even though she cannot claim it in court. There's a counterfactual version of this question, which asks whether, absent the time bar, Ledbetter could claim compensation under Title VII. That is a legal question, but the Court did not answer it, since it had no significance once the Court decided that Ledbetter's claim was time-barred.

There is, however, another question we can ask, which is not counterfactual. We can ask whether Ledbetter has a right to compensation that is not enforceable in court. I said already that she does. Quite apart from what any statute says, it is wrong to pay a person less because of her sex. And quite apart from the particulars of our legal practices, we ought to right our wrongs when we can. If Goodyear asked me for advice, I would tell them that they owe Ledbetter back pay plus interest, that they should pay it promptly, and that they should apologize, both for the original wrong and for taking so long to set it right.

It is possible, I suppose, that the justices who rejected Ledbetter's claim would agree with me. But I doubt that they ever entertained the question, since it runs beyond their writ. I said at the start that lawyers are apt to insist that they traffic in law, not morality. They are wrong about that. Law is a moral practice. When a plaintiff asserts a right in court, she is making a claim about what she is owed. But when lawyers distinguish law from morality, they are gesturing toward a distinction that plays an important role in our lives. We are entitled to enforce some of our rights in court, but not all of them. And we can be called to account for some of our wrongs in court, but not all of them.

In his last essay about law, Ronald Dworkin suggested that our legal rights are the rights that we are entitled to enforce in court.[48] I am hesitant to put things that way, at least absent explanation, because I think there are many ways to distinguish legal rights from the rest, depending on what we wish to emphasize. No doubt, a right is legal (in a sense) when it is enforceable through legal institutions. But a right can be legal in other senses too. For instance, a right might be legal in the sense that its source lies in the actions of legal institutions.[49] Or a right might be legal in the sense that legal officials are properly concerned with it.[50] There is overlap between these ways of thinking about what makes a right legal. Some rights tick all three boxes; perhaps those rights are paradigmatically legal. But the senses in which a right might be legal can come apart. For instance, some rights are not enforceable in court, but we nevertheless think legal officials ought to take them into account when deciding how to act. That is apt to be true whenever officials are protected from suit by an immunity or whenever the subject matter of the suit is regarded as nonjusticiable—perhaps because it involves state secrets or presents a political question to be resolved by the political branches without the supervision of courts.[51]

Among those who share the view I have set forth—that legal rights are just rights of the ordinary moral sort—there is much debate about how best to distinguish legal rights from the rest. I think that debate misguided; we should be happy to allow that there are different senses in which a right might qualify as legal. That said, Dworkin's distinction—between rights that are enforceable in court and those that are not—has practical significance for everyone who lives with law. It matters which of your rights you can enforce in court (or other adjudicative institutions) and which you can't. The other distinctions have their uses, but they are lawyers' distinctions, far removed from the concerns of most laypeople, at least most of the time. So from now on, when I talk about legal rights, I will speak as Dworkin suggests.[52] I will say that legal rights are the rights that we are entitled to enforce in court. You should, however, keep in mind that we might distinguish legal rights from the rest differently, depending on our aims and interests.

What's Distinctive about Law?

Once we put a spotlight on the rights that are enforceable in court, we can see why lawyers are likely to distance what they do from ordinary moral argument. Indeed, legal argument differs from ordinary moral argument in several dimensions. To start, the stakes are often higher, because there are institutions that stand prepared to act on the outcomes of the arguments, and in ways that can be awfully disruptive. Second, our legal rights and obligations are affected by those institutions' involvement. We witnessed that earlier, when we saw that a plaintiff's rights might depend on the statutes, regulations, and precedents that issue from legal institutions. But there are other ways in which institutional involvement affects people's rights and obligations. To rattle off two: Many of our legal obligations are over- or underinclusive as against the evil they aim to avoid, since legal institutions prize rules that are easy to articulate and administer. And the severity of the consequences that are often attached to legal wrongs generate notice requirements, so that obligations cannot be enforced unless the penalties for noncompliance have been announced in advance. Those sorts of requirements are not completely foreign to our everyday moral lives, but they are far less frequent.

We will return to some of these issues later, but I want to highlight one more way legal argument differs from ordinary moral argument, in part to suggest that we not make too much of it. Legal rights and obligations have distinctive sources. They typically trace to statutes, regulations, and precedents, so those are, unsurprisingly, the first places a lawyer will look to ascertain what rights a litigant might have. (This is why some are attracted to the idea that the source of an obligation determines whether it is legal.) Indeed, in a well-developed legal system, it may be that most, if not all, of the rights that are enforceable in court will rest, in some fashion, on the prior actions of legal institutions. It doesn't have to be that way. In some places, courts enforce customs that develop outside legal institutions. And some transitory courts (like the International Military Tribunal, which conducted the Nuremberg Trials) have enforced obligations that, at least arguably, did not rest on the prior actions of legal institutions.[53] But these are marginal cases. In the main, the rights and obligations that courts enforce are ones that were created by the actions of legal institutions.

Some people are taken by the fact that we create law.[54] And it's true. We do. But that does not mark law off from morality, since much of morality is made by us too. Indeed, most of the obligations that I have trace to decisions that I made. In a few minutes, I will call my father. I would feel obligated to call him in any event—he is not well—but I owe him a call at 9:00 p.m. tonight, because that's when I said I would call. In the morning, I must rouse my children in time to get them to school; that's my responsibility because they are mine, and they are mine as a result of decisions I made. Life is full of obligations we would not have but for the choices that we make. And our choices are not the only ones that matter. In a bit, I'll set this draft aside and grade my students' exams. I'm obligated to submit their grades shortly because the faculty committee responsible for such matters set a deadline, which is fast approaching. As I said before, there may be parts of morality that do not depend on what we do, but an awful lot of morality does. Legal rights and obligations are a part of that part of morality.

There are two further reasons that we should not make too much of the idea that legal rights and obligations have distinctive sources. First, the sources are not actually distinctive, as we have nonlegal obligations that trace to the actions of legal institutions. If the state were to lower the speed limit on the highway near my house, I might owe it to the people I carpool with to pick them up a bit earlier.[55] This is not a legal obligation in the sense we have adopted; it cannot be enforced in court. But the explanation of why I have the obligation runs through the actions of legal institutions. Second, even though our legal rights and obligations are, in some sense, traceable to the actions of legal institutions, they are traceable to much else besides. When legal institutions succeed in imposing obligations, they do so in virtue of moral principles that empower them to do so. In any given case, their power might trace to consent, or the value of democracy, or simply to their capacity to do something that morality demands be done.

Those involved in legal practices rarely spend much time thinking about why legal institutions have the power to determine our rights and obligations, at least not when they approve of them. They simply take it for granted that they do. (Though, as we shall see later on, questions about why they have that power burble up from time to time, even among those who take it for granted.) Of course, people might be wrong to take it for granted. As I've said, there is no guarantee that any legal practice will affect our rights and obligations at all, let alone in the way intended. The point I want to make is not that, in any given case, there are moral principles that empower legal institutions to determine people's rights and obligations. Rather, it is that legal institutions succeed in creating rights and obligations only if there are such principles.

Taking Stock

I started with the suggestion that law is a moral practice. Once that claim is clarified, I do not think it can be denied. There is no question that we employ legal practices in an effort to adjust who owes what to whom. I also suggested that litigation poses moral questions and that the rights and obligations contested in court are rights and obligations in the ordinary moral sense. Those are claims that can be denied. Indeed, they are often denied, in favor of the view that law is a separate normative system, similar to but separate from morality. We'll consider that view in Chapter 3. But first, we should further develop the idea that law is a moral practice. Once again, we can turn to Hank for help.

CHAPTER TWO

A Tale of Two Textualists

A Tiny Textualist

Hank eventually hit on another strategy for resisting the rule that required him to try all the food on his plate. One night for dinner, we served pesto pasta, sausage, and vegetables. Hank took a few bites, wincing all the while, then asked if he could have yogurt instead.

"Did you try the pasta?" Julie asked.

"No," Hank said. And then, with a sly smile, he added: "The pasta is in a bowl, not on my plate."

That was the moment at which Hank started to think like a lawyer. I was stunned—and proud. And for a split second, I was not sure what to say. We had always told Hank that he had to try the food on his plate. Now, this tiny textualist was holding us to that. He had tried the sausage and vegetables, which were, in fact, on his plate. But the pasta was in a bowl, so he did not have to try it.

Or so he thought. Was he right? There's no question that the pasta didn't fall within the rule we had articulated. But the way that we phrased the rule was an accident. Most nights, we served Hank's food on a plate, and that affected what we said. But we certainly intended that Hank try the food he was served, no matter how it was served. Had we thought about it, we would have told Hank just that. But we never thought about it, because we almost always served dinner on a plate, not in a bowl.

In that split second of silence, I made a quick calculation. We could let Hank off the hook and amend the rule going forward, so as to make clear that he must try all the food he is served, however it is served. Out of appreciation for Hank's clever lawyering, I was tempted to do just that. But I resisted the temptation. No amendment was needed; Hank was already required to try everything he was served. *That* was the rule we had adopted—and that was the rule that Hank was bound by—even though it was not the rule that we had announced.

Why do I say that? Sometimes, we have reasons to be fussy about language—to insist that people speak precisely and hold them to just what they said. But just as often—maybe even more often—there are reasons to be flexible and honor what was meant, though it may not have been said. Hank had little reason—and no right—to be fussy about our language. He was not structuring his affairs in reliance on the rules we had articulated. He was four years old; he had no affairs to structure. Of course, reliance is not the only reason to be fussy about language. As we'll see shortly, there are other reasons to insist that authorities speak precisely. But for now, I'll simply assert: none of them apply to parental authority.

At this point, some will be tempted to object: the rule in our house, they might say, just is whatever rule we articulated, not the rule we intended to impose, or the rule we would have imposed had we thought about it. Why would that be? Well, you might try to vindicate this view by appeal to Hart's picture, which we glimpsed back in the Introduction. Hart, you will recall, argued that every legal system has a rule of recognition—a rule for recognizing other rules of the system. The rule of recognition is constituted by a social practice; it exists because officials apply the rule and see themselves (and others) as obligated to do so. Though the Hershovitz household is not a legal system, Hart might have offered a similar analysis of the rules in our house. The rule of recognition, he might have said, is whatever rule Julie and I apply—and see ourselves as obligated to apply—in identifying the rules of our house. If our rule is that the rules of the house are what we say they are, then Hank would be right: the rule we announced required Hank to try the food on his plate, so we'd have to amend the rule if we wanted to insist that he try food served in a bowl too.

But Julie and I might have a different rule of recognition. We might, for instance, take the rules of the house to be the rules we intended to impose, whether or not we adequately articulated them. If that was our rule of recognition, Hank would be wrong. We intended that he try the food he was served, however it was served. The upshot is that Hank and his defenders cannot settle the argument simply by appeal to Hart's picture. To know whether he must try food served in a bowl, we'd have to figure out what the rule of recognition in our house is. And that presents a problem. Up to that point, nothing that Julie and I had ever said, thought, or done distinguished between these two rules of recognition. To that point, no one had ever noticed a difference between the rule we had announced and the rule we intended to impose, so we had never had occasion to resolve the question which rule governed in cases where they came apart. As between these two rules of recognition, our practice was indeterminate, with the consequence that there was (at that moment) no answer to the question whether the rules of the house required Hank to try food served in a bowl.

Hart was alive to the possibility that a rule of recognition could be indeterminate.[1] When it is, he said, officials have to make a decision. If the decision they make sticks, then it will establish the right answer going forward, even though the decision was neither right nor wrong when it was made. But that's not how the situation seemed to anybody in our house. Hank thought that he was in the clear, since the pasta was not on his plate. And I thought that he was required to taste it, since it had been served to him. In other words, both of us thought that the rules of our house resolved the question, though we disagreed about what the resolution was.

Of course, we could have been wrong about that. Hart's picture could be right, and our confidence could have been confused. But there's another way to see our dispute that makes our attitudes make sense—and doesn't require appeal to a rule of recognition, fixed in some fashion by past practice. Hank and I both acknowledged that, on many occasions, I had said he had to try the food on his plate. We simply disagreed about the moral significance of what I'd said. That is, we disagreed about the rights and responsibilities generated by my acts of legislation. As I re-counted in the Introduction, Hank once doubted that what I said counted at all. Now, he was tacitly conceding that what I said did count. Indeed, he took the view that what I said was all that counted. I said "plate," and this was not a plate, end of story. Or, at least, that's what Hank thought. I had a more complicated view. I thought that what I said mattered—there would be no requirement had I not said anything at all about what Hank was required to eat. But I also thought that what I meant mattered, even if it was not just what I said.

To meet the challenge Hank posed in the Introduction—when he flatly denied that what I said counted—I needed to make a case for my authority, and earlier I attempted to sketch one. To meet Hank's textu-alism, I'd need a different argument; that is, I'd need an argument for thinking that my act of legislation imposed a broader requirement than the one I had articulated. And that's just what I offered Hank when my stunned silence stopped. I told him that I was impressed by what he said. He was lawyering, just like his dad. But then I explained that we had told him that he had to try the food on his plate because, most nights, his food was on a plate. The point of the rule, I explained, was to make sure that he tried the food we served, and indeed, that was all along the rule we intended to impose, even though it was not the rule we an-nounced. I also explained that grown-ups sometimes get to insist that the people who make the rules speak precisely. But kids don't get to in-sist on that, I explained, because parents make rules to help kids, so what they mean matters more than what they say.

I don't know how much of that Hank followed. He acquiesced more quickly than normal, giving the pasta a quick bite. I'd like to think that's because he sensed that his argument wasn't sound. More likely, he was hungry. Or bored. Or both.

A Not-So-Tiny Textualist

Hank is a tiny textualist. (Or, at least, he was. I hope I nipped that in the bud.) Justice Scalia was not a tiny textualist; indeed his outsize person-ality almost singlehandedly brought the position to prominence, if not quite dominance, among American lawyers. Nobody was a more forceful advocate of the idea that the words of a statute matter—and that nothing else does, at least when the words are clear. Why did Scalia think so? Happily, we don't have to guess. He wrote a book, called *A Matter of Interpretation*.[2] Hart is nowhere to be found in it, not by name and not in spirit.

In the book, Scalia argues that "[t]he text [of a statute] is the law, and it is the text that must be observed."[3] He says that he agrees with Justice Holmes, who once offered the following report: "Only a day or two ago—when counsel talked of the intention of a legislature, I was indiscreet enough to say that I don't care what their intention was. I only want to know what the words mean."[4] Why did Scalia think that the words of a statute—and not the intentions with which they were adopted—determine people's rights and duties? If he had Hart in mind, he might have offered an argument about the rule of recognition in the United States. That is, he might have argued that judges in the United States accept a rule according to which the meaning of a statute is determined by its text, and not the intentions with which it was adopted. On Hart's view, that is the only thing that could establish that the text—and the text alone—determines the legal significance of a statute. If judges had the opposite practice—if they routinely looked for legislative intent, perhaps treating the text as important but inconclusive evidence of it—then Hart would say that the rule the legislature intended to adopt was the law, whether or not it was expressed in the text.

So what is the shared practice among legal officials in the United States? As Scalia explains, there is none. The situation in American courts, he says, is "accurately described" by Henry Hart and Albert Sacks's famous treatise, *The Legal Process:* "Do not expect anybody's theory of statutory interpretation, whether it is your own or somebody else's, to be an accurate statement of what courts actually do with statutes. The hard truth of the matter is that American Courts have no intelligible, generally accepted, and consistently applied theory of statutory interpretation."[5] That would not have bothered our Hart (that is, H. L. A., not Henry).[6] In absence of a generally accepted rule for determining the law generated by an act of legislation, he would have thought the law indeterminate.[7] Presumably, he would have seen Scalia's book as an effort to persuade judges to adopt a textualist approach, so as to render the rule of recognition determinate going forward. But while Scalia certainly did aim to persuade judges (and lawyers more generally), he aimed to sway them toward a view that he thought right already, notwithstanding the absence of a generally accepted rule for identifying the meaning of a statute. He was emphatic: "The text is the law, and it is the text that must be observed."[8] And he was not shy about declaring decisions that departed from this view "wrong" for failure "to follow the text."[9]

This was not just bluster. Hart's partisans sometimes suggest that lawyers, like Scalia, insist that there is law, even where there are no shared tests for identifying it, simply in the hopes of hoodwinking people.[10] The thought is that if they can con enough people, or at least the right people, then they can make the law what they want it to be, by bringing about the agreement necessary to render the rule of recognition determinate. But Scalia was not attempting to hoodwink anyone. Right at the start, he acknowledges that textualism is not a consensus view—far from it. He discusses decisions he disagrees with, at length, some of which he dissented from. And he acknowledges that the views he opposes are so firm a feature of the legal firmament that lawyers routinely brief them to the Supreme Court. In fact, he quotes a brief he found particularly irksome because it addressed legislative history *before* it took up the text of the statute. "Unfortunately, the legislative debates are not helpful," the brief declared, "[t]hus, we turn to the other guidepost in this difficult area, statutory language."[11] That sentence is, perhaps, the apotheosis of everything Scalia opposed, so much so that one wonders whether it was written to make him mad. But the point is that Scalia never denied that the view he decried had an awful lot of adherents, even among the members of his own Court. He simply thought his opponents wrong.

In insisting that textualism determined the content of the law, notwithstanding the lack of agreement about it, Scalia implicitly rejected Hart's picture. But he did offer an argument for his textualism, and tellingly, it took just the form that I've suggested it should have. Scalia offered a moral argument, grounded in the nature of democracy and a claim about the proper role of a judge within it. It's worth examining his argument in some detail, since it will help us to see that the question how acts of legislation affect people's rights and responsibilities is, at bottom, a moral question.[12]

Scalia opens his book with a description of what judges do when they decide common-law cases.[13] The description is defamatory, but it is important to repeat it since it is the backdrop for Scalia's argument about the right way to read statutes. According to Scalia, the common-law judge plays "king—devising, out of the brilliance of [his] own mind, those laws that ought to govern mankind" and then imposing them on the litigants.[14] The image of the great common-law judge, he explains,

> is the man (or woman) who has the intelligence to discern the best rule of law for the case at hand and the skill to perform the broken-field running through earlier cases that leaves him free to impose that rule: distinguishing one prior case on the left, straight-arming another one on the right, high-stepping away from another precedent about to tackle him from the rear, until (bravo!) he reaches the goal—good law.[15]

The mindset of the common-law judge, he says, is to ask, "What is the most desirable resolution of this case, and how can any impediments to the achieving of that result be evaded?"

As I said, this description is defamatory.[16] There are, no doubt, judges for whom it's apt. But a great many common-law judges (and all the great ones) are engaged in the project described in Chapter 1: trying to work out the rights and responsibilities of the parties to a case, in light of the past history of their political communities, which (in common-law countries) includes a great many decisions that bear on those rights and responsibilities. They treat those past decisions not as impediments, but as something akin to commitments and, therefore, constraints on the decisions that the judges make. They do not always agree on what those constraints are and why. But the common law is an extended conversation about (among other things) just that. Indeed, even judges who deserve Scalia's description surely sense that they are going about things the wrong way, for if they really were kings, free to do as they pleased, they would not have to pretend to care about yesterday's cases.

I have a sunnier view of the common law than Scalia does. I'd like to think that's because I am more intimately familiar with it, as a result of teaching and writing about tort law. As Scalia points out, the docket in the federal courts is almost completely devoid of common-law cases, and when they do arise, it is typically through diversity jurisdiction, which puts the federal judge in the odd position of predicting how a state court would resolve the case.[17] So Scalia did not have many occasions to wrestle with contested questions in the common law, at least not in the way that a common-law judge would. But ultimately, it does not matter whether you share Scalia's cynicism about common-law judges or accept my sunnier view. What matters is that Scalia saw in common-law judges the very attitude he insisted was inappropriate for statutory interpretation. "[A]ttacking the enterprise with the Mr. Fix-it mentality of the common-law judge is a sure recipe," he insisted, "for incompetence and usurpation."[18]

Those are strong words. What backs them up? Scalia starts by observing that judges often say their aim in interpreting a statute is giving effect to the intent of the legislature.[19] But, he continues, judges do not seem to be interested in the actual intentions of legislatures (or even legislators). Rather, he says, they "look for a sort of 'objectified' intent—the intent that a reasonable person would gather from the text of the law, when placed alongside the remainder of the *corpus juris*."[20] Among other things, he points out, judges interpret statutes in light of previously enacted laws, on the almost certainly counterfactual assumption that the present legislature was aware of those laws and intended to legislate in a manner consistent with them.[21] This emphasis on objective intent—as opposed to actual, or subjective, intent—makes sense, Scalia says, because "it is simply incompatible with democratic government, or indeed, even with fair government, to have the meaning of a law determined by what the lawgiver meant, rather than by what the lawgiver promulgated."[22] Indeed, he says that this is "one step worse than the trick the emperor Nero was said to engage in: posting edicts high up on the pillars, so they could not easily be read."[23]

This is the first appearance of democracy in Scalia's argument, but not the last, for he does not endorse the search for objective intent. The worry that we might be "bound by genuine but unexpressed legislative intent," he explains, "is only the *theoretical* threat. The *practical* threat is that, under the guise or even the self-delusion of pursuing unexpressed legislative intents, common-law judges will in fact pursue their own objectives

and desires, extending their lawmaking proclivities from the common
law to the statutory field."[24] He adds:

> When you are told to decide, not on the basis of what the legislature said,
> but on the basis of what it *meant,* and are assured there is no necessary
> connection between the two, your best shot at figuring out what the leg-
> islature meant is to ask yourself what a wise and intelligent person *should*
> have meant; and that will bring you to the conclusion that the law means
> what you think it ought to mean—which is precisely how judges decide
> things under the common law.[25]

Now, it is worth noting that this passage is a sequence of non sequiturs.
The possibility of a gap between what a legislature said and what it meant
does not imply that what it said does not matter, even if all you are interested in is figuring out what it meant. There is typically a tight connection
between the two. Moreover, the best way to figure out what someone
meant is not to ask what you think they should have meant. You are,
after all, different people, with (at least, potentially) different values, aims,
and access to information. To make sense of a speaker, you do need to assume that she's reasonable—but reasonable in light of what you know
about her values, her ambitions, her beliefs, and so on. Most of us have
no trouble figuring out what people mean when they speak, even if we
would not have said or meant what they did. The fact that Scalia sees
nothing but temptation in the task of looking for legislative intent might
tell us more about him than that task.

In any event, Scalia does see temptation, and he can, to be sure, point
to cases where judges seem to succumb to it. His parade of horribles starts
with *Church of the Holy Trinity v. United States.*[26] In that nearly never celebrated case, the Court confronted a statute that made it unlawful to "encourage the importation or migration of any alien . . . into the United
States, . . . under contract or agreement . . . made previous to the importation or migration of such alien . . . to perform labor or service of any
kind in the United States."[27] A church challenged a fine imposed pursuant to the statute on account of the fact that it had imported an im-
migrant to serve as rector. Though the plain terms of the statute seemed
to cover the case, the Court concluded that the legislature could not have

intended to prohibit the importation of clergy. In fact, there is evidence to suggest that the legislature considered the question and had that intent.[28] So *Church of the Holy Trinity* is indeed an awful decision. Whether it is representative is another question. Scalia thinks yes; I think no. But thinking the answer yes, Scalia returns to democracy, announcing that "[i]t is simply not compatible with democratic theory that the laws mean whatever they ought to mean, and that unelected judges decide what that is."[29]

We should unpack that sentence carefully. Here again, Scalia invokes democracy—indeed, democratic theory. He does not tell us why it is incompatible with democracy for laws to mean whatever they ought to mean, but it is not hard to figure out what he had in mind.[30] The last phrase—about "unelected judges"—is the tell. Scalia is worried that the People—the demos, if you prefer—would not have control of the law if unelected judges could pour any content they liked into it. In a democracy, Scalia thinks, that task belongs to the legislature, which is accountable to the People through the electoral process. Since the alternatives to textualism strike Scalia as invitations for the judges to substitute their own preferences for the decisions made by the People's representatives, he insists that the "[t]he text is the law, and it is the text that must be observed."[31]

The argument is a touch too dramatic for my taste. I don't think that *Holy Trinity* (or the many nontextualist opinions from which Scalia dissented) damaged democracy to any significant degree. Moreover, Scalia overlooks something significant about authority. Sometimes the best way to honor someone's authority is to do what she meant, rather than what she said.[32] Imagine, for a moment, a mother who calls home and tells her child to take out the trash. A short while later, she calls back frantically: "Did I say take out the trash? I meant the recycling. The recycling truck is coming." Now, imagine that her kid replies, "Yeah, Mom, I knew what you meant. I put the recycling out." That is a good kid, and importantly, it is a kid who paid heed to his mother's authority. Had he done what she said—knowing all along that it was not what she meant—he would have been at least as defiant as if he had done nothing at all, maybe even more so.[33] As a first cut, then, we might suppose that democracy requires deference to the decisions that democratic authorities make, whether or not they are adequately articulated in the legislation that they produce.

To reach the opposite conclusion, we'd need to suppose that there is something that sets democratic authorities apart, such that deference to their authority demands doing just what they said, no matter what they meant. Scalia's worry about unelected judges usurping the authority of democratically constituted legislatures is supposed to push us in that direction. But it is simply not true that any attempt to figure out what an authority meant inexorably leads one to substitute one's own judgment for the authority's. In a moment, we'll see an illustration of that—a case in which one of Scalia's conservative colleagues deferred to legislative intent when interpreting a progressive piece of legislation that he almost certainly thought misguided. So Scalia's main argument is not so impressive.

There are, however, other arguments that might mark democratic authorities as different. Democratic authorities are political authorities, and we might think it particularly important for political authorities to provide people notice about the rules that will be applied. As you'll recall, Scalia invoked Nero posting edicts atop pillars to make this point. And it is a good point, at least up to a point. There are circumstances in which notice is important. When the criminal law creates malum prohibitum, it is not fair to punish people unless they had notice of the prohibition.[34] Similar, but different: when courts establish rules for the interpretation of insurance contracts, it is important that insurers know them, so that they can properly price their products. But the considerations that make it unfair or unwise not to provide notice of the rules that will apply are local and limited. In other contexts, it might be helpful to leave the rules a bit obscure.[35] Or if not helpful, at least not so bad, since no one has need to rely on the rules. In the case that we will come to in a moment, *King v. Burwell,* no one was harmed by implementing congressional intent, though an awful lot of people would have been harmed by sticking to the language of the statute. So the notice-oriented argument for textualism is not so impressive either, except perhaps in local and limited domains.

There is, however, another argument for textualism. Scalia does not state it so clearly, but it is implicit in much that he says. Representative democracy is predicated on the idea that representatives are accountable to the People for what they do. The People will not be able to police their representatives if they cannot identify the law that they make. So, we might think, it is important that the law be transparent, and one way to promote that is to insist that the law just is what the text of the laws adopted say. Alas, this argument is not so impressive either. In the circumstances of modern democracies, it is not easy for people to ascertain the law, even if we understand the law simply to be a set of texts. There are too many texts to keep track of. It can be difficult to locate the ones that are relevant. And they are often written in ways that are obscure even to lawyers. Moreover, judicial decisions that clarify the meaning of legislation can themselves provide occasions for the People to exercise democratic control, as the swift reaction to *Ledbetter* (discussed in Chapter 1) illustrates. All things considered, it may be better if the meaning of an act of legislation is transparent to laypeople at the moment of its adoption, but democracy is hardly dead if its meaning unfolds more slowly.

That's enough about Scalia's argument—well, almost. Before we go on, I want to make two more observations about it. First, as Ronald Dworkin once noted, Scalia cannot escape the search for legislative intent. "Any reader of anything," Dworkin pointed out, "must attend to semantic intention." As Dworkin explained,

> the same sounds or even words can be used with the intention of saying different things. If I tell you (to use Scalia's own example) that I admire bays, you would have to decide whether I intended to say that I admired certain horses or certain bodies of water. Until you had, you would have no idea what I'd actually said even though you would know what sounds I had uttered.[36]

Semantic intentions are intentions to say something (in speech or writing), and as Dworkin observes, Scalia is open to considering them—and not just to resolve ambiguities that trace to words with multiple meanings. Scalia says he is also willing to correct scrivener's errors—slips of the pen, so to speak, that result in the text saying something other than what was intended.[37] The intentions that Scalia resists relying on, Dworkin explained, are intentions (or expectations or hopes) about the consequences of legislation. And, interestingly, Dworkin agreed that judges ought not appeal to those sorts of intentions in deciding what a statute demands.

I would not have been so quick as Dworkin to concede that point, since it strikes me that there are more distinctions to be drawn here.[38] There is a difference between the rule that one intended to impose and the hopes or expectations one had about how that rule would apply. The former, I think, might deserve deference on at least some occasions, as my attitude toward my dispute with Hank indicated. In just a second, we'll turn to *King v. Burwell,* which illustrates the point even better. (Scalia dissented.) But Dworkin's point aside, Scalia deserves credit for offering the right sort of argument in support of his textualism. The dispute between Scalia and his critics—several of whom sat on the same bench as he did—was about the moral significance of an act of legislation. That is, it was about the way in which—and the reasons for which—acts of legislation adjust people's rights and duties. The answer is not to be found in a shared practice; there is none, and even if there was, the shared practice could be mistaken. The only way to answer the question is to mount an argument about how and why legislation makes a moral difference, and that's just what Scalia did, through his appeal to democratic theory.

That brings us to the last point. On first glance, there is something odd in Scalia's argument. He is hyperconcerned about judges who would, in deciding cases, impose their own moral views on the litigants, rather than follow the law as written. Why? Well, he's got a moral view about the nature of democracy and the proper role of a judge within it. According to that view, judges should set aside their views about what good law would be. And they should decline to ascertain the law the legislature intended to adopt, lest they have a chance to smuggle their own views in under that guise. In other words, Scalia relied on *his* moral views to conclude that judges must not rely on *their* moral views in deciding cases.

Is that inconsistent? No. The moral views Scalia draws on are different than those he deems irrelevant. In fact, he's right to say that a judge ought not impute to litigants the rights and duties that she thinks they ought to have. As we saw in Chapter 1, the question posed in court is what rights and duties the parties do have, and nothing guarantees that those are the rights and duties they ought to have. That said, judges *must* rely on their moral views to resolve the cases that come before them.

They have to decide how acts of legislation (and other bits of our political history) bear on the rights and responsibilities of the parties. The questions posed in court are moral questions, since they are questions about who owes what to whom. There is no way to answer them but through moral argument.[39]

A Tale of Two Buttons

We got deep in the weeds with Scalia's case for textualism. Let's liven things up by digging into the details of a statute! No, seriously—it's worth working these ideas through in the context of a case. In fact, it's worth working through the entire picture presented so far, so we'll take a moment to build up to the case. I want you to imagine that you are presented with two buttons and told the following. If you push Button A, then eight million people who presently have health insurance will lose it because it will become, for them, unaffordable. This will have knock-on consequences. Some of those people will be in the midst of medical treatment they cannot pay for themselves; if they cannot cobble together the funds to continue—from family, friends, or charity—then that treatment will cease. For some of those people, the consequences will be dire, up to and including death. But other catastrophes will unfold slowly, as people put off medical care or skip it entirely so as to avoid bills that are no longer covered by insurance. As a result, many people will lead sicker, shorter lives than they would have had you not pushed Button A. Happily, there is another button, and you only have to push one. If you push Button B, you are told, nothing will happen; those eight million people will maintain their health insurance.

Which button would you push? If that's all you knew, you might think that there's a clear-cut case for Button B. But you suspect that there's more to the story, so you ask: Why will health insurance become unaffordable for the eight million if I push Button A? And then you learn that the government subsidizes their health insurance. If you push Button A, those subsidies will stop. All the consequences just mentioned will come to pass, but the government will save the money that it pays out in subsidies, so it will be available to be put to other purposes—investments in roads or schools, retirement security, restoration of polluted lands—the possibilities are nearly endless. Or, instead, the government could cut taxes and raise less revenue.

Now what seemed like a simple choice might strike you as a harder one, and you might want more information as you think it through. You face a policy question—how much money to raise and how to spend it—which is similar to the questions that legislatures face every day. Of course, a legislature has many more buttons to push. But the job is the same: decide which button is best to push.

Now I want you to imagine a different backstory for those buttons. The setup is still the same. If you push Button A, eight million people will lose their health insurance, since it will become, for them, unaffordable. If you push Button B, nothing will happen. The subsidies that make their health insurance affordable will continue to flow. But this time you are not asked which button you think it best to push. Rather, you are told, a group of people say that you owe it to them to push Button A—that they have a right that you do so—and your job is to figure out whether they do indeed have that right. If they do, you should push Button A; if not, Button B.[40]

This was more or less the choice presented to the Supreme Court in a case called *King v. Burwell*.[41] The Supreme Court pushed Button B, over the vigorous dissent of Justice Scalia, who would have pushed Button A. Which button would you have pushed? Unless you know a lot about the case, I hope you think, "I don't know yet." Because I have not told you much, if anything, that bears on the question whether the plaintiffs had a right that the Court press Button A. What does bear on that question? To answer that, we need to know more precisely what their claim was, and that requires that we learn a bit about a statute called the Patient Protection and Affordable Care Act (more popularly known as the ACA, or Obamacare). Pursuant to the ACA, the government subsidized the purchase of health insurance for some people who could not otherwise afford it. The plaintiffs in the case came to court seeking an order declaring them ineligible for the subsidies.[42] Why would anyone do that? Well, another provision of the ACA required that anyone who could afford health insurance purchase it or pay a penalty for failure to do so. The plaintiffs did not want to purchase health insurance. If they were declared ineligible for the subsidy, then according to the statutory formula, they would no longer be able to afford it, and they would be released from the requirement to buy it.[43] If that sounds a bit convoluted, it was. In a typical case, the plaintiff asserts that she has a right and the defendant denies it. Here, the plaintiffs asserted that they lacked a right—that they were ineligible for the subsidies. The defendant, Sylvia Burwell, who was then the secretary of health and human services, insisted that the plaintiffs had the right they disclaimed.

Now, you know a bit more about the dispute. Do you know which button you would push? I hope the answer is still no, but it's worth pausing to ask why you should care about any details beyond the ones I've already given you. If you push Button A, you seriously disrupt the lives of millions of people, quite likely killing some of them. If you push the other button, none of that happens. Moreover, there's another institution—Congress—that could move the money to other purposes if it thought it wise to do so. Congress is also capable of gathering information to decide whether it is wise, and if it decides that it is, it has tools for managing the transition so as to limit the downside for those affected. You, on the other hand, have just these two buttons. So, you might think, the case for Button B is strong. But notice that nothing in what I've said so far answers the question you were asked to answer: whether the plaintiffs have a right to an order declaring them ineligible for the subsidies.

Or does it? Here's a line of argument that suggests we already know enough to know the answer. The order the plaintiffs seek would disrupt the lives of millions of people. How on earth could the plaintiffs have a right to do that, given that the only thing at stake for them is their wish not to purchase something they ought to purchase anyway?[44] The plaintiffs are being selfish, you might think, so they cannot have a right to the order that they seek. That's not a terrible argument. Until, that is, you notice that there is more at stake here than whether eight million people lose their health insurance. What else is at stake? Well, remember way back at the start when I said that we need to find ways to live together, notwithstanding the fact that we disagree about how to live? Around here, the political process set out in the Constitution plays that role. Congress decides what revenue to raise and how to spend it, subject to a few limitations spelled out elsewhere the document. Maybe Congress should not have that power; maybe there should be more limitations. But, as I said before, we have no prospect of agreeing on any better process, at least not now. And that gives us reasons to respect this one.

There are also reasons to think that our process is roughly the right one—or rather, the right sort of one—in that it is, broadly speaking, democratic. I will not rehearse the reasons to make decisions democratically; you probably know them as well as I do.[45] There are problems with our particular democracy—lots of them. But there is also value in a system that, among other things, holds regular elections, provides opportunities to participate in the political process, and guarantees both free speech and a free press. That value provides reason to defer to the system's outputs, even as we work to improve it. Or so I think. As you'll see in a moment, the justices of the Supreme Court agreed, at least implicitly. And that's not a surprise, since it would be hard to get that gig if you did not think the system broadly legitimate. But it might not be. Later on, we'll consider systems that are so awful no one has any reason to respect them. I do not think ours is, at present, one of them, though there are reasons to worry that we are trending in that direction. But for now, I'll proceed as if we do have reasons to respect the decisions that Congress makes, since I think it plausible that we do, at least in the vast majority of cases.

As I said, the Constitution grants Congress the power to decide how to spend the money that it raises. So the question whether the plaintiffs in *King* had a right to receive subsidies depends on whether Congress granted them that right. The plaintiffs said no, Congress did not grant them that right. Their argument was straightforward. The ACA directed states to establish health care exchanges.[46] If any state failed to do so, the Act had a fallback provision: it directed the secretary of health and human services to "establish and operate such Exchange within the State."[47] The subsidies at issue were called "premium assistance credits," and a provision deep in the bowels of the Act set the amount of those credits. According to the provision, the dollar value of the credit depended on the number of months that a taxpayer was enrolled in an insurance plan "through an Exchange established by the State under section 1311 of the Patient Protection and Affordable Care Act."[48] The plaintiffs argued that they could not purchase health insurance through an exchange *established by a state,* since their home state, Virginia, had declined to establish an exchange under the Act. Virginia had an exchange, but it was established by the secretary, rather than the state. Therefore, the plaintiffs said, they were ineligible to receive premium assistance credits.

As you might guess, Justice Scalia found that argument persuasive. Indeed, he marveled at the fact that the case had reached the Court at all:

> This case requires us to decide whether someone who buys insurance on an Exchange established by the Secretary gets tax credits. You would think the answer would be obvious—so obvious there would hardly be a need for the Supreme Court to hear a case about it. In order to receive any money under § 36B, an individual must enroll in an insurance plan through an "Exchange established by the State." The Secretary of Health and Human Services is not a State. So an Exchange established by the Secretary is not an Exchange established by the State—which means people who buy health insurance through such an Exchange get no money under § 36B.[49]

He concluded: "Words no longer have meaning if an Exchange that is not established by a State is 'established by the State.'"[50]

That's a compelling argument. So why was Scalia dissenting from a decision written by his conservative colleague, Chief Justice Roberts? Roberts agreed with Scalia that, when "statutory language is plain, we must enforce it according to its terms."[51] But, he observed, "oftentimes the 'meaning—or ambiguity—of certain words or phrases only becomes evident when placed in context.'"[52] So, he explained, "when deciding whether the language is plain, we must read the words 'in their context and with a view to their place in the overall statutory scheme.'"[53] Roberts then went on to argue that the phrase "established by the State" was in fact ambiguous. I will not detail all his arguments here, since they are rather detailed.[54] Roughly, Roberts argued that, if you construed the phrase "established by the State" in the way that the plaintiffs did—as excluding state exchanges established by the secretary—other provisions of the Act became almost nonsensical. Far from operating as a backstop, exchanges established by the secretary would turn out not even to count as "Exchanges" under the Act, and no one would be qualified to purchase health insurance on them.[55] He concluded: "The phrase may be limited in its reach to State Exchanges. But it is also possible that the phrase refers to *all* Exchanges—both State and Federal—at least for the purposes of tax credits."[56]

Having concluded that the phrase could be read either way, Roberts looked to the structure of the Act to clarify its content. He pointed out that the ACA adopted three major reforms of the individual insurance market. First, the Act barred insurers from denying coverage or charging a higher rate on account of an applicant's health. (These policies are called *guaranteed issue* and *community rating*.) As attractive as that sounds, if those policies were adopted on their own, they would pose a serious problem: if people know that they will not be denied coverage or charged higher rates on account of their health, they might wait until they are sick to purchase health insurance. In insurance lingo, that's called *adverse selection,* and it results in a less healthy insurance pool than you would have absent guaranteed issue and community rating. Insurers' costs would go up, so they would raise rates. That would drive more healthy people from the pool, which means rates would have to go even higher, leading even more healthy people to leave the pool . . . and so on, until the whole thing collapsed of its own weight. This process has a cheerful name; it is a called a *death spiral.*

To head off death spirals, the ACA adopted a second reform. It mandated that all individuals maintain health insurance or pay a penalty; that gave healthy people an incentive to participate in the insurance pool. But the mandate poses another problem: some people cannot afford insurance. Thus, the third reform: subsidies to help those who could not afford coverage on their own. As Roberts explained, "these three reforms work together to expand insurance coverage,"[57] which was the main aim of the ACA.

Absent the subsidies, the reforms would not work. The subsidies mattered on their own. But they also mattered because the mandate to purchase coverage had an escape hatch for people who would have to spend more than 8 percent of their income on premiums.[58] The evidence suggested that, in 2014, nearly 90 percent of people who purchased insurance through a federally established exchange did so with tax credits, and nearly all of them would have been exempt from the mandate to pur-

chase coverage without them.[59] Absent the subsidies and an effective mandate, the guaranteed issue and community rating requirements would
push federally established exchanges into death spirals. Indeed, the Court
cited one study that predicted that "premiums would increase by 47%
and enrollment would decrease by 70%."[60] Moreover, the Act would have
spillover effects on markets outside the exchanges, since the ACA required
"insurers to treat the entire individual market as a single risk pool."[61]

Roberts concluded: "It is implausible that Congress meant the Act to
operate in this manner."[62] But that was not the only reason that he had
for thinking that Congress meant to make subsidies available on all state
exchanges, whether established by the state itself or by the secretary of
health and human services acting in its stead. On the plaintiff's view of the
statute, he pointed out, "Congress made the viability of the entire Affordable Care Act turn on the ultimate ancillary provision: a sub-sub-sub
section of the Tax Code. We doubt that is what Congress meant to do."[63]
Had Congress meant to limit subsidies to exchanges created by the states,
he suggested, it would have made the intention apparent, not left it to be
inferred from the formula for calculating the size of subsidies.

Roberts wrapped up by acknowledging that we should be wary of
attempts to infer intent from the context and structure of a statute, "lest
what professes to be mere rendering becomes creation and attempted interpretation of legislation becomes legislation itself."[64] "In a democracy,"
he said, "the power to make laws rests with those chosen by the people."[65]
"In every case," he added, "we must respect the role of the Legislature,
and take care not to undo what it has done."[66] But, he concluded, "[a]
fair reading of legislation demands a fair understanding of the legislative
plan. Congress passed the Affordable Care Act to improve health insurance markets, not to destroy them. If at all possible, we must interpret
the Act in a way that is consistent with the former, and avoids the latter."[67]
On the basis of his understanding of the legislative plan, Roberts (and
the majority he wrote for) decided that the plaintiffs had the right they
disclaimed.

Scalia would have none of this. He called it "interpretive jiggery-
pokery,"[68] and he offered a point-by-point rebuttal. Once again, I won't
detail the details. They matter. But the dispute came down to competing
visions of the Court's role vis-à-vis Congress. "Only by concentrating

on the law's terms," Scalia argued, "can a judge hope to uncover the scheme of *the statute,* rather than some other scheme that the judge thinks desirable."[69] That's an echo of his argument from *A Matter of Interpretation,* though it's a bit dissonant here, since Roberts (a Republican appointee) almost surely did not think the scheme laid out in the ACA desirable. But Scalia did not rest there. Responding to Roberts's frank acknowledgment that the drafting of the Affordable Care Act did "not reflect the type of care and deliberation that one might expect of such significant legislation,"[70] Scalia insisted that it was not the Court's "place to judge the quality of the care and deliberation that went into this or any other law."[71] "Much less," he continued, "is it [the Court's] place to make everything come out right when Congress does not do its job properly. It is up to Congress to design its laws with care, and it is up to the people to hold them to account if they fail to carry out that responsibility."[72] He concluded: "Rather than rewriting the law under the pretense of interpreting it, the Court should have left it to Congress to decide what to do about the Act's limitation on tax credits to state Exchanges. . . . The Court's insistence on making a choice that should be made by Congress both aggrandizes judicial power and encourages congressional lassitude."[73]

Pause now and ask: Who in this debate is deferential to Congress? Roberts, who aims to implement Congress's plan, as best he understands it, though it almost surely would not have been his plan had he been in Congress? Or Scalia, who thinks that Congress should be stuck with the consequences if it did not "do its job properly" and express its intent in its text? I don't mean to suggest that deference to Congress is the sole metric by which we should judge who has the best of this argument; that itself is a conclusion that requires an argument. But these passages put Scalia's paean to democracy in a different light; the modest judge has turned into a schoolmarm, who will do what Congress said, rather than what it meant, just to teach it a lesson and lessen its lassitude.

Plainly, I think that Roberts has the better of the argument. But the outcome of the argument is not my primary concern.[74] What matters, for our purposes, is the form that the argument took. Scalia and Roberts did not disagree about the words of the statute or whether Congress had enacted it. They disagreed about the significance of the fact that Congress had enacted a statute with the words that it did.[75] Scalia thought that the words mattered—and indeed that they were all that mattered, since their meaning was clear. Congress said "exchange established by a state," and this was not an exchange established by a state, end of story. Hank would be proud. Roberts's view was more complicated. He thought that what Congress said mattered—there would be no subsidies had Congress said nothing about them. But he thought that what Congress meant mattered too, even if it was not just what it said.

This was a moral disagreement. It was a disagreement about the rights and responsibilities generated by an act of legislation. Absolutely everyone at the Court accepted that Congress had the power to grant the plaintiffs the right they disclaimed. (Or, if they had any doubts about that, they kept them to themselves.) The question was whether Congress had effectively exercised that power. And the justices divided over that question because they had competing visions of democracy and the proper role of judges within one. Both sides could point to past decisions that supported their views, but no side could point to a consensus—or anything close to one—about the way in which, and the reasons for which, acts of legislation generate rights and responsibilities. But that does not mean that neither side was right, because neither side's arguments depended on the existence of consensus, or anything close. The arguments stood or fell on their moral merit, which should be no surprise since the claims asserted in court are moral claims—claims about who owes what to whom.

There is nothing unique about *King*, except perhaps that it made manifest the moral underpinnings of the legal claims, since they were so deeply contested. That is characteristic of the cases that reach the high Court. Where everyone agrees about people's rights and duties, cases settle or are settled in lower courts. Some people think that there is no law in the cases that reach the Supreme Court, on account of the fact that they are so deeply contested.[76] But disagreement about what the law is does not imply that there is no law, since the existence of rights and responsibilities that courts are obligated to enforce does not (at least, not generally) depend on consensus about them.

That is why it makes sense for judges like Roberts and Scalia to make claims about what the law is—about what people's rights and duties are—notwithstanding the fact that their colleagues disagree. Indeed, seeing that legal disputes are, at bottom, moral disputes, helps explain their depth and persistence, since morality is something that we disagree about, deeply and persistently. But it is important to be clear: The moral disagreements that play out in court are not disagreements about the rights and responsibilities that people ought to have. (Roberts and Scalia probably agreed on that: no subsidies for health insurance.) And they are not arguments about how best to fill gaps in the law. (Roberts and Scalia probably would have agreed about that too, had either of them seen a gap and thought it his job to fill it.) Rather, they are disagreements about the rights and responsibilities that people actually have.

CHAPTER THREE

Not a Set of Norms

Do Justice, Justice

There's a story that lawyers pass around, endlessly, which is supposed to tell us something about the relationship between law and morality (though just what it is supposed to tell us differs depending on who does the telling).[1] Ronald Dworkin, who was a law clerk for Learned Hand, one of the characters in the story, told it this way:

> When Oliver Wendell Holmes was an Associate Justice of the Supreme Court he gave the young Learned Hand a lift in his carriage as Holmes made his way to the Court. Hand got out at his destination, waved after the departing carriage, and called out merrily, "Do justice, Justice!" Holmes stopped the cab, made the driver turn around, and rode back to the astonished Hand. "That's not my job!" he said, leaning out the window. Then the carriage turned and departed, taking Holmes back to his job of allegedly not doing justice.[2]

Hand, however, told the story differently:

> I remember once I was with him; it was a Saturday when the Court was to confer. It was before we had a motor car, and we jogged along in an

old coupe. When we got down to the Capitol, I wanted to provoke a response, so as he walked off, I said to him: "Well, sir, goodbye. Do justice!" He turned quite sharply and he said: "Come here. Come here." I answered: "Oh, I know, I know." He replied: "That is not my job. My job is to play the game according to the rules."[3]

Dworkin sets us up to be shocked that Holmes—a man who goes by the title *Justice*—does not see it as his job to do justice. He casts Hand as the hero for encouraging the Justice to do just that. Hand, however, wants us to know that he was in on the joke, or at least anticipated it.

It does not matter which version of the story was true—probably Hand's, though even he may have massaged the facts to fit the point he was making. What interests me is the last bit of what Holmes said in Hand's telling of the story: "My job is to play the game according to the rules." There are many ways to read that statement, and we should be careful not to overread it. If I had to guess, Holmes was counseling a kind of restraint.[4] That is, he was denying that, as a justice, he had a roving mandate to pursue justice in the cases that came before him.

If that is all Holmes meant, then what he said is consistent with the picture presented so far. I argued that litigation poses moral questions, but the moral questions posed in court are quite narrow: in most cases, the question is whether the plaintiff has the right she asserts. A person can have a right that she ought not to have, or lack a right that she ought to have, so there is no guarantee that enforcing a person's rights will be a way of doing justice.[5] Moreover, it can be wrong to stand on your rights, and one way in which it might be wrong is that doing so could promote injustice. In recent years, white supremacists marched through Charlottesville, Virginia, to protest the city's decision to remove Confederate monuments. The largest of those protests turned violent; one person was killed and several more injured when a white supremacist drove a car into a crowd of counterprotesters.[6] But even if the protests had remained peaceful—and therefore protected by the First Amendment—they might well have worked injustices, on account of the messages the marches sent. As Leslie Kendrick, a law professor who teaches the First Amendment at the University of Virginia, in Charlottesville, explains, "free speech is not free, and we do not split the check evenly."[7] The costs, she observes, "fall disproportionately on African-American, Jewish, Muslim, and other minority members of the community. They are the ones who absorb these very public, very ugly assertions that they are worth less than other Americans."[8]

Charlottesville tried to move the march that turned violent, modifying the organizer's permit at the last minute, so that the white supremacists would be required to gather in a park more than a mile from the site originally planned.[9] The organizers challenged the modification in court, arguing that it violated their First Amendment right to free speech.[10] The suit posed a very particular question to the court. The question was not whether permitting the march to proceed in its original location would promote justice. And the question was not whether we ought to have the First Amendment, or even whether it ought to protect hate speech. Rather, the question posed to the court was whether the white supremacists had a right to march in the planned location in light of the fact that we do have the First Amendment, as well as a long history of applying it to particular cases, some not so different from this one.[11] The court said yes, in part because it was convinced that the city modified the permit because it disapproved of the content of the white supremacists' speech.[12] Now, the court might not have been right to find that the white supremacists had the right they asserted; it dismissed the city's safety concerns, which were tragically vindicated.[13] But right or not, the court was answering the moral question put to it, rather than trying to decide whether, all things considered, reinstating the permit promoted justice.

I do not know whether Holmes would endorse this picture of the judicial task, but it is consistent with his insistence that his job was not to do justice, but rather "to play the game according to the rules." Some people, however, see a different point in what Holmes said. They take him to say law is just a set of rules—like a game—with only a contingent connection to justice or morality more generally.[14] And that way of reading Holmes links up with the dominant view among philosophers of law. They think that law is a set of rules, and many of them think that those rules could have any content whatsoever (or, if not quite that, certainly content that is morally defective). To be honest, I rather doubt that this was the point that Holmes was making to Hand. The idea that law is a set of rules did not become dominant until Hart wrote *The Concept of*

Law—several decades after this exchange, and partly in reaction to
Holmes's suggestion that the law is nothing more than a prediction about
what courts will do.[15] But it does not matter much whether Holmes
meant to say that law is a set of rules. Some people see that in what he
said, and I am more interested in the view than whether Holmes held it.
In this chapter, we are going to explore why people think that law is a
set of rules. We'll see that there are, on occasion, good reasons to talk
about law as if it's a set of rules. But we'll also see that we have to be
careful with that sort of talk, as it can lead to confusion. Sometimes, we
end up talking past each other, as there are many different sets of rules
associated with our legal practices. Worse yet, the image of law as a set
of rules can obscure the fact that law is a moral practice.

Norms, Not Texts

Lawyers talk a lot about *the law*. They tell us what the law requires. They
tell us what it permits and prohibits. Sometimes, they tell us the law is silent
on a question. Sometimes, they tell us the law is unclear. What are they
talking about? A layperson might think that they are talking about the stuff
written down in law books, and sometimes lawyers do speak that way.
Dworkin liked to tell another story about Hand—from the first day of
his clerkship, when Hand was explaining the job. "Most of my colleagues have their clerks look up the law," Hand told Dworkin. "But I
know where the law is better than you do, because I wrote most of it."[16]
Now Hand did not actually write most of the words in the law books
that lined his shelves, but he wrote a surprising number of them, and his
words were among the most important, given the work he did to re-
work the law in so many fields. That said, this story suggests that some
talk about the law (even among lawyers) refers to a set of texts.[17] When
Hand said that he'd written most of the law, Dworkin reports, he was
gesturing at those books on his shelves.

But there's another way that lawyers talk about the law, and some
simple observations can help us see it. The books that line the shelves of
law offices contain statutes that have been repealed, as well as cases that
have been overturned. The case reports also include lots of what lawyers

call dicta—observations or opinions about the law that are not binding, since they were tangential to the case at hand. The statutes often contain preambles, or other precatory language, whose relevance to the law is disputed. And, sometimes, courts decide that statutes do not quite mean what they say, or mean more than what they say. All this suggests that there's something else we might refer to when we talk about the law— something that is related to the stuff written down in law books, but not identical to it.

What could that be? Well, most philosophers would say that the law is a set of norms. What are norms? They are standards, against which we might assess an action or attitude (or, for that matter, anything else—an object, an event, and so on). Rules are norms, since you can use them to assess action. As you know, one of the rules in our house is that Hank must try everything on his plate. Each night at dinner, Hank gives us the opportunity to assess whether he has done what the rule requires. He does that because we have another rule, which says that he must ask permission to leave the table, and he observes this second rule more consistently than the first. Rules are, perhaps, the most familiar kind of norm, but there are many others: among them, principles, plans, orders, and even recipes.[18]

No one thinks that the law is a set of recipes. But Hart argued that the law is a set of rules.[19] Shapiro argues that it's a set of plans.[20] And Dworkin, at least at times, seemed to say that the law was a set of principles (or perhaps a set of rules *and* principles).[21] At other times, however, Dworkin resisted the thought that the law is a set of norms.[22] I think he was right to resist it, but not because norms do not play a central role in law. Obviously, they do. Litigation is often a fight about norms—which ones matter and how they apply to the case at hand. And one point of legislation, it is plausible to think, is to make new norms binding. Against that background, it is not surprising that many would conclude that the law is a set of norms—rules, principles, plans, or perhaps some combination of the three.

And that thought—that the law is a set of norms—has structured debates in jurisprudence for several decades. If you think that the law is a set of rules, plans, or principles, then it is natural to wonder what makes something a member of the set. That is, it is natural to wonder how the norms that constitute the law are themselves constituted.[23] This is the question that stood at the center of what became known as the Hart-Dworkin debate. And lots of philosophers—not just Hart and Dworkin—developed theories at different levels of detail. On some of those theories, the content of the law is determined by social facts about legal practices (that is, facts about what people have said, done, or thought as part of those practices). Morality does not play any role in determining the content of the law. That's the thesis that goes by the name *legal positivism*.[24] On other theories, the content of the law is determined, at least in part, by moral facts (that is, facts about people's rights and responsibilities, how they ought to act, what's good or bad). Some call those *natural law* theories, but that label has been used for so many different ideas—some quite distant from this debate—that it's probably best just to call these views *antipositivist*.[25] Ultimately, I don't think these labels are helpful, because I think it misleading to assume that there is a single set of norms properly called the law of a community. But before I make that case, I want to think a bit about how norms are created. Since rules are the most familiar sorts of norms, we will work with them, but we'll do so without prejudice to the idea that principles and plans play an important part in law.

How Do You Make a Rule?

How do you make a rule? They aren't hard to think up. Here's one:

> The Pickle-Hopping Rule: Before eating a pickle, you must hop six times.

One reason rules aren't hard to think up is that there are an infinite number of them. Indeed, there are an infinite number of pickle-hopping rules (just count up from six—you will never run out). Did I make the Pickle-Hopping Rule just now, when I wrote it down? I don't think so—at least, not yet. To make a rule, you have to make it for somebody or for some purpose. I could make the Pickle-Hopping Rule for my children, either generally or as part of a game. It would be odd to make it one of the rules of our house, and it is hard to imagine what game worth playing would include it. So there may be little point in making the Pickle-Hopping Rule. But my point is that I haven't made it yet. At best, I made it up, when I wrote it down.

But maybe I did not even do that. Maybe the Pickle-Hopping Rule exists independently of me, so the most I can claim is to have discovered it in the space of possible rules. Which should we say? Did I make up the rule or discover it? There does seem to be a sense in which we make up rules. After all, they can be challenging to craft. But then, crafting a rule might simply consist in searching the space of possibilities, so as to identify the one that works best. And it does seem like the higher-number pickle-hopping rules are simply there, waiting for us to think of them, once we've got one pickle-hopping rule in hand. To be honest, I have no idea what I would say if I thought I had to say one thing. But as is so often the case with these sorts of conundrums, the solution is to say more than one thing. There's a sense in which I made up the rule *and* a sense in which I discovered it. That is, there is a sense in which the rule did not exist until I dreamt it up, and a sense in which it existed independently of anything that I did.

How could that be? How could the rule both exist and not exist at the same time? The answer is that there is more than one way in which something might exist. Harry Potter did not exist until J. K. Rowling dreamt him up. That implies that he exists now, and surely, he does—but not in the same sense that you and I exist. Harry Potter exists in the way that fictional characters exist. You and I exist in the way that corporeal characters do. I'd like to think that I exist in a thicker or more robust way than Potter does. But I worry about awarding myself that honorific, since Potter has sold way more books than I ever will. Still, I will speak as if there are thicker and thinner ways of existing, since I think that sort of language captures something important. Potter's existence is thicker than the existence of characters who are simply present in the space of possible characters, though no one has ever dreamt them up. And my existence is thicker still than Potter's.[26]

Rules can also exist in different ways. The thinnest way in which a rule might exist is to be present in the space of possible rules. All possible rules exist in that sense, whether or not anyone has ever engaged them or ever will. But there are thicker ways in which a rule might exist, and some of them, at least, depend on some sort of engagement. There are lots of ways to engage rules—positing, presupposing, printing, enforcing, entertaining—and those are just some *p*'s and *e*'s.[27] In fact, I'll posit some rules right now. To this point, you've just been reading this book, without any rules to guide you. But I'll now introduce the Rules of This Book:

1. This book must be read in one sitting, while eating popcorn.
2. You must agree with everything that this book says, or you must keep quiet about it.
3. After you read this book, you must write a favorable review.
4. If you have read this far, you must send me half of your next paycheck.

The Rules of This Book did not exist until I wrote them down, except in the thin sense that they were present in the space of possible rules. Now, they exist in a thicker way. I've grouped them together and given them a designation. We can talk about them by name and ask lots of questions about them. Here are a few: How many rules are there? (Four.) Whose interests do they serve? (Mine.) Should you comply with the rules? (Yes, especially the part about the paycheck.) Will the rules be enforced? (Probably not, but do you really want to risk it?)

Obviously, I'm having a little fun here. I don't really think that you have any reason to comply with the Rules of This Book. Indeed, I wrote them to be ridiculous, so that there would be no doubt about that. And that points the way to another sense in which rules might exist. They might be *binding* or *authoritative*. That is, people might have reason to comply with them, such that their behavior is, at least in some dimension, defective if they don't. We will take up that mode of existence in a moment, but before we do, I want to pause and ask one more question about the Rules of This Book: Should we be positivists about them? Should we think that their existence and content is determined solely by social facts? For sure, we should.[28] What is the alternative? We just said that the Rules of This Book exist, in the most robust sense they do, only because I wrote them down. Moral facts play no part in the explanation of why the Rules of This Book are what they are.[29] So, we could be nothing other than positivists about the Rules of This Book.

Keep that in mind. It will be important later. But let's think a bit more about rules that exist in the sense that they bind us to do as they direct. The Rules of This Book don't exist in that sense, because I lack the power to make rules of this sort bind you. Authors do, at least sometimes, have the power to create rules for their readers. Among academics, it's common to see draft papers with the phrase "Please do not quote, cite, or circulate" printed prominently at the top. This is an order posing as a request because it sounds more polite that way. But the presence of the phrase creates a rule for readers, requiring them to obtain permission if they want to quote, cite, or circulate the draft. The rule is not absolute in the sense that it must be followed whatever the circumstances. There may well be good reason to break the rule. If, for instance, the paper is defamatory, you might do well to send it to the person defamed. But the fact that authors have the authority to restrict distribution of their drafts means that they can make rules for their readers in a different sense than I made the Rules of This Book.

Indeed, it is only when rules are made in this sense that it makes sense to talk about breaking them. If you are not eating popcorn right now, you are not doing what the Rules of This Book require, but it would seem odd to say that you are breaking those rules, given that they don't bind you. Likewise, with the Pickle-Hopping Rule. If you did not hop six times last time you had a pickle, you didn't break the rule. That's not because you didn't know about it; you can break a rule you don't know about. It's because the Pickle-Hopping Rule doesn't bind you; it's not authoritative for you. You have no reason to comply with it whatsoever.[30]

How do you make a rule that is authoritative? Often, they are made through the exercise of a normative power. A normative power is a power to change someone's normative situation through an act that aims at bringing about that change.[31] When I made the rule that Hank must try everything on his plate, I was exercising a normative power that is partly constitutive of my authority as parent. As I suggested earlier, I hold that power because it is indispensable aid to discharging the duties that attach to parenthood. The normative power that an academic has to set the terms on which her drafts are distributed is grounded differently. According authors that authority improves academic discourse, since it lowers the stakes of presenting work in draft form. That encourages people to share their ideas at an early stage, so that they can get help developing them, without the worry that embarrassing mistakes will be transmitted widely. This rationale for an author's authority limits its scope. I once read a draft that flipped the standard phrase: "Please circulate promiscuously," it said. I admired the bravado, but I did not feel bound to share the draft. The author had the authority to bar me from sharing her draft, had she wanted to do so, but she had no authority to conscript me in her efforts to disperse it.

Sometimes, however, we make rules that are binding accidentally, or incidentally. This is possible because of a more general moral phenomenon: we can change our normative situations without intending to do so (or in ways other than intended). For instance, if I carelessly crash into you, I'll have an obligation to apologize, ask after your well-being, and perhaps also to help you with (or compensate you for) your injuries. I have those obligations because my action—crashing into you carelessly—triggers moral principles that apply to all of us.[32] We should apologize for our wrongs and seek to set them right.

This sort of triggering can generate authoritative rules. Suppose there's a coffee machine in the break room. No one ever set any rules for its use, but over time, people coalesced around a practice. If someone finished a pot of coffee, she would start a new one. Perhaps just one or two people did so at the start; others noticed, and then they did the same. They may have encouraged each other to do so or criticized people who didn't. Eventually, when new employees started, people might have told them: "The rule around here is that the person who finishes the coffee starts a new pot." This story ends with the articulation of a rule, but that rule may well have been authoritative before it was articulated. Fairness, I'm inclined to think, requires participating in practices like this, so long as the benefits and burdens are shared in roughly equal measure.[33] But what's important to see is that articulation, on its own, would not be enough to make the rule binding, unless the person who announced the rule had the authority to do so. Absent that authority, there is an authoritative rule here, if there is, only in virtue of the fact that the shared practice triggers principles about the fair distribution of burdens and benefits.

The Rules of the House (Revisited)

I want to return to our first example—about the rule that requires Hank to try everything on his plate—because it will help us to see the significance of the ideas just introduced. And I want you to recall the form that Hank's protest took. When I reminded Hank that the rule in our house requires that he try everything on his plate, he said, "THAT IS NOT A RULE. THAT IS NOT A RULE IN OUR HOUSE." Now, we could imagine Hank putting his point differently. He might have said, "Yes, that's the rule, but I don't have any reason to comply with it." Of course, he didn't have the vocabulary to say that, so it's no surprise that he didn't put his point that way. But if he had said that, he would have been making a different point from the one he actually made. He would have been acquiescing to my claim that there is a rule in our house that requires him to try everything on his plate, and he very much wanted to deny that.

Should he acquiesce? Well, it depends what we mean when we talk about the rules of the house. There are many sets of rules that are associated with our house and, in particular, our parenting. Here's a small sample of those sets:

- The rules that Julie and I articulate
- The rules that Julie and I intend to impose
- The rules that Julie and I enforce
- The rules that Julie and I threaten to enforce
- The rules that Julie and I think are authoritative for Hank
- The rules that Hank follows
- The rules that Hank accepts as authoritative
- The rules that are authoritative for Hank

Depending on the conversation, it might make sense to refer to one or more of these sets as "the rules of our house." For instance, a family therapist might ask us what the rules are in our house, and it might not be clear at first which set she is interested in. So the ensuing conversation might play off different senses in which we could talk about the rules of the house. Julie and I, for example, might assume that she's interested in the rules that we articulate; if so, we might tell her that lights must be out by 8 p.m. If she then asks whether lights typically are out by that time, and we tell her, "No, most nights it's closer to 9 p.m.," then she might reply, "Well, it's not really a rule of the house, is it?" When she says that, she makes clear which of those sets she's interested in—the rules we enforce, rather than the rules we articulate. But either set could be called "the rules of our house," and so could several others.

Hank's interest—at the moment of protest—is in the last set. When he denies that there is a rule in our house that requires him to try everything on his plate, he's denying that there is an authoritative rule of that sort. I know that for two reasons. First, I know it because I know what Hank knows. And he knows that we articulate that rule, that we enforce it, and that we think it authoritative for him. So it's not plausible to think he is quibbling with whether there is a rule in any of those senses. But I also know it because of the role that his denial plays in our conversation. He denies that there is a rule in an effort to rebut my assertion that he must try everything on his plate. What he's denying is that there's a rule that provides him a reason to do so, and from our list above, only the last set carries immediate implications about the reasons that Hank has.

The Baby and the Bonnet

In *The Concept of Law*, Hart introduced the idea of a social rule. Roughly, he said a social rule exists among a group whenever members of the group converge in their behavior, see their convergence as setting a standard that ought to be followed, criticize one another for deviating from that standard, and see the criticism as warranted in light of the deviation.[34] (If this is starting to sound similar to the coffeepot case, there's a reason for that—we'll get to it in a moment.) When Hart introduced the notion of a social rule, he was trying to explain the difference between things people did out of habit and things they did because they accepted a rule that required them to do so. Lots of people go to the movies on Saturday night, Hart observed. But they do so, he suggested, out of habit.[35] They don't see the failure to go to the movies on Saturday night as a deviation from a standard with which they ought to comply, so they don't pressure one another to go or criticize the failure to do so. That stands in contrast, Hart argued, to the attitude people take toward men removing their hats in church. In that case, people do see the convergent behavior as setting a standard with which they ought to comply, so they pressure one another to remove their hats and criticize the failure to do so.[36]

The idea of a social rule played an important part in Hart's account of law, since the rule of recognition—which I mentioned in the Introduction—is a social rule.[37] We'll think about Hart's theory of law in a bit. But before we get there, I want to think more about men removing their hats in church. In one of his first rejoinders to Hart, Dworkin extended Hart's case. "Suppose," he said, "that the members of the community which 'has the rule' that men must not wear hats in church are in fact divided on the question whether 'that' rule applies to the case of male babies wearing bonnets."[38] Hart argued that a social rule exists only where there is convergent behavior. So if the community were split down the middle on the question whether male babies must remove their bonnets, there would be no social rule and, hence, no requirement either way.[39] Nevertheless, Dworkin suggested, members of the community could sensibly insist that male babies are (or are not) required by rule to remove their bonnets. And they could do so even in the face of disagreement, he said, because the rules they would be invoking were "normative rules," not social rules.[40]

What is a normative rule? The label is odd. Rules are norms, so *all* rules are normative, in the sense that we've been using the term (that is, they can be used to assess an action, an attitude, and so on). To make Dworkin's point clearer, I want to translate what he said—and what Hart said—into the framework we've developed in this chapter. So think again about our churchgoers. There are many sets of rules that are associated with the way they dress in church. Here are a few:

- The rules they articulate
- The rules they accept
- The rules they follow
- The rules they enforce
- The rules that are authoritative

Hart gave us a theory of the second set—the rules they accept. And if you pay careful attention to *The Concept of Law*, you'll see that's exactly what he set out to do. His social rule theory is presented as answer to this question: "What is the acceptance of a rule?"[41] Throughout the book, he talks about the acceptance of rules. But his language often slips, and he suggests that the social rule theory describes the conditions under which rules exist.[42] I don't think this slip is illicit, since rules do have a kind of existence in virtue of being accepted. But, as we learned before, that's not the only kind of existence that rules can have.

When Dworkin talks about normative rules, he's talking about rules that exist in a different sense. In fact, he's talking about the fifth set on the list above—the rules that are authoritative. Now, I should say: Hart may have meant to offer a theory of those rules too.[43] His social rule theory was intended to explain the existence conditions for moral rules, which he seemed to see as a species of social rules.[44] For Hart, then, a rule couldn't be morally binding unless it was accepted.[45] Dworkin observed that authority and acceptance can come apart—hence, the need for a distinction between normative and social rules. And the key to his argument against Hart was his further observation that when people contest what ought to be done, they are arguing over the rules that are authoritative, not the rules that they accept (that is, over normative rules, not simply social ones).

There might, of course, be a relationship between those two sets of rules. One might hope that people would accept the rules that are authoritative. But the relationship could run in the opposite direction too. In some circumstances, rules could become authoritative partly because they are accepted.[46] The coffeepot story is plausibly one such case. There might be several fair ways to distribute responsibility for making coffee. The responsibility might be assigned to the most junior employee. (At the Supreme Court, the most junior justice takes notes at the conference and opens the door if someone knocks.) If there's not much turnover, that might not be fair. But if there are enough new hires to make the responsibility short-lived, then it might be a fine way to distribute the burdens and benefits of making coffee. Alternatively, responsibility could rotate among employees on a regular schedule. The fact that, in our example, employees accept the rule that the person who finishes the pot should start a new one is, therefore, part of the explanation of why that rule is authoritative. If they accepted a different rule, it is possible—perhaps even likely—that the rule they accepted would be authoritative instead.

As Dworkin pointed out, the rule requiring men to take off their hats in church is plausibly another case in which the rule is authoritative in part because it is accepted. Men remove their hats as a show of respect, but one could just as well show respect by covering one's head (that's what my people do), so long as the proper social practice was in place.[47] What about male babies and their bonnets? Recall that, on Hart's theory, there is no rule that covers the case, since there is no convergent behavior. But the rules that are authoritative might differ from the rules that are accepted. And as Dworkin suggested, one way in which they might differ is that they might require more than people currently see themselves as required to do. They are apt to do so if the rationale that renders the accepted rule authoritative extends to cases that are not covered by that rule. For instance, the people who think that male babies must not wear bonnets probably think so because they believe that their parents show a lack of respect by refusing to remove them.[48] And the people who think it fine for a male baby to wear a bonnet might think that parents should worry about whether their babies are comfortable, rather than whether they are showing respect through what they wear. That is a dispute about whether the rationale for men removing their hats in church extends to babies. For our purposes, it does not matter who would have the better of the argument. What matters is that the argument makes sense—and might have an answer—because what is at stake is the rule that is authoritative, rather than the rule that is accepted.

So Many Sets of Norms

Let's think about law again. A while back, I said that the dominant view among philosophers is that the law of a community is a set of norms. But we've now seen enough to know that there are many sets of norms that will be associated with any community's legal practices. Here are just a few:

- The norms that are expressed in legal materials (constitutions, case reports, statutes, and so on)
- The norms that are accepted by legal officials
- The norms that are accepted by laypeople
- The norms that are enforced by legal officials
- The norms that are followed by legal officials
- The norms that are followed by laypeople
- The norms that are authoritative

Which one of these sets counts as the law of a community? Maybe none of them. Hart suggested a different, more complicated set: the rules validated by a rule that legal officials accept (that is, the rules picked out by the rule of recognition). But the truth is that several of these sets could be called the law of the community, depending on the conversation.[49] A sociologist might be interested in Hart's set or perhaps the simpler one constituted by the norms that legal officials accept. A historian of an ancient legal system might take an interest in the norms that are expressed in legal materials, since she might not have access to the information needed to construct any other set. An economist might take an interest in the norms that are enforced, since incentives are mainly a function of enforcement or the threat of it.

What set is a lawyer interested in? If she's any good, more than one. A lawyer has to take an interest in the norms that are enforced. She has an obligation to watch out for her client's interests, and she can't do that if she can't predict the consequences that will follow from the courses of conduct that her client is considering. She must also take an interest in the norms that are authoritative, since that will be the topic of conversation when she goes to court. But since her job is to be an advocate for her client, she'll need to pay attention to the norms that legal officials accept—even if she does not think them authoritative—since the success of her arguments may depend on the application of those norms.

Still, you might ask: Which of these sets is the law? There's a sense in which the last set—the norms that are authoritative—has the best claim to the title. As Chief Justice Marshall announced in *Marbury v. Madison*: "It is emphatically the province and duty of the judicial department to say what the law is."[50] When a court says what the law is, it says which norms are authoritative. Now, there are lots of caveats to insert here. We glimpsed them in Chapter 1, and we'll explore them further in the chapters that follow. Courts make mistakes about which norms are authoritative. If a court makes a mistake, there will be consequences. For the parties, for sure, since their case will be resolved by application of the wrong norms. But the mistake might also adjust the norms that are authoritative going forward, depending on the practice of precedent in the jurisdiction.

All that said, I would not insist that the law is the set of authoritative norms. Indeed, I'm tempted to say that the original sin among philosophers of law is the rigid insistence that *this* and not *that* set of norms counts as the law of a community.[51] When someone says that the speed limit on the highway is not the speed posted on the sign, but rather a speed several miles per hour above that, I know just what she means. She is pointing out that you can get away with driving faster than the posted limit, since cops rarely write tickets for people traveling close to that speed. In other words, she is calling attention to the norms that are enforced. The problem comes when someone insists (as some who style themselves "legal realists" are wont to do) that the law just is the set of norms that are enforced, and nothing else.[52] That's a problem because it obscures facts that we need to keep in view. For instance, if a cop does ticket someone driving just a mile or two over the limit, courts will not hear his complaint that the law "really" permits him to drive up to ten miles an hour over the limit. That's because the courts aim to apply norms that are authoritative, not the norms that are generally enforced.

Hart took Holmes to task for his suggestion that the law is just a prediction about what courts will do. Courts appeal to the law, Hart pointed out, to justify the decisions that they make, so the law cannot just be the set of norms they are likely to enforce; a law has to exist independently of its enforcement if it is to play a role in justifying it.[53] Hart offered his own suggestion: the law is the set of rules validated by a rule that judges accept. But that's not what is at issue in court either. What's at issue is the norms that are authoritative. But before we insist on saying that the law is just the set of authoritative norms, we should remember that Hart's and Holmes's sets are helpful to highlight—and not just helpful for academics, but for lawyers, on the ground, doing their jobs.[54] As I said before, a lawyer advising her client better know a lot about the norms that will be enforced. And a lawyer heading to court better know a lot about the rules that are validated by the rule of recognition that judges accept.[55] But though that may inform the arguments she advances, the arguments themselves will be aimed at establishing which rules are authoritative. All three sets are important to the work that lawyers do. And all three could plausibly be called the law of the community, depending on what we were trying to convey. So, I suspect, could several other sets.

The Problem with Positivism

As I said before, legal positivism is the thesis that the content of the law is determined by social facts about legal practices. But now that we see that "the law" might refer to any of several sets of norms, we need to ask which set of norms legal positivism is a thesis about.[56] If positivism were a thesis about the norms that are expressed in legal materials, or the norms that are enforced, or the norms that are accepted, it would be true, but trivially so. The questions what norms are expressed, enforced, or accepted just are questions about social facts.[57]

If positivism is a thesis about Hart's set—the rules validated by a rule that judges accept—then it is not trivially true; indeed, it might be false. That's because the rule of recognition that judges accept might include moral criteria for determining which further rules are valid members of the set. That possibility is what led to the development of the view known as *inclusive legal positivism*.[58] It holds that the content of the law is *ultimately* determined by social facts, since the content of the rule of recognition is determined by a social practice among legal officials. But it denies that the content of the law must be *exclusively* determined by social facts, since that practice might involve applying moral criteria.[59]

Once that possibility was noted, philosophers who stuck to the original thesis—that the content of the law is determined solely by social facts—were labeled *exclusive legal positivists*.[60] And they had to construct their sets differently than Hart did, since the inclusive legal positivist thesis is true of Hart's set. There have been several efforts in this direction. Scott Shapiro, for instance, says that the law is a set of plans, made pursuant to a master plan for planning.[61] Given the way that Shapiro thinks of plans (roughly, as norms that are the objects of intentions to act in accord with them or to have others do so),[62] you won't be surprised to learn that the exclusive positivist thesis is true of that set (the question what norms people intend to comply with is a question about social facts). All the action, it turns out, depends on what set of norms is picked out as the law.

The problem for positivism is that the thesis—in both its forms—is false when it comes to the set of norms that is contested in court. As I've said several times now, courts attempt to ascertain and apply the norms that are authoritative. But norms are authoritative, if they are, only in virtue of moral principles that establish their authority. Of course, social facts matter too, since morality is sensitive to social facts. But the question what norms are authoritative is never just a question about who said or did what. We learned that lesson way back with Hank. And it holds for law just as well as the rules of our house.

This wouldn't be a problem if positivists had no pretensions to say anything about the norms contested in court. But Hart did, and many who have followed in his wake did too. Hart thought that the law had gaps—that there was no legally correct answer to any question not covered by a norm in the set he described.[63] So to resolve a case posing such a question, the judge would have to draw on norms that were not part of the law. That makes sense if you identify the law with the set Hart described. But a court's task is to apply the norms that are authoritative, not the norms in Hart's set. And there could be an authoritative norm covering a case, even if none is validated by the rule of recognition that judges accept. This was part of the point Dworkin aimed to make through the case of the baby and the bonnet. As we saw, the dispute among parishioners as to whether male babies must remove their bonnets could have a right answer, notwithstanding the fact that no accepted rule covered the case. So too with legal disputes: judges, Dworkin was fond of pointing out, can often see that they do not share tests for identifying legal rules, but nevertheless persist in asserting that there are such rules, even absent shared tests. The assertion makes sense—and might be true or false—because it is a claim about the rules that are authoritative, not the rules that are accepted.

There are two ways to resist the conclusion that positivism is false as applied to the set of norms that are contested in court. First, you could reject my characterization of that set. You might deny that courts aim to apply the set of norms that are authoritative; rather, you might say, they aim to apply the set of norms that is "legally authoritative." The trick here is to suppose that slipping in that qualifier—*legally*—shifts the set in question back to one of the ones about which positivism is plausibly true. But the qualifier should not distract us from the reasons we have for thinking that courts aim to apply norms that are actually authoritative, not just treated as such. Law is a moral practice. Court is a place we go to contest what we owe each other. And courts issue orders that interfere with people's lives, often in substantial ways. They appeal to norms to justify the decisions they make, and only authoritative norms (that is, norms that we have reason to follow) can supply a justification. Of course, you could slip in the qualifier again and say that courts aim to be "legally justified," rather than justified, full stop. Indeed, you can play this game endlessly. But it is endlessly unsatisfying. If "legally justified" is a stand-in for "justified according to the rules legal officials accept," it is no justification at all.[64]

Alternatively, you could concede that courts aim to apply norms that are authoritative—and that morality determines which norms those are. But you might insist: the norms that morality designates as authoritative for courts are members of a set whose content is determined solely by social facts. Joseph Raz held a view like this. He believed that judges should act in ways that are morally justified. But morality, he thought, at least sometimes directs judges to apply the law, which he conceived as a set of norms whose membership was socially determined.[65]

Why conceive law that way? In Raz's view, morality assigns law a task. Law is supposed to modify what morality requires of us in morally desirable ways. It might make morality more concrete, specifying how much tax we should pay, rather than suggesting that we should pay our fair share. It might help coordinate our conduct by setting a speed limit, so we can drive more safely. Or it might create valuable institutions, like corporations or administrative agencies. In Raz's view, law can modify morality only if it's something separate from it—a socially determined set of norms.[66]

It's just that last bit I disagree with—the bit about socially determined norms. Because the rest of the picture Raz paints fits perfectly with the idea that law is a moral practice—a practice through which we attempt to create, extinguish, enforce, articulate, arrange, and rearrange our moral rights and responsibilities. The difference is that Raz imagines that our legal practices affect what morality requires by creating a set of norms that morality instructs us to apply (assuming, that is, that the norms we create are morally legitimate). In contrast, I think our legal practices affect what morality requires directly.[67] They don't do so by creating a set of norms ("the law"), which might (or might not) be morally binding. In fact, I think it's misleading to suppose that our legal practices create a set of norms called "the law."

I'll explain why in a moment. But I want to pause to emphasize how close Raz's picture is to the one I've been painting—and to the one that Dworkin put forth too. Raz and Dworkin are commonly thought to occupy opposite ends of the positivist-antipositivist spectrum. But the differences between their views are subtle. Both agree that judges are moral actors, making moral decisions.[68] And both agree that the norms that courts apply are binding, if they are, only in virtue of moral principles that make them so.[69] The main difference is that Raz believes that morality sometimes directs judges to leave morality behind and make decisions according to something separate from it ("the law"), whereas Dworkin denies that morality cedes control that way.[70]

Is this difference significant? In some way, perhaps, but I'm skeptical. Both would allow that morality sometimes tells us to drive at the speed posted on the sign, to honor the terms of a contract, or to disburse funds in accord with the formula specified in a statute. Dworkin draws our attention to the role that morality plays in determining what standards we should apply. Raz emphasizes the way that social facts inform that choice. But on both pictures, what we should do (and what courts should do) depends on a melding of the two. This is one reason I prefer to avoid labels like *positivist* and *antipositivist;* they make it hard to see what ostensible opponents share in common.

Not a Set of Norms

To this point, I've argued that the law is not *a* set of norms. There are many sets of norms associated with our legal practices, and depending on the conversation, any number of them could be helpfully labeled "the law." But I have reservations about construing the law as a set of *norms,* in the way that Hart and Raz did. And Dworkin did too (even though at times, he seemed to argue that the law was a set of principles, or perhaps a set of principles and rules). At the end of *Taking Rights Seriously,* Dworkin had this to say about some of his critics:

> They believe that rules can be usefully said to exist, and they believe in something Hart calls the 'existing law', which consists in a special and numerable list of legal rules (and possibly other sorts of standards) that at a given moment do exist. The existing law, so conceived, has two functions: it alone can provide answers to questions about the legal duties of citizens and other legal persons, and it alone can impose obligations upon judges to accept these answers as dispositive of law suits.[71]

Dworkin then recounted how Hart once described a clash between the "Nightmare" and the "Noble Dream," labels he attached to positions prominent among American legal theorists.[72] According to the Nightmare—which Hart saw in the work of American legal realists, like Holmes, Karl Llewellyn, and Jerome Frank—existing law is an empty set.[73] There are no rules; judges do what they like and dress it up in fancy language. According to the Noble Dream—which Hart attributed to Dworkin—there's a rule for every conceivable case.[74] Hart counseled a middle ground: the law contains many rules, but it does not have a rule for every case that could possibly come up.[75]

Dworkin joined Hart in his rejection of both the Nightmare and the Noble Dream. But that was because he rejected the underlying picture, which supposed that the law is a set of norms. Since Hart subscribed to that picture, Dworkin thought his sensible-sounding middle ground misguided too. Here's what Dworkin said:

> I hope to persuade lawyers to lay the entire picture of existing law aside in favour of a theory that takes questions about legal rights as special questions about political rights, so that one may think that a plaintiff has a certain legal right without supposing that any rule or principle that already 'exists' provides that right. In place of the misleading question, whether judges find rules in the 'existing law' or make up rules not to be found

there, we must ask whether judges try to determine what rights the parties have, or whether they create what they take to be new rights to serve social goals.[76]

I hope you will see the similarity between the picture that Dworkin presses in this passage and the one presented in Chapter 1 and Chapter 2. I argued that courts attempt to resolve questions about the rights and obligations of the parties before them. Here, Dworkin agrees, and he adds that you can have a right—or presumably, an obligation—without a preexisting rule that assigns you that right or obligation.

This would be unremarkable if it were an observation about our rights and obligations outside court. Children are masters of mischief, and their capacity to misbehave in ways that do not run afoul of previously articulated rules knows no bounds. The youngest child of a friend of mine recently pulled down his brother's pants in public. You won't be surprised to learn that his parents had never made a rule prohibiting public pantsing. You also won't be surprised to know that they regarded this as a punishable offense nonetheless. That's not how the criminal law works. The principle of legality permits punishment only if a law clearly defines an offense prior to its commission.[77] Why? Lots of people think it has something to do with fairness. They say that it's not fair to punish people if they were not told in advance what conduct would expose them to punishment. I'm not sure about that. I don't think, for instance, that my friends were unfair to their son. He didn't need someone to tell him that public pantsing is wrong; he's old enough to figure that out for himself. And for lots of criminal offenses—at least the ones that are mala in se, or wrong in themselves—the same would be true for any competent adult. Moreover, another principle of criminal law holds that ignorance of the law that makes your conduct criminal provides no excuse, even if your ignorance is itself excusable.[78] That suggests that fairness is not the driving force behind the principle of legality. So what is? I think the principle of legality is a tool for constraining the exercise of state power. If the state could articulate the elements of crimes ex post, then it could put anyone in prison, simply by defining something they'd done as a crime. To guard against that, we insist that the state announce how it will use its power to punish in advance.

But whether I am right about that or not, the practical implication of the principle of legality is clear enough: the state can't punish someone unless a rule that preexists the offense prohibits it. In what sense does the rule have to exist prior to the offense? In two senses: the rule has to have been articulated—though jurisdictions differ on just where and how—and the rule articulated has to be authoritative. Here, then, the picture of preexisting law has some purchase. But the principle of legality has limited scope. There is no counterpart principle in the common law that permits the imposition of liability only if a rule has announced the grounds for liability in advance. Judges in civil cases do worry about notice, and counterintuitively, notice concerns may carry more weight in civil than criminal law, partly because predictability is important for insurance markets. But in a civil suit, a plaintiff can be held to have a right—and a defendant a corresponding obligation—simply on the grounds that there are good reasons to recognize that right, even though no rule assigning it has ever been articulated before.

There is, I suppose, a sense in which rules assigning rights that there are reasons to recognize can be said to exist, even if no one has ever engaged them before. They exist precisely because those rules are authoritative. A court judgment would be defective if it did not meet the standards set by those rules. But when Hart and others (like Raz) invoke "existing law," they are picturing a set of norms that exists because of some sort of engagement—articulation, acceptance, or validation by a rule of recognition that is accepted.[79] And nothing of that sort is needed to support a right or obligation, except in special cases covered by the principle of legality (or some other sort of clear statement rule).[80]

Dworkin thought it misleading to ask "whether judges find rules in the 'existing law' or make up rules not to be found there."[81] One reason the question is misleading is that "existing law" could, as we have seen, refer to many different sets of norms. It could refer to rules that are articulated in legal materials, that are picked out by a rule of recognition, or that have in some other fashion been engaged by legal officials. But, as I just noted, talk about "existing law" could equally well refer to the rules that are authoritative, whether or not anyone has ever engaged them. When a court applies a rule from the latter set, it makes it a member of (one or more of) the former sets. So it will sometimes be possible to describe one and the same judicial act as finding a rule (in the set of authoritative rules) and making a rule (by, say, adding it to the stock of announced rules). Or, to put the point a bit differently, fidelity to the law in one sense might create law in another sense.

For that reason, picturing the law as a set of norms risks confusion. We seem to be talking about one thing when in fact we are talking about many. We can avoid the confusion by setting aside the idea that "the law" names a special set of norms, which we look to when we have legal questions. In its place, we simply need to remind ourselves that legal questions are questions about our rights and responsibilities. To answer them, we consult records of our legal history—statutes, regulations, case reports, and the like—because the decisions those materials reflect bear on our rights and responsibilities. At no point do we need an answer to the question that has preoccupied philosophers of law: how the set of norms that constitutes the law is itself constituted. Rather, we need an account of the moral differences that legal practices make, so that we can see how they affect our rights and responsibilities, and so that we can pick out the rights and responsibilities that courts are properly concerned with. *That,* as we saw in Chapter 1 and Chapter 2, is what lawyers argue about in court.

Pardon Me

Several years ago, I was having lunch with law professors, and the question whether the president could pardon himself came up. I pay careful attention to the way that people talk about the law in situations like this, since I want to know what they say when they aren't pressed to take sides on questions in jurisprudence. After we marveled at the fact that Donald Trump had made this an important question, and not just an academic one, people started to work their way toward an answer. One of my colleagues, who teaches constitutional law, began by observing that the law is not clear. "Why is that?" I asked. Well, he said, you won't find an answer in any of the materials that people look to when they have legal questions. He's right about that. No president has ever tried to pardon himself, so there are no judicial opinions on whether such a pardon would be valid. The Constitution doesn't squarely address the question either.

It pronounces that the president "shall have Power to grant Reprieves and Pardons for Offences against the United States, except in Cases of Impeachment."[82] But it does not say whether the president has the power to pardon himself.

"So can the president pardon himself?" I asked. "No, of course not," he said. And everyone at the table agreed. Some mentioned the principle that no one may be a judge in their own case. Others observed that, if the president had the power to pardon himself, he could do absolutely anything—take bribes, murder a member of Congress, abuse a child—and immunize himself from all consequences other than removal from office.[83] That's a repugnant conclusion, more at home in a monarchy than a democracy, but repugnant even there.

I've had this conversation with many people since, and some take the opposite view. They point out that the Constitution includes a limitation on the pardon power: it does not extend to impeachment. And since the Constitution does not mention any other limitations, they suggest, we should infer that there are none. This sort of argument goes by the name *expressio unius est exclusio alterius* (the expression of one thing is the exclusion of the other). It is an instance of a broader idea that, in some circumstances, we can draw an inference from the fact that something wasn't said. Of course, the strength of the inference you can draw depends on just how strong the expectation is that, if something was meant, it would have been said.[84] For the reasons my colleagues supplied, the idea that a president could pardon himself is so ludicrous that it would probably not occur to anyone that the limitation needed to be spelled out, lest it be overlooked. So the inference is weak here. But regardless of where people line up on the ultimate question, nearly everyone notes the law is unsettled, adding that they have no idea what a court would do if confronted with the case.

I'm not recounting these conversations because I want to explore the pardon question in detail. Rather, I'm reporting them because they illustrate just how flexible our talk about law is. "The law is not clear," my colleague said, meaning that no rule covering the case is announced in the Constitution or other legal materials, like case reports. The fact that the law is not clear, in that sense, did not prevent him from having an opinion about whether the president has the power to pardon himself: no, most certainly not. But my colleague also said that the law is not settled, in the sense that no rule is widely accepted, so we can't be confident how a court would resolve the case.

That's three different judgments—the law is not clear, the law is determinate, the law is not settled—all of which we express by talking about what the law is, but each of which invokes "the law" in a slightly different sense. If you don't see that our talk about law is supple in this way, then you are apt to fall prey to an *ism*—positivism, realism, or some other flavor of the day. Each of those isms captures something important about law. That's why they stick around. But none of them captures everything that is important. And if we treat them as theses about the single set of norms properly called the law of a community, all of them are false. There is no such set.

CHAPTER FOUR

An Immoral Practice?

———•◦•———

From Pointless to Pernicious

I bought my first book of law when I was ten. I spotted it at the school book fair, and the title tickled me. It was called "Donkeys Can't Sleep in Bathtubs and Other Crazy Laws."[1] The title was inspired by a Brooklyn law that, as you might guess, prohibited donkeys from sleeping in bathtubs.[2] The book was little more than a list of laws, each more absurd than the last. Or at least that's how they were presented. One suspects that most of the laws had a point when they were promulgated, and part of the fun of the book lies in guessing what that point might have been. Someone, you can be sure, did let a donkey sleep in a bathtub, and the result was not nearly as amusing as that sounds.

In some cases, it's not hard to figure out what the point of the law was. For instance, the book reports that in Washington, DC, "you can be put in jail if you are cruel to animals."[3] The only mystery there is that the author thought to include that in a book of crazy laws. But some of the laws on the list do seem pointless: "You may not carry your lunch in a pail on the streets of Riverside, California."[4] And others are pernicious: "In Mississippi, the state librarian has to be a woman."[5] Now, it is important to note that there are no sources cited in the book, and I cannot locate most of the laws described. Many of them, I suspect, are apocryphal.

But not all of them. The Mississippi Constitution did, for a long time, deem the position of state librarian open to "any woman, a resident of the state four years, and who has attained the age of twenty years."[6] That provision—which was written into the state constitution in 1890—remained on the books until 1978. If it were still there today, it would be struck down as a violation of the Fourteenth Amendment's guarantee of equal protection. But for most of the life of that law, courts did not take gender discrimination to pose an equal protection problem, so Mississippi was, as a practical matter, free to exclude men and stereotype women.

That's not good, but it pales in comparison to many other provisions of Mississippi law in that period. A statute adopted in 1888 demanded that "all railroads carrying passengers in this state, other than street railroads, shall provide equal, but separate, accommodation for the white and colored races."[7] And, of course, segregation extended far beyond the rail. Another law—which is still on the books, even though it's not enforceable—establishes a separate camp for "Negro 4-H club members . . . for the purpose of teaching the Negro boys and girls of Mississippi standards of better farm and home making, the importance of and the methods of conservation of our natural resources, and the development of character and leadership and training for citizenship."[8] The last phrase is more than a bit maddening, given how hard Mississippi worked to deny Black people the benefits of citizenship. The state adopted a scheme of residency requirements, literacy tests, and poll taxes, which the Mississippi Supreme Court acknowledged were nothing more than "expedients to obstruct the exercise of the franchise by the negro race."[9] Mississippi was not alone in this; disenfranchisement was widespread in the days of Jim Crow. And of course, segregation followed slavery, which was supported by some of the most objectionable laws imaginable.

I have argued that law is a moral practice. But legal practices are often immoral. Indeed, the more awful an atrocity, the more certain you can be that law played a role, since mass internment, enslavement, and execution are not the work of a few souls. They are the work of states, typically carried out through law, so as to ensure widespread participation, or at least acquiescence. Doesn't this fact, undeniable as it is, prove that law is not a moral practice? Doesn't it show that the morality of law is contingent and, indeed, dubious, given how much misery law inflicts, even in places that disclaim slavery and genocide? We may have moved past the worst horrors in our history, but still we struggle with mass incarceration, police brutality, and disenfranchisement—all, to one extent or another, artifacts of law. Faced with this, you might insist that law—at least as we know it—is an immoral practice, not a moral one.

And you would be right, in a way. But not in a way that undercuts my claim that law is a moral practice. To say that law is a moral practice (in the relevant sense) is simply to say that we employ law in an effort to adjust who owes what to whom. And all of the laws listed above—the silly and the sinister, the arbitrary and the awful—were issued with just that ambition. To say that law is a moral practice, then, leaves open the possibility that many legal practices (including our own) are deeply immoral, as slavery and segregation surely were.

If it seems odd to insist that law is a moral practice while, at the same time, acknowledging the immorality of many legal practices, it is important to note just how modest the claim is. I'm not saying that all law is morally good, simply in virtue of the fact that it's law. As we'll see, many legal practices have moral merit, even when they are morally defective. But I wouldn't say that all or even most do. The moral merit of any legal practice is contingent. But that just puts law on a par with lots of other practices that are moral in the relevant sense. For instance, the moral merit of any particular promise is contingent; a promise can be commendable or contemptible. But promising is a moral practice—a practice that aims at rearranging what we owe each other—and you wouldn't understand what promises are if you did not understand that. Immoral laws pose no more problem to seeing law as a moral practice than immoral promises pose to seeing promising as a moral practice—which is to say, they pose no problem at all. Indeed, we can learn a lot about law and immorality by thinking about bad promises, so it's worth revisiting (and expanding on) some of what we explored earlier.

Bad Promises

When you promise, you communicate an intention to take on an obligation, and if all goes well, your doing so actually generates that obligation.

Just now, you asked me to feed your fish while you are out of town. I said I would, and as a result I have an obligation that, just a moment ago, I did not. I owe it to you to feed your fish, and I'll wrong you if I don't. I might be able to mitigate the wrong—or even eliminate it entirely—by seeking your approval to substitute someone in. But the promise adjusted our moral relationship. Had I never promised to care for your fish, I would not owe it to you to do so.

So far so good, but suppose your fish wasn't what you wanted help with. You've chained a chimpanzee to the wall in your basement, and you want me to feed him while you're out of town. I'm appalled to hear about his captivity; it's cruel to keep a chimp under such conditions. But I nevertheless agree to care for him. Do I owe it to you to do so? This is a trickier case, since I've agreed to assist you in doing something dreadful. Maybe I shouldn't have made the commitment. It might have been better to call you out on the spot and notify the authorities responsible for animal welfare. Or perhaps, in the circumstances, it was best for me to keep quiet, since it might be easier to rescue the chimpanzee if you remain unsuspecting. But whether I should have made the promise or not, it seems that what I ought to do is find a way to end the chimp's captivity.

Will I have broken my promise if I do? Well, I certainly won't have done what you expected, even if the chimp has been fed. But promises are like rules: you can't break them unless they're binding. And it is arguable that my promise is not binding—that I'm permitted to rescue the chimp by turning him over to people that can properly care for him. You are not, after all, in a position to demand that I feed the chimp rather than rescue him, since you have no right to hold the chimp in such cruel conditions. Suppose, however, that I don't rescue the chimp but don't feed him either. This would be a terrible way to treat the chimp, and wrong on account of that. But it would, I think, also wrong you by breaching the commitment I made to feed him. You have a legitimate interest in keeping the chimp alive, even if you don't have a legitimate interest in keeping him captive. You were entitled to rely on my promise, and I let you down, on top of treating the chimp cruelly.

Or, at least, that's how I see the situation. You might see it differently, but once again, it doesn't matter exactly how this shakes out. What matters is that we see again what we saw earlier. A promise that ought not to have been made might have moral consequences. Indeed, it might be binding. That is, we might owe it to others to do just what we promised to do, even though we shouldn't have promised to do it. This fact—that a commitment that ought not to have been made sometimes ought to be kept—will turn out to be important when we think about law. As we shall see, a statute that ought not to have been passed—or a decision that ought not to have been made—might nevertheless have moral consequences. Indeed, people might be obligated to do as the statute or decision directs. But I do not want to turn to law just yet. Promises are one-offs, so there's a limit to how much we can glean about law from them. But there are more systematic moral practices, with more thoroughgoing immorality, that can help us think about law.

Morality and the Mafia

In 2007, Italian police arrested Salvatore Lo Piccolo. He was believed to be the leader of Cosa Nostra, the Sicilian Mafia. Among his papers, the police found a typewritten list. It was labeled "Rights and Duties," though the popular press called it the Ten Commandments of the Mafia.[10] Here's the list:

1. No one can present himself directly to another of our friends. There must be a third person to do it.
2. Never look at the wives of friends.
3. Never be seen with cops.
4. Don't go to pubs and clubs.
5. Always being available for Cosa Nostra is a duty—even if your wife's about to give birth.
6. Appointments must absolutely be respected.
7. Wives must be treated with respect.
8. When asked for any information, the answer must be the truth.
9. Money cannot be appropriated if it belongs to others or to other families.
10. People who can't be part of Cosa Nostra: anyone who has a close relative in the police, anyone with a two-timing relative in the family, anyone who behaves badly and doesn't hold to moral values.

This list is remarkable—for its retrograde take on gender, its insistence on availability (even if your wife is about to give birth), and perhaps most of all its exclusion of anyone who "doesn't hold to moral values."[11] This from an organization whose primary pastimes include protection rackets, drug trafficking, and bribery.

The history of this list is obscure. We don't know whether it was issued as an edict or offered simply as a summary of the rights and duties of Mafia members. If it was issued as an edict, then its author intended that Mafia members have the rights and duties described (at least in part) in virtue of the issuance of the edict.[12] Let's assume that the list was, in fact, issued as an edict. Did the edict make it the case that Mafia members had the rights and duties described? I rather doubt it. The members might have had some of the duties described even absent the edict, though given the way they are framed, even that is dubious. For instance, wives ought to be treated with respect, quite apart from what the edict says. After all, wives are people, and people ought to be treated with respect. Singling out wives, however, sends a different message. The author of the list almost certainly had—and intended to convey—demeaning views about when, why, and how women ought to be respected. But even if I am wrong about that, the edict almost surely didn't make a moral difference. Though we don't know much about the history of the Lo Piccolo list, it is hard to imagine an argument that would establish the authority of its author to impose duties of this sort.[13]

The most likely candidates would point to the oaths that people swear when they join the Mafia.[14] After all, consent can, in the right circumstances, ground authority. When you sign up for a soccer team, for instance, it is plausible that you are obligated to do as the coach directs, so long as you remain a member of the team. There are limits, of course, both substantive and jurisdictional. On the substantive side, the coach won't have authority to demand that you do things that put you in serious danger. On the jurisdictional side, the coach will have authority over the way the team plays and practices, but not over how much players save toward retirement. Consent is an important part of this story. You wouldn't have an obligation to defer to the coach if you did not agree to be part of the team. But consent is not all that matters, and indeed, you may not be free to withdraw your consent and leave the team, if doing so would harm people who have relied on you to play your part.

One could imagine telling a similar story about the Mafia, and I suspect many mafiosi would do just that. But consent can make a difference only in the right circumstances, and these are not those. There are better ways to spend your time than soccer (baseball, for instance). But there is value in soccer. It is fun to play. It provides a nearly never-ending opportunity to develop physical capacities. And it allows one to be part of a team, working toward a common goal, with all that entails, from character development to camaraderie. Some of the same might be said of the Mafia. Its members are, in a way, a team, working toward a common goal, and some of them, at least, have the opportunity to develop physical capacities. But in soccer, these goods are not parasitic on pain caused to others.[15] Whatever value might lie in the close friendships that members of the Mafia form (and I do think they might be valuable), members of the group do not owe their allegiance to the aspects of the practice that aim at inflicting pain on others, even if they agreed to participate in them. The goods simply do not warrant the pain, in part because they can be pursued through other activities (like soccer) that do not systematically harm others.

Or at least that's how I see the situation. Once again, it does not matter much whether I'm right. And indeed, what interests me is the fact that many mafiosi, it seems safe to assume, see the situation differently. They think that they really do have rights and duties of the sort set out in the Lo Piccolo list. Why? There are many stories that the mafiosi might tell themselves, and my guess is that most are told at one time or another. For instance, the mafiosi might think that the Mafia hierarchy has authority over its members in virtue of the oaths they swear when they join up. Or they might think that the mutual regard they show each other generates an obligation for each to do his part to support the common scheme.[16] These views could, of course, be combined. And they might find further support in archaic notions of honor, which have wide appeal in macho settings like the Mafia.

In all this, the mafiosi would be misguided, and if they asked, I'd be happy to explain why. I wouldn't expect to persuade many of them. As Upton Sinclair said, "It is difficult to get a man to understand something, when his salary depends upon his not understanding it!"[17] So much the more so, I would guess, when his life depends on it. But even so, I suspect that the immorality of what the Mafia does is manifest to some of its members. And I'd guess that some of them see that this undercuts the claims they might make on one another. I want to spend some time thinking about these members of the Mafia: the queasy ones, the ones who participate but doubt that their practices have the moral force more committed mafiosi take for granted. There are almost surely degrees of unease among this cohort. There are those who are, in the main, comfortable with what the Mafia does, but sometimes question the brutality with which it does it. They may reject—privately, if not publicly—some of the demands that are placed on them. But some of their brethren are more disillusioned. They see the practice for what it is, and though they may not see a way out, they do not think that they owe anything to their partners in crime.

Suppose for a moment that you are one of the more disillusioned members of the Mafia. Your orientation toward the institution might be primarily pragmatic. You'll show up when expected, but not because you see yourself as bound to do so; you simply don't want the hassle (or worse) that comes from going AWOL. When your superior asks you a question, you won't think that you owe him the truth, as the Lo Piccolo list says you do, but you might give it anyway. Or you might not. Sometimes, it will be safer to keep your mouth shut, especially if an honest answer will out you. When you fail to speak the truth, you might wonder whether you'll get away with it. But you won't wonder whether you have failed to discharge an obligation. Sometimes, however, you might see yourself as having genuine obligations in virtue of your membership in the Mafia. You might, for instance, think that you are obligated to participate in mourning rituals or care for the family of a fallen mobster.

In all this, you'll straddle two stances toward the rights and duties of Mafia membership. Much of the time, you'll take a sociological stance. That is, you'll take an interest in the rights and duties that others take you to have or, somewhat different, the rights and duties that are apt to be enforced. When you interact with others who see those rights and duties as genuine, you'll tailor much of what you say to suit their views, so as not to cause conflict. That might lead you to speak about these rights and duties as if they're genuine, even though you don't think they are. But sometimes, you'll occupy a straightforwardly moral stance. That is, you'll take an interest in what your rights and duties actually are. You'll do this when you are in the terrain where it is plausible you have obligations. But you might do it more generally. Indeed, it is possible to take both stances at once, treating rights and duties that others take you to have as if they're genuine, while at the same time insisting, if only to yourself, that they're not.

Indeed, most of us take a mixed stance toward the moral claims that others make. Of course, most of us are not mafiosi. But we all interact with people who hold different moral views than we do. And all of us—or at least those who have more than the minimum social savvy—account for that in various ways. Sometimes we do what others demand, even when we don't think we are obligated to do it. Sometimes we are upfront about our objections, and sometimes we aren't. Sometimes we shade our arguments, so that we can appeal to premises our interlocutor accepts, even if they're not premises that we accept. Sometimes we adjust our own claims, so that they'll have a greater chance of success, even if we find ourselves asking for something less than (or different from) what we think we are owed. We can do all of this (and more) without abandoning the moral stance. In fact, we can't do it unless we occupy the moral stance, since we must decide what demands to make on others and assess demands that people make on us. But when we anticipate moral conflict, we almost always temper the moral stance with a sociological one, so that we attend not just to our rights and responsibilities, as best we can discern them, but also to the way that others see them.

The fact that we mix moral and sociological stances in this way deserves more attention than it gets, since it raises serious ethical questions. Just how far may we go in shading our arguments to improve their odds for success? When, how, and why should we accommodate the views of others, even though we think them mistaken? Lawyers confront special versions of these questions every time they step into court, since they come as advocates, not disinterested seekers of truth. We'll think about lawyers later on. For now, it's enough to see that we can—and do—mix moral and sociological stances throughout much of our moral lives. The Mafia is an extreme case, as its manifest immorality makes it hard for most of us to take anything other than a sociological stance toward the moral claims that its members make on one another. But though the case is extreme, it is not extraordinary. Most legal systems have more to recommend them than the Mafia, but not all do, and even the best leave a lot to be queasy about.

The Difference That Law Makes

By this point, it is probably not difficult to piece together what I think about laws that make us queasy—or worse, laws that shock, offend, abuse, or terrorize. Indeed, I have said most of it already. Law is a moral practice—a practice that aims at adjusting what we owe each other. But there is no guarantee that any attempt to do so will succeed in bringing about the change intended. The mere fact that a statute says that people have some right or responsibility is no guarantee that they do. Lots of legal documents are little different from the Lo Piccolo list. They purport to assign rights and duties, but they fail in that. The authors of the document may not have authority over those they purport to govern. Or they may have authority but exercise it so poorly that people are not bound by the decisions that they've made. But what's interesting about law is not how (and how often) it fails to make the moral difference intended, but how (and how often) it succeeds, even when its content makes us queasy. Indeed, we should think a bit more about the reasons that law makes a moral difference, as that will put us in a better position to assess the moral significance of starkly immoral laws.

Law matters morally for lots of reasons, and we've seen several of them already. Way back in the Introduction, when we considered the Constitution, we noticed legal documents can make a moral difference even when the people drafting them do not have authority over those they purport to govern. The rules articulated in the Constitution do not (at least not now) owe their authority to the authority of the people who drafted them (if in fact they ever did). Why are we bound by them now? Earlier I suggested the Constitution binds us because we need to find ways to live together notwithstanding the fact that we disagree about how to live. Of course, there are lots of constitutions that could help us do that, and it's easy to imagine better ones. What makes our particular Constitution authoritative—for us, here and now—is the fact that most of us are willing to defer to it. Some people are willing to defer to the Constitution because they admire the document or the people who drafted it. Some are willing to defer out of small-*c* conservatism; they worry about the risks of attempting to replace the Constitution with something better. And some are willing to defer simply because others do. Of course, not everyone is willing to defer to the Constitution, and some contest its authority. But it is hard to overstate the significance of the fact that so many of us are willing to defer—and share a sense of what deference requires across many cases. This allows us to resolve most disagreements about how power will be exercised peacefully.

That is the foundation of the Constitution's authority. Or so it seems to me. But the substance of the claim matters less than its shape. I don't want to defend the Constitution so much as to set out reasons we might have to recognize its authority. And I'm happy to allow that there are reasons running in the other direction. The peace that the Constitution provides is purchased at the price of the oppression that it permits (plus an awful lot of inefficiency and inanity). If those costs are high enough, the Constitution might lack authority, such that we aren't bound by the political process it structures. But if the Constitution is the best we can do now—and if it is better than stepping into the abyss—then it has authority, and it passes that authority on to the decisions that are made pursuant to it, at least within limits. When Congress decides, for instance, what the tax rates shall be, we are bound by its decision because that is the sort of question for which we require peaceful ways of resolving conflict.[18] On the merits, there may be little to recommend the decision that Congress made. But unless the merits are way out of whack, there will be much to recommend compliance, even as we work to revise the decision through the procedures the Constitution provides. In this way, many of the laws that Congress produces are authoritative, even if the details are less than desirable.

Again, there are limits. Some immorality is so momentous that it is worth casting the system aside and seeking something better, even if that risks the abyss. Nazi Germany and Taliban Afghanistan were clear-cut cases, as was the Confederate South. Those regimes were so oppressive, and offered so little hope for redemption, that they could not claim authority on the ground that they helped people to live together peacefully. Indeed, they did the opposite. Many of the legal documents produced in those places had the moral status of the Lo Piccolo list. They failed to generate the rights and duties they purported to put in place. Of course, many of the people who populated those legal systems would not have conceded that. We'll circle back to them in a bit. But first I want to highlight other ways in which law might make a moral difference.

I said that we need to find ways to live together, even when we disagree about how to live. Law can help us do that, but that is not all that it can help with. Life is full of coordination problems—situations in which we need to settle on a solution, so that lots of us act in the same way—and law can help. It can make solutions salient and encourage compliance, through carrots and sticks. Traffic laws are a paradigm case. We have reasons to drive on the same side of the road as everyone else, reasons to coordinate our behavior at intersections, and even reasons to ensure that curbs are clear on at least some occasions, so that streets can be cleaned. When traffic laws help us solve these problems, they have a source of authority that is independent of the authority of the legal system as a whole. I don't know much about the traffic laws in Nazi Germany, but I do not find it difficult to imagine that they were authoritative—that people really did owe it to one another to drive on the right side of the road and stop at stop signals—even though the regime that enforced those rules could claim no right to rule.

There are lots of coordination problems for law to solve: zoning ordinances, pollution permitting schemes, and fishery rules, among other sorts of laws, play a part in coordinating behavior. But there are other ways in which individual laws—or interlocking sets of them—might come to have authority, independent of the authority of the regime that issues them. They might have authority because they help us to discharge collective responsibilities. For instance, it is plausible that we owe it to each other to ensure access to education, health care, and a decent standard of living. Law can play a part in securing all those goods, by establishing institutions to promote or provide them. When it does so, the relevant laws may be authoritative in virtue of the fact that they discharge these collective responsibilities. There is no guarantee that they will be authoritative; the taxes that support those institutions might be unfairly distributed or otherwise oppressive. But if the laws are not oppressive, then they can be authoritative, whether or not we have reason to respect the regime that issued them.

The arguments I've advanced so far at least potentially have purchase in any place that has legal practices. Wherever there are people, there are reasons to resolve disagreements peacefully, solve coordination problems, and discharge collective responsibilities. But these are not the only ways in which legal practices might make a moral difference, and others may be more weighty in the places that they apply. In particular, there are special ways in which democratic law might make a moral difference. For instance, Seana Shiffrin argues that we are morally required to develop democratic institutions, since only they recognize and respect our fundamental equality.[19] When law is genuinely democratic—and not just democratic on the surface, as when votes are employed to provide a patina of legitimacy for authoritarian regimes—then the laws produced have a special claim to our allegiance.[20] As Shiffrin explains, by adhering to democratic law, we express our commitment to the project of governing together as equals, even when we might have preferred that we'd reached different decisions together.[21]

Shiffrin's point is reminiscent of Jeremy Waldron's insistence that democratic decisions demand "a certain sort of . . . respect—that *this,* for the time being, is what the community has come up with and that it should not be ignored or disparaged simply because some of us propose, when we can, to repeal it."[22] There are surely limits to that respect. As Shiffrin emphasizes, dissent can be vital to democracy too, precisely because it can destabilize "a particular law's claim to represent *us.*"[23] There is, she says, a "symbiotic" relationship between participation "in elections following the law *and* vocal protest."[24] Given that, it may be difficult to discern just what moral difference democratic law makes in a particular case. But any attempt to account for the moral difference that legal practices make must allow for the possibility that democratic legal practices make a difference that other legal practices don't.

These are all just sketches of arguments. We would need to develop them in more detail to make the case that we have any particular right or duty as a result of our legal practices. And that work cannot be done in the abstract. If you want to know, for instance, whether the mandate to purchase health insurance in the Affordable Care Act succeeds in generating the obligation that it purports to impose, there is no way to answer the question without thinking through (among other things) the details of our democracy, the details of the statute and the legal framework it is embedded in, the economics of health insurance, and the nature of our collective responsibility to care for one another. The details of our democracy matter for multiple reasons. To start, they matter for the reason that Shiffrin gives; by working together in democratic institutions, we express our mutual regard for each other's equal membership in our community. That message is undermined if we do not then defer to the decisions those institutions make.

Of course, our actual democratic institutions fall short of Shiffrin's ideal, and that surely matters when we think about what deference we owe to the decisions they make. But the details of our democracy matter for more prosaic reasons too. The Constitution does something we desperately need done; it provides procedures through which we can and do peacefully resolve political disagreement. To that end, the Constitution establishes a Congress and specifies its legislative powers, which are restricted to the subjects listed in Article 1, Section 8.[25] So to the extent that the validity of the ACA's mandate rests on the authority of Congress pursuant to the Constitution, it matters whether Congress exercised one of the powers specified therein.

In imposing the mandate, Congress took itself to be acting pursuant to its power to "regulate Commerce . . . among the several states." When the mandate was challenged, the Supreme Court decided that the Commerce Clause did not grant Congress the power to impose it. But the Court nevertheless upheld the mandate on the ground that it could be construed as a tax, which Congress clearly had the authority to impose.[26] Both aspects of that decision were controversial. Some justices thought that the mandate was a proper regulation of interstate commerce, and they could point to several prior court decisions about the scope of that power in support of their view. Others denied that the mandate counted as a tax. But no one at the Court denied that the Constitution mattered.

That's no surprise, since it would be difficult to become a justice if you did not think (or at least act as if) the Constitution matters. That's an important fact about the sociology of the institution, which (in part) accounts for the limited range of arguments that are advanced in court. There's little reason to tell the justices that the Constitution lacks authority, even if you think that true. The chances that they will agree with you approach zero. But it is worth noting that someone who doubts the Constitution's authority might nevertheless think herself obligated to comply with the mandate to purchase health insurance. As I said before, it is plausible that we owe it to one another to ensure access to health care, and the mandate to purchase health insurance plays an important role in the only practice with any hope of doing so. This argument for thinking the mandate valid is not the sort of argument that would move a court to enforce an obligation to purchase health insurance. Judges of all stripes (not just justices) are apt to think the Constitution authoritative, so they are apt to think that the decisions Congress makes matter when (and only when) it acts pursuant to a power provided by the Constitution. If Congress lacked the power to impose the mandate, the courts would not permit the government to enforce it. If they did, they would undermine the procedures that the Constitution provides for resolving political disagreements. But when the rest of us wonder what we are obligated to do, arguments of this sort surely matter. They can augment arguments from the legitimacy of the system as a whole or fill gaps when that is in doubt.

Law and Immorality

We are now in a position to think through the moral significance of starkly immoral laws, like the ones that supported slavery and segregation. And what's immediately apparent—at least from our vantage point—is that the legal practices that produced these laws were not capable of making a moral difference in any of the ways just outlined. Slavery and segregation were brutal practices, so the laws associated could not claim authority on the ground that they helped people to live together peacefully. Those laws did not solve significant coordination problems or help people to discharge collective responsibilities. And though they were produced by regimes that were nominally democratic, part of the point of those laws was to deny Black people membership in the political community. So when we look back at the Fugitive Slave Act or the Mississippi statutes that aimed at the segregation of public spaces, we ought to think them just like the Lo Piccolo list: they purported to create rights and duties, but they failed in that. (Instead, they triggered duties to resist the regime the statutes sought to create, to repeal them, and so on.)

Many of the people who participated in the legal practices that produced those statutes did not see it that way. And, no doubt, they told themselves stories that supported their sense that people really did have the rights and obligations those statutes purported to put in place. The stories were every bit as misguided as the ones that the mafiosi would tell, even more so. The White people who enacted these laws told themselves that Black people were inferior, that they were not capable of self-governance, and that God had ordained White people to exercise dominion over other races. These "justifications" (and countless others) were simply slanders, but those in the grips of them would have had no trouble believing that the laws associated with slavery and segregation did, in fact, generate the rights and duties they purported to impose. And what's striking in reading old cases is the lack of shame people felt about their participation in these practices. Recall, for instance, the Mississippi Supreme Court's acknowledgment that several statutes were simply "expedients to obstruct the exercise of the franchise by the negro race."[27] They simply did not see what they were up to as immoral.

Others did, even at the time. Many of them stood outside the system, but some played a part in it.[28] They are cousins of the queasy members of the Mafia, and like them, they spread across a spectrum. Many were racist, though they found one reason or another to object to slavery or segregation, in whole or in part. Further out on the spectrum stood abolitionists and civil rights pioneers, who regarded slavery and segregation as a scourge precisely because they saw Black people as equals. Like our queasy members of the Mafia, the folks on this spectrum had to straddle two stances—moral and sociological.

They had to ask themselves what they were obligated to do, in light of legal practices associated with slavery and segregation. That's a moral question, and the answer would have depended on the details of the practices in question, as well as on the role that the person asking played within those practices. Or, at least, it might have. It is hard to say in the abstract, as we've seen already that people might be obligated to participate in practices that are, in one way or another, morally corrupt. In the case of slavery and segregation, I'm inclined to think that no one had an obligation to play any part. But it is not hard to see why some might think otherwise, even as they objected to the practices. A district court judge, for instance, might have thought that questions about whether to maintain slavery were above his station, such that he should defer to the decisions that Congress and higher courts had made. That's a moral view about the role he ought to play in the practice, and though I think it misguided, I also think it intelligible, especially given that lower court judges ought to defer to Congress and higher courts on nearly every question that comes before them.

Whatever answer a judge (or official of another sort) might give to the moral questions he faced, he also had reasons to take an interest in the ways that others would answer them. Some of these sounded in self-interest—a judge might lose his job, or suffer an even worse fate, if his rulings departed too far from the views of his colleagues. But judges would have had less selfish reasons to tailor their actions and attitudes to match those of their colleagues. Though a state judge in the antebellum South would not have lasted long if he refused to treat Black people as property, he might have been able to soften their mistreatment, if only in particular cases. To be in a position to do that, the judge would have to say an awful lot that he did not think true and do an awful lot that he did not think justified. The question whether a judge ought to stay true to his own beliefs, even if he might lose his job, or dissemble so as to preserve the possibility of small-scale resistance is difficult, and it's no surprise that many people struggled to decide what to do in circumstances like this. But as important as that ethical question is, the point for us is simply to see that judges (and other legal officials) may, like members of the Mafia, find themselves in circumstances in which it makes sense to adopt a sociological stance toward the practices they participate in.[29]

I've focused on legal officials so that we could see how similar their position might be to the one occupied by queasy members of the Mafia. But those outside the legal system equally well have reasons to adopt both moral and sociological stances toward legal practices. They have reasons to adopt a moral stance, because legal practices might affect their moral situations, even when the practices are immoral. And they have reasons to adopt a sociological stance, since they need to be able to anticipate how others (inside the legal system and out) will interact with them if they are to successfully navigate the social world. The more immoral legal practices are, the more the sociological stance will come to the fore. Those who saw slavery and segregation for what they were had no reason to take them seriously as sources of obligation. But they did have reason to pay careful attention to the obligations that others thought those practices generated, as their lives may have depended on acting as if those obligations were genuine.

Philosophers spend a lot of time worrying about the worst legal systems. (Shiffrin once joked that the capital of Jurisprudence is Riyadh.)[30] It is important that we think about oppressive legal systems and the distinctive problems they pose to those who must live with them. But even as we notice that adopting a sociological stance can help us cope with bad legal practices, we should remember that the moral stance is vital too. As we've seen, some aspects of immoral practices may generate genuine obligations. But beyond that, it is important that we maintain a clear-eyed sense of the shortcomings of our legal practices. To do that, we have to treat them as potential sources of obligations and note the ways in which they fall short.

CHAPTER FIVE

Stop! In the Name of Law

Misleading Questions

I started Chapter 1 with a slur. I said that philosophers are ham-handed when they write about the moral consequences of legal practices. I should take that back; it's a bit too harsh. If you read philosophical reflections on particular domains of law—criminal law, tort law, the First Amendment—you'll find lots that's worthwhile. But the philosophical literature on the moral consequences of law in general is decidedly less helpful.[1] There are, to be sure, sharp insights in it. But the field is preoccupied by misleading questions of marginal importance. Indeed, one of them popped up on Twitter recently, in a poll posted by a philosopher of law: "If your government enacts an unjust law," John Tasioulas tweeted, "do you have a moral obligation to obey it?"[2] Most respondents (nearly 70 percent) said no, but a handful said yes (14 percent), and another chunk said maybe (17 percent).[3] The last group is right; you can't answer Tasioulas's question without knowing something—anything—about the law in question. Suppose, for instance, that the law at issue establishes an income tax, which is unjust. It is tempting to think that you aren't obligated to pay it. But suppose that the reason that the tax is unjust is that it demands too little of wealthy people like you. If that is the only respect in which the law is unjust, then you probably are obligated to pay what it says you owe. You would have been obligated to pay more, if the law had demanded it, so there's little reason to think that the injustice involved lets you off the hook, even if others have cause for complaint.[4]

This is not a criticism of Tasioulas or the people who responded to his poll. It's hard to do philosophy in 280 characters or less. But it's worth encouraging lawyers and laypeople to think about the relationship between law and morality, and Tasioulas did just that. In the comments, people asked clarifying questions, drew distinctions, and staked out simple views. The problem for philosophers is that the scholarly conversation about the moral significance of legal practices is consumed with questions that aren't all that much better than the one Tasioulas posed. The main debate revolves around a question that appears in the title of a famous article by M. B. E. Smith (though Smith was far from the first to ask the question): "Is there a prima facie obligation to obey the law?"[5] Smith is a skeptic. Though he holds out the possibility that the answer is yes, he says that none of the arguments so far offered suggest that it is. I want to work through the details of Smith's argument, so that we can see the problems with the ways that philosophers tend to think about the moral consequences of legal practices—and put ourselves on a better path.

Smith starts by explaining what he means when he asks whether we have a *prima facie obligation* to obey the law.

> I shall say that a person *S* has a prima facie obligation to do an act *X* if, and only if, there is a moral reason for *S* to do *X* which is such that, unless he has a moral reason not to do *X* at least as strong as his reason to do *X*, *S*'s failure to do *X* is wrong.[6]

That is a mouthful; let's make it more bite-sized. Smith's definition has two parts. First, Smith says a person is *obligated* to do a thing if (and only if) it would be wrong for her not to do it. Second, he says that a person has a *prima facie* obligation to do a thing if (and only if) there are reasons that make it wrong not to do it, in the absence of sufficiently strong countervailing reasons.[7] Finally, Smith says he wants to know whether there is a *general* prima facie obligation to obey the law. "Everyone," he observes, "even the anarchist, would agree that in many circumstances individuals have specific prima facie obligations to obey specific laws. Since it is clear that there is in most circumstances a specific prima facie obligation to refrain from murder, rape, or breach of contract, it is plain that each of us has a specific prima facie obligation not to violate laws which prohibit these acts."[8] This is also true, he suggests, when breaking the law would have "seriously untoward consequences."[9]

Add all that up, and Smith says his question amounts to this: "Is there any society in which mere illegality is a moral reason for an act's being wrong?"[10] That is a good question, and in a moment we'll explore Smith's answer. But I want to pause to say that I like this question an awful lot better than the one Smith started with. His original question—Is there a general prima facie obligation to obey the law?—is misleading on many fronts. First, it presupposes that we can identify the content of the law independently of ascertaining its moral force. Second, it encourages us to look for a general mechanism by which our legal practices might make a moral difference, rather than to attend to all the disparate ways different aspects of them might do so. And third, by framing the inquiry in terms of obedience, the question suggests that authority is the mechanism by which law makes a moral difference, when it is just one mechanism among many.

It's worth pausing over these problems, since, as I said, scholarly conversation about the moral significance of our legal practices has long been preoccupied with the question Smith poses. So let's start with the first—the presupposition that we can identify the law independently of ascertaining its moral force. There are, to be sure, ways of talking about law for which this is true. As I said in Chapter 3, sometimes talk about "law" refers to a socially determined set of rules: the rules that are printed in legal materials, the rules that are accepted by legal officials, the rules that are enforced, and so on. Smith's original question poses no problem when we talk about law in one of these ways. It makes sense to wonder whether we are obligated to do what a statute says or whether we are obligated to stop at a stop sign. Since legal positivists think that law just is a socially determined set of rules, it is no surprise that when it comes time to ask about the moral significance of law, they take the central questions to be whether, when, and why we are obligated to obey those rules.

But as we've seen, there's another way that we talk about law. I've argued that law is a moral practice and that legal claims are moral claims.

When I say that you have a legal obligation to pay me $500, I'm saying that you owe me $500, and moreover, that I could claim it in court if it came to that. This just is a claim about what you are obligated to do, and if it is true, there is no further need to ask whether the legal obligation has moral force. On this way of talking, when we conclude that a person has a legal obligation to stop at a stop sign, it is built into our conclusion that the person has a moral obligation to stop, since legal obligations just are obligations of the ordinary moral sort. That doesn't mean that the person should stop. I don't even think it implies that the person will have acted wrongly if they don't (though to vindicate that claim, I'll need to persuade you to think of obligations differently than Smith does). We'll return to this case in a bit, since stop signs are, oddly, a staple of the literature on the moral significance of legal practices. The point I want to make for now is this: when legal claims are moral claims, there is no gap between the judgment that someone is legally obligated to do a thing and the judgment that she is morally obligated to do it. The moral inquiry is internal to the legal judgment, not something that comes after it.[11] Smith's question, then, is simply inapposite when we talk about law this way, and as we've seen, this is one of the central ways that we talk about law.

Second, Smith tells us that he wants to know whether we have a general prima facie obligation to obey the law, as opposed to specific obligations to obey specific laws. It would, of course, be helpful to know if we have a general obligation to obey, so there is no harm in asking, at least when we talk about law in one of the ways for which the question makes sense. But as Smith shows, the arguments that are typically offered are awful (more on them in a moment), and the quest for a general obligation distracts us from more productive questions we could ask about the ways in which particular legal practices affect our obligations. Smith's acknowledgment that we might be obligated to obey specific laws hardly helps, since his examples (murder, rape, breach of contract) suggest that what he has in mind are laws that happen to coincide with what morality would have required anyway.[12] What's missing—from Smith's article and from the philosophical conversation more generally—is systematic discussion of the ways in which, and the reasons for which, different sorts of legal practices shape our obligations.[13]

Finally, Smith's question is troublesome for its invocation of obedience. Asking whether we are obligated to obey the law suggests that the primary way in which law makes a moral difference is through the exercise of authority. Obedience is, after all, a way of responding to orders. I am happy to allow that legal actors sometimes have authority and that they sometimes issue orders that people are obligated to obey. That is one way in which legal practices can make a moral difference. But it is not the only way in which legal practices can make a moral difference. As we have seen time and again, legal practices shift social facts in ways that are morally significant. Indeed, in the Introduction, I suggested that the authority of the Framers plays no role in explaining why we are bound by the rules set forth in the Constitution. We are bound by those rules, if we are, because we have a pressing need to resolve political conflict peacefully, and the present willingness of people to defer to those rules provides us a way to do that.

But it is not just the Constitution that owes its moral force to something other than an exercise of authority. As Mark Greenberg has observed, the moral force of judicial decisions, at least in common-law countries, extends far beyond the authoritative orders issued therein.[14] A court case ends with a judgment in favor of the plaintiff or defendant. The judgment authoritatively resolves that dispute and only that dispute. But the decision reached might bear on the rights and responsibilities of people not party to the case.

The reasons for that are not distinctively legal. Not so long ago, a student approached me to ask whether he could have an extension on his paper assignment. The deadline was close to one for a different class, and he had unexpected responsibilities to a client in a law clinic too. I said yes and extended his deadline by a few days. Shortly thereafter, another student approached me with a similar tale of woe. This time my decision was easier, but not because (or at least not just because) I'd already thought through the reasons for and against. It was easier because I've got an obligation to treat my students equally, so the fact that I'd decided to extend the deadline for the first student counted heavily in favor of extending the deadline for the second student. And that was true notwithstanding that, in making the first decision, I'd said nothing about the rights and responsibilities of anyone other than the student who had made the request. The second student, I thought, had a right to an extension, even though no authoritative act assigned her that right. She had it simply because equality demanded that I treat her the same way I treated the other student.

This is how a lot of legal rights and obligations are generated. A decision is made in one dispute, and equality then requires that we resolve others in the same fashion. Integrity operates a bit differently. It demands that we treat people in accord with a set of principles that is coherent—and plausibly (if not actually) correct.[15] Suppose a third student asks for an extension, citing legal work that she does for a public interest organization, unconnected to any law school class. She's differently situated from the first two students, so she cannot appeal to equality to claim a right to an extension. But that does not make my earlier decisions irrelevant. The fact that a distinction can be drawn between the cases does not mean that it is a good one. If the principle that justified the earlier extensions applies to her as well, she is entitled to the benefit of those decisions. But if it does not—if, for instance, the earlier decision was justified by the need to avoid conflicts between educational demands— then she is not. Again, lots of legal rights and obligations are generated in this fashion.

For all I know, Smith would be happy to allow that, and I want to be clear, nothing about his question precludes the possibility. Rather, the point I want to make is that the philosophical conversation about the moral significance of legal practices is impoverished, in part because it is preoccupied with the question whether, when, and why it generates obligations of obedience, when in fact many of the obligations that law generates are not obligations of obedience to an authority's directives.

As I said at the start of Chapter 1, the most sophisticated inquiries into the moral consequences of our legal practices are not to be found in the philosophical literature. They are located in judicial decisions and the briefs that inform them, since serious inquiry into the moral consequences of legal practices is down-in-the-weeds sort of work. That work is done in response to particular claims—that the plaintiff has a right, that the defendant committed an offense, and so on—and the particulars of the claim and the community's political history matter. Philosophers can help, of course, and some do, both at the retail and wholesale levels. But the time is long past to put Smith's question to bed—at least his first question. His second question isn't so bad.

Bad Answers

But wait, that doesn't make sense. Smith said that his questions were equivalent. So how could the second ("Is there any society in which mere illegality is a moral reason for an act's being wrong?") be better than the first ("Is there a prima facie obligation to obey the law?")? In a moment, I'll argue that there's a way of understanding Smith's questions on which they are not equivalent. It is not Smith's way. And since I want to explore Smith's argument, I propose that we continue to treat his questions as equivalent. Once we see how the argument works, I will suggest another way to read the questions. So back, then, for a moment, to Smith's first way of framing his inquiry.

Is there a general prima facie obligation to obey the law? As I said before, Smith is a skeptic, since he thinks that none of the arguments that philosophers have advanced so far suggests that the answer is yes. He considers several potential sources for an obligation to obey: gratitude for benefits conferred by the state, considerations of fair play that require us to play our part in cooperative endeavors from which we benefit, consent, and consequentialist arguments that all goes better if we are all obedient. He rejects every one of these arguments, and rightly so. As arguments for a general obligation to obey, they aren't impressive (though, as Smith allows, they might have purchase in particular cases).

Why aren't these arguments impressive? Really, you ought to read Smith (as well as John Simmons, who offers even more comprehensive rebuttals).[16] But here's a super-quick rundown. Many of us receive benefits from the state for which we ought to be grateful. But it is far from clear—indeed, it seems doubtful—that blanket obedience to the state is the best way for us to display that gratitude. And it is not clear that we must display gratitude in the very best way, anyway, so long as we display it in some sufficient way. The blanket bit poses a problem too. Perhaps gratitude would warrant doing what the state directs when it advances the state's interest without costing us too much relative to the benefit conferred. But, in lots of cases, obedience to the law does little to advance the state's interests, and when it doesn't, it would seem odd to insist that gratitude toward the state demands that we defer anyway.

Fair play fares no better. It's plausible that we are, on occasion, required to contribute to cooperative schemes (as in the coffeepot case from Chapter 3). The argument is most compelling when benefits and burdens are shared in roughly equal measure. But our legal practices don't allocate them even roughly equally. Moreover, fair play has bite only when obedience would further the aims of the enterprise. But there are lots of cases in which obedience to the law doesn't do anyone any good. Indeed, modern legal regimes are designed to tolerate a bit of disobedience. In fact, they are often parasitic on it; in some places, the police are funded by traffic fines. So if you take fair play seriously, doing one's part might demand a bit of disobedience—or so I suggest, tongue not completely in cheek.

The other arguments can be dispatched even more quickly. Consent flounders on the fact that nearly none of us has done anything that could plausibly count as consent to be governed by the law of the state in which we live. And the consequentialist arguments don't add up. Surely there is some lawbreaking that has good consequences and, indeed, good consequences that could be anticipated ex ante, such that even a sophisticated rule utilitarianism would carve out exceptions to a general rule that required obedience (were such a rule even warranted in the first place).

Of course, there's more to say about all these arguments; each has their partisans, who would push back on my too-quick critique.[17] And further arguments might make more progress toward establishing an obligation to obey the law.[18] But we won't chase them down, because what really interests me is what comes next in Smith's argument. After rejecting all the standard rationales for an obligation to obey, Smith makes a surprising claim: even if some yet-to-be-advanced argument were to establish a general obligation to obey the law, it would be a trivial obligation—so trivial, in fact, that we would do well to ignore it and "refuse to count an act as wrong merely because it violates some law."[19]

To make his case, Smith offers two tests for determining the weight of an obligation:

First . . . a prima facie obligation is a serious one if, and only if, an act which violates that obligation and fulfils no others is seriously wrong; and second . . . a prima facie obligation is a serious one if, and only if, violation of it will make considerably worse an act on which other grounds is already wrong.[20]

By neither of these tests, he tells us, would a prima facie obligation to obey the law count as serious. Applying the first test, he imagines failing to stop at a stop sign when no one else is around. If the prima facie obligation to obey the law is "of substantial moral weight," then the failure to stop must, Smith says, be "a fairly serious instance of wrongdoing."[21] "But clearly it [is] not," Smith says. "If it [is] wrong at all . . . it [is] at most a mere peccadillo."[22] Applying the second test, Smith argues that "acts which are otherwise wrong are not made more so—if they are made worse at all—by being illegal."[23] Defrauding someone, he explains, "is hardly worse morally by being illegal than it would have been were it protected by some legal loophole."[24]

I'm not sold on Smith's tests. As to the first: I take it that I have an obligation not to cheat on my taxes and that this is a serious obligation—not, to be sure, the most serious, but not trivial either. There are, however, more and less serious sorts of cheating, and some of the less serious sorts might even be trivial. (Suppose you win a few dollars on a scratch-off lottery ticket but fail to declare the income.) The fact that some breaches of an obligation are trivial does not imply that the obligation itself is trivial.[25] As to the second test: if it turns out that Paul Manafort conspired with the Russian government to throw the 2016 election to Donald Trump, the fact that he failed to declare income to facilitate doing so would not make what he did much worse than it would be on other grounds, even if the tax evasion itself was far from trivial.[26] Tax evasion (on any significant scale) is seriously wrong, but it hardly makes a difference when we consider just how wrong it is to interfere with a presidential election.

Still, I think Smith is right. The fact that the law prohibits an act does not much affect whether the act is wrong, if it has any effect at all. Or, at least, it does not do so directly. Murder is wrong regardless of what the state has to say about it. Playing hopscotch is not, though legend has it that Missouri prohibits it on Sunday.[27] There are, to be sure, actions that are wrong that would not be wrong if the law did not say so. But the saying so is not what makes the difference. Rather, it is the practice in which the prohibition is embedded. It is common for cities in snowy places to have rules about where one can park during a snowstorm. Flouting those rules is wrong, but not simply because the city says that they must be followed. It is wrong because of a complicated set of social facts, which includes, among other things, the fact that snowplows will attempt to remove the snow; the fact that your parking in a prohibited area will slow them down or stop them entirely; the fact that most people will observe the rules, so that your failing to do so is likely to pose a problem that the plows would not face otherwise; the fact that your neighbors need to go places, even when it snows; the fact that snow impedes emergency vehicles; and so on. Parking offenses are textbook mala prohibita, but it is not the prohibita that makes the mala. Or, at least, it does not do so by itself.[28]

So I agree with Smith: the mere fact that an act is illegal does not tell us much, if anything, about how wrong that act is. Smith says this shows that the obligation to obey the law is, at best, a trivial obligation. (At worst, there is no such obligation.) And that makes sense if you think about obligations the way that Smith does. Remember, Smith told us that he says that a person is obligated to do a thing if (and only if) it would be wrong for her not to do it. This is a common way of thinking about obligations, but it is not the only way. And indeed, it is not the way that we were thinking about them until we encountered Smith. Way back in Chapter 1, I suggested that rights and obligations are relationships. If I am obligated to pay you $500, then I owe it to you. And as we saw, there are many aspects to that owing. If I can't pay you (or simply won't), then I ought to tell you in advance and seek your release. If I fail to pay you without receiving a release in advance, then I ought to apologize and make it up to you as best I can. And, of course, other things being equal, I ought to pay you what I owe you.

But, of course, other things might not be equal. The fact that I owe you $500 does not guarantee that it would be wrong not to pay you; all it guarantees is that I would wrong you if I don't. If I need the money to pay for my child's medical care, then wronging you would be the right thing to do.[29] Likewise, if I know that you plan to use the money in a plot to commit murder, then I'd do no wrong in refusing to pay you, even if (and this is a big if) I would wrong you in doing so. This serves as a reminder that we can ask two questions about any act: (1) Is it wrong? and (2) Will anyone be wronged by it? Smith interprets the question whether we have a general prima facie obligation to obey the law as inviting the first sort of inquiry. When he rephrases it, he comes out with this: "Is there any society in which mere illegality is a moral reason for an act's being wrong?" No, Smith says, and he's right about that. But we could instead interpret the question to invite the second sort of inquiry. That is, we could understand the question to ask whether illegal acts are wrongs, not whether they are wrong.

I think that is the better way to render the question.[30] But I won't insist on it, because, as you know, I think it misleading to talk about obligations to obey anyway. I will, however, insist on this: when we inquire into the moral consequences of legal practices, we should take account of all the ways in which legal practices might make a moral difference. Smith gets only a part of the picture in view, and a minor part at that. The primary purpose of legal practices is not to make acts wrong, or more wrong than they would otherwise be. Rather, it is to rearrange our moral relationships. And as we are about to see, that is something law can do.

The Standing to Punish

A case will help me make my case. In *State v. R.Z.M.*, the Oklahoma Court of Criminal Appeals reviewed a complaint that alleged that a sixteen-year-old boy assaulted a sixteen-year-old girl.[31] They had been drinking, and she became so intoxicated that she had to be carried to the defendant's car. Later in the evening, the boy brought the girl to her grandmother's house, and from there, she was taken, unconscious, to the hospital, where her blood alcohol content measured a staggering 0.34. A sexual assault exam showed that the boy's DNA was present near the girl's mouth, and the prosecution alleged that he had penetrated her there. Most people would probably call that rape, but Oklahoma law defines rape so as to require "vaginal or anal penetration."[32] Another provision of Oklahoma law, however, establishes the offense of forcible sodomy. The language in that statute is archaic and offensive. It defines sodomy as "the detestable and abominable crime against nature," without explaining just what that is.[33] But the phrase has long been interpreted to encompass oral as well as anal penetration.[34] So the state prosecutor charged the boy with forcible sodomy.

The trial court dismissed the charge, and the Oklahoma Court of Criminal Appeals affirmed that judgment. Why? Well, if the boy did penetrate the girl's mouth, then he committed sodomy. But the offense he was charged with was *forcible* sodomy, and the statute set out four circumstances in which sodomy counts as forcible, none of which covered the case. Here is the relevant provision:

B. *The crime of forcible sodomy shall include:*
  1. Sodomy committed by a person over eighteen (18) years of age upon a person under sixteen (16) years of age; or
  2. Sodomy committed upon a person incapable through mental illness or any unsoundness of mind of giving legal consent regardless of the age of the person committing the crime; or
  3. Sodomy accomplished with any person by means of force, violence, or threats of force or violence accompanied by apparent power of execution regardless of the age of the victim or the person committing the crime; or
  4. Sodomy committed by a state, county, municipal or political subdivision employee or a contractor or an employee of a contractor of the state, a county, a municipality or political subdivision of this state upon a person who is under the legal custody, supervision or authority of a state agency, a county, a municipality or a political subdivision of this state.[35]

Viewing this provision in isolation, you might be tempted to argue that intoxication is the sort of "unsoundness of mind" that renders a person incapable of giving consent, especially if the person is intoxicated past the point of consciousness. But the statute that defined rape includes an almost identical provision plus two others that explicitly address intoxication and consciousness. The additional provisions provide that anal or vaginal penetration constitutes rape "[w]here the victim is intoxicated by a narcotic or anesthetic agent, administered by or with the privity of the accused as a means of forcing the victim to submit,"[36] or where "the victim is at the time unconscious of the nature of the act and this fact is known to the accused."[37] The presence of those additional phrases in the rape provisions suggests that "unsoundness of mind" refers to conditions akin to mental illness, rather than intoxication or lack of consciousness. And if that is right, then what the boy did (or rather, was alleged to do— from now on I'll drop the qualifier for ease of exposition) did not fit within the statute's definition of forcible sodomy. That's just what the trial court decided when it dismissed the charges. The Court of Criminal Appeals did not even bother to publish its opinion affirming the judgment, presumably because it regarded the outcome as obvious.

The decision sparked outrage, but not because commentators took the case to be wrongly decided. Michelle Anderson—one of the foremost scholars on the law of rape—said the decision was "appropriate," even as she argued that Oklahoma law was "archaic" and "entirely out of step with what other states have done . . . and what Oklahoma should do."[38] Anderson did not explain why she thought the decision appropriate, but it's not hard to figure out what she had in mind. As we saw in Chapter 3, criminal law is constrained by the principle of legality, which requires that the law define an offense before people are punished for it. As I suggested before, the point of the principle is not that people must be told what conduct is wrongful in order for it to be permissible to punish them. I doubt that even this child needed to be told that what he did was wrong, but even supposing that he did, promulgating it in a piece of legislation and printing it in Title 21 of the Oklahoma Statutes Annotated would probably not have been an effective way of conveying it to him. Rather, the point of the principle of legality is to constrain the state—to make it say how it will use its power to punish in advance, so as to guard against all the ways it might abuse people if it had the power to define crimes ex post. The decision in R.Z.M. was a straightforward application of the principle of legality; the outrage was that the Oklahoma statute was so sloppily drafted that it did not make what the boy had done criminal.

The Oklahoma legislature sprang into action, amending the statute so as to include intoxication and lack of consciousness in the definition of forcible sodomy. Here's the question I want to ask: Did the amendment make a moral difference? It certainly did not make what the boy did wrong. Forcibly sodomizing someone who is not conscious is wrong, regardless of what the law has to say about it, so what the boy did was wrong already. And I don't see any argument for thinking that the amendment made what he did worse than it was. Amendment aside, what the boy did was seriously wrong, and I don't feel the slightest inclination to blame him less than I would someone charged with similar conduct after the amendment was adopted. The boy was let off because of a legal loophole. But as Smith taught us, loopholes do not bear on blameworthiness.

Does that mean the amendment was morally inert? No, most definitely not. But it does mean that we have to look elsewhere for the moral difference that it made. Where? Well, way back at the start, I suggested that legal practices are tools for adjusting our moral relationships. So instead of looking to the wrongness of what the boy did, we might instead look to the relationships that people had in respect of it. The first thing to say is that the boy wronged the girl. She had a right not to be treated the way she was. She would have had that right regardless of what the law had to say about it. But as it happens, Oklahoma law recognizes that right, and it grants her a further right to enforce it through a civil suit for battery. That's good, but not good enough, in part because sexual assault victims rarely file civil suits, and in part because people who do what the boy did ought to be punished, harshly, not just made to pay damages. The state failed in its effort to punish the boy because it had no right to do it. Indeed, the boy had a right not to be punished, on account of the principle of legality. But once the amendment passed, all that changed. The moral concern that underwrites the principle of legality abated, at least for future defendants, and with it any bar to punishing people who do what the boy did. In other words, the amendment extinguished the right that the boy exercised when he moved to have the charges against him dismissed, and in doing so granted the state the standing to punish people who commit the acts described in the amended statute.

Laypeople are often bothered by legal technicalities. But technicalities—like the principle of legality—often reflect moral constraints on the way the state operates. The cost of the principle of legality is high. The boy ought to have been punished. Since he was just a boy, one hopes that his parents or school stepped into the breach. But even if they did, the punishments they imposed were surely inadequate. It would be hard for a parent or school to impose a punishment commensurate to this wrong, at least not without violating the law themselves. And if they dispensed any punishment at all, they probably did so privately. But in cases like this, punishment ought to be public, since it has expressive work to do. In addition to condemning the defendant, punishment affirms the value of the victim by confirming that the way she was treated was wrong. It also tells people tempted to do what the defendant did that their conduct will not be tolerated and, at the same time, reassures potential victims their community cares about the wrongs they might suffer. The fact that none of this happened in *R.Z.M.* is tragic, and it's no wonder that people are frustrated when technicalities get in the way of responding to wrongdoing properly. But these costs are worth bearing because the alternative is dire: a state that can punish anyone at will for an offense made up after the fact.

The principle of legality is not the only technicality that reflects moral constraints on the state. Indeed, a state must do much more than satisfy that principle if it wants the standing to punish. Many of the requirements that we take to be constitutive of due process reflect these moral constraints. To have the standing to punish, the state must notify the accused of the charges against him. It must give him an opportunity to defend himself. It must provide a right to a public trial, so that others can monitor the fairness of the proceedings when guilt is in dispute. And much more.[39]

Identifying the conditions a state must satisfy in order to have standing to punish could hardly be more important, especially in a society that incarcerates a shocking proportion of its population. There is lots in the literature on criminal law and procedure that bears on the question (though it is not always presented through the lens of that question). If I seemed impatient with Smith earlier, it is because I think he seriously misconstrues the point of our legal practices. Criminal law may rarely make conduct wrong, or more wrongful than it would otherwise be. But that is not the moral difference that it most commonly seeks to make. The main point of the criminal law is to put the state in a position to punish—to give it the standing to do so, by removing rights that defendants would otherwise have against it. That is a moral difference that it can and often does make, as *R.Z.M.* and its aftermath illustrate.

Amusing the Gods

Forcible sodomy is wrong, regardless of what the state has to say about it. So perhaps it is not surprising that, with the right background in place, the state can acquire the standing to punish it. But what about acts that are not wrong, regardless of what the state has to say about them? Can the state acquire the standing to punish them too? The answer is yes, at least sometimes, and the standard stop sign case can help us see why. So picture yourself driving, all alone, through a desolate place, approaching an intersection with a stop sign. The day is clear, and the landscape is flat. There are no obstructions—no trees, no buildings, no billboards, no signs of any sort, save that lonely stop sign, standing as a sentinel on the side of the road. You, for your part, have vision that would make a pilot proud, and you are paying careful attention. There are no cars, no trucks, no vans, no vehicles of any sort, for as far as you can see, which is plenty far. There are no people, no pets, no animals—just you, all alone, approaching that stop sign and wondering: should you bother to stop?

To stop, you'll have to slow down, put stress on your brakes, and burn a bit of extra gas to bring yourself back up to speed. What would you get out of it? Nothing, and nobody else will either. So why would you stop? Well, there is that sign that says stop. And standing behind that sign is a complicated social practice. Do the sign and the practice it is embedded in bear on what you ought to do? Well, let's think about the practice. Presumably, some legislative authority established an administrative agency, which employees traffic engineers. They decided to put a stop sign at this intersection. They might have done so for safety reasons, or to smooth traffic flow, or some combination of the two. But whatever reasons they had for thinking that there ought to be a stop sign at this intersection aren't operative now—you are the only car around, so there's no traffic to smooth and no safety risk either.

There's more to the practice, of course. Passing the stop sign without stopping is an offense, and if the police were to catch you doing it, they would write you a ticket. The ticket would have a fine attached, and your insurance company would be apt to raise your rates, once it learned that you were ticketed. But there are no police around. It is possible, of course, that there's some detection device that you can't see—a sensor in the road, perhaps, linked to a camera that will record your license plate if you fail to stop. But that seems the slimmest of possibilities, and we could eliminate it if we set this story before the advent of those sorts of sensors.

As we've set up the story, there is nothing about the situation that warrants stopping, and you know that. So if you do stop, you're either risk averse or a rule fetishist. Either way, you'll give the gods a good laugh. Or so some philosophers say. Are they right? Well, the setup of the story is not realistic. As I've told the tale, there's no one around, and you know it. But there are not many cases where we can be so confident in our judgment. The day may not be so clear, your eyesight may not be so good, the land might not be so flat. But even if all that and more work out in your favor, you may not know that, and finding out comes at a cost. Joseph Raz made this point long ago:

> We all know the benefit from allowing traffic lights to regulate one's action rather than acting on one's own judgment. But we tend to forget that a significant part of the benefit is that we give up attempting to form a judgment of our own. When I arrive at a red traffic light I stop without trying to calculate whether there is, in the circumstances, any reason to stop. From our vantage point we have invented an example in which the question does not arise since the answer (there is no reason) is plain. But for the man in our example the question does arise; he has to discover whether there is no reason to stop. And if he is to inquire in this case, he has to inquire in many other cases. For us it looks ridiculous to hear him say, "I am bound to follow authority regardless of the merits of the individual case," for we know in advance what the merits are and forget he has to find that out, and not only now but in many other cases as well. Only when it is justified to prevent this, is it also justified to accept authority in this respect, even if once in a while this makes one look ridiculous to the gods.[40]

Raz is right. The fact that there is no first-order reason to stop does not preclude the possibility that there is a second-order reason to decline to form a judgment on the merits of the case and simply defer to the presence of the stop sign.[41] If the costs of finding out whether there are first-order reasons to stop are high enough, you should stop. And they don't have to be very high to be high enough, since stopping has so little cost.

Raz's story helps us to see why it can be rational to stop. Does that mean that it's wrong not to stop? I don't think so, at least not if you have properly judged the case. If stopping does not serve anyone's interest, it is hard to criticize you for failing to stop, even if we think you shouldn't have wasted your time trying to figure out whether you should. (If you didn't try to figure out whether it was safe, then your failure to stop was risky and wrong for that reason.) The presence of the stop sign does not destabilize this judgment, nor does the practice behind it. As we saw with Smith, the law does not bear much on blameworthiness, except in cases where it creates the possibility of new sorts of wrongs (like parking in the wrong spot in a snowstorm, or failing to pay your taxes), and this is not one of those cases.

Are you obligated to stop? That's a different question. On Smith's way of thinking about obligations, the answer is no. Recall that, on Smith's view, a person is obligated to do a thing if (and only if) it would be wrong for her not to do it. So once we've decided that it is not wrong not to stop, we've also decided that you aren't obligated to do it. But as we've seen, there's another way to think about obligations, a way that I've suggested is more suited to thinking about law. On this way of thinking, obligations are relationships. And as we've seen several times now, the fact that a person is, in this sense, obligated to do a thing does not mean that she ought to do it, or even that it would be wrong not to do it. All it means is that not doing it would constitute a wrong to the person to whom she owes the obligation.

The reason for this is that when you have an obligation, you ought to do what it requires, all else equal. But all else is not always equal. Sometimes, as we've seen, the right thing to do is to wrong someone, as when I default on my debt to pay for my kid's medical care. Defaulting on my debt constitutes a wrong, and because it does, I ought to explain, apologize, and pay as soon as I'm able, perhaps with interest. But it is a wrong I ought to commit. We can construct a similar case by supposing that you've got a pressing reason not to stop at the sign; perhaps you are rushing your child to the emergency room. In that case, the right thing to do is to ignore the sign. But that is not our case. In our case, your reasons not to stop are not at all pressing. You'll get where you are going a tiny bit quicker, put a tiny bit less stress on your brakes, and burn a tiny bit less gas, but all that matters at most a tiny bit. Still, the case is constructed so that there is absolutely nothing weighing on the other side, and if we take that aspect of it seriously, then I think it plausible that you ought not to stop. But as Raz reminds us, we ought not take it too seriously, because outside the hypothetical, there are almost surely costs, even in situations that are similar. Ultimately, however, I don't think it is a terribly interesting question whether you ought to stop. The point here is simply that there is nothing inconsistent in thinking that you have an obligation to stop but ought not do it.

Are you obligated to stop? I am happy to say that you are, at least assuming that all the other facts necessary to support the obligation are in place (that, for instance, the traffic code was promulgated by the proper procedures; that the sign was put there by the proper authorities, not as a fraternity prank; and so on). To whom do you owe the obligation? If there were other people around, then you would owe those people an obligation to stop. If you promised your spouse that you wouldn't take the slightest risk of getting another traffic ticket, then you would owe them an obligation to stop. What about the state? Do you owe the state an obligation to stop? Again, I am happy to say that you do. I think that fact is what we mark when we describe crimes as offenses against the state. And I think crimes are offenses against the state even when they have victims. The victim in *R.Z.M.,* for instance, had a right not to be penetrated while unconscious. The act wronged her. Had the statute not been so sloppily drafted, the act would also have been an offense against the state. That label signals that the state had a right that the act not be done, separate from victim's right. And that means that the defendant did indeed owe the state an obligation not to commit the offense.

This is a point that must be made with some care, as it can cause confusion. To say that those subject to the laws of Oklahoma owe the state an obligation not to forcibly sodomize someone is not to say that the state itself is harmed by forcible sodomy, or that the interests the state vindicates in a criminal prosecution are its own. The victim is the primary person harmed, and her interests are the primary interests vindicated. But sometimes, we hold rights so that we can vindicate the interests of others. The genius of the trust lies in its formalization of that fact, through the splitting of legal and beneficial ownership.[42] As legal owner, the trustee holds an array of rights and is owed the obligations that correspond to them. But she holds them so that she can vindicate the interests of the beneficial owners. Something similar, I think, is true with crimes. The state holds a right that those subject to its jurisdiction not commit offenses against it, but the state does not hold that right because it serves the state's interests (though, with respect to a narrow class of crimes, like tax evasion and treason, it does). Rather, the state holds the right because it allows the state to vindicate the interests of the victim (when there is a victim), as well as the interests of others interested in the crime: people who care about the victim, people who might be victims, people who suffer secondary harms, and so on. Indeed, the fact that criminal law can vindicate this broader set of interests is one reason that we ought to have it, even if (and this is not always true) tort law provides an adequate mechanism of vindicating the interests of victims.

All that said, I will not insist that we owe the state an obligation not to commit criminal offenses. Some people find it odd to say so, and though I don't, I'm happy to rest on a weaker claim: when the criminal law works as intended, the state has the standing to punish criminal offenses. Consistent with the way that I treated *R.Z.M.,* I shall say that the state has the standing to punish an offense if (and only if) the defendant does not have a right not to be punished by the state. In *R.Z.M.,* the defendant had a right not to be punished by the state because his act was not defined as an offense in advance of its commission. Future defendants in similar forcible sodomy cases will not have that right, so the state will have standing to punish them (absent other rights they might hold).

What about our stop sign case? Does the state have the standing to punish you if you don't stop? I think that it does, but that doesn't mean the state should exercise it. If the facts are as transparent to the state as they are to you, then perhaps the state should let you off with a warning, or least a reminder, that things are not always as they appear. But, of course, the facts may not be transparent. A sensor or camera might capture your failure to stop, without showing that your doing so posed no danger to anyone, that you were aware of that fact, and so on. It is sensible, then, for the state to punish you even when you can protest, truthfully, that you posed no risk to anyone. Indeed, if we hold that the state does not have standing in cases like this, then we leave it hostage to the accused's description of the facts, which may often be inaccurate.

The upshot is that the state sometimes has standing to punish you when you've done nothing wrong—nothing you ought not to have done. My suspicion is that cases like this are not so common; remember how carefully constructed this case was. There are lots of offenses for which this is hardly a risk. It is hard to murder someone without having done something wrong. That's in part because the law is sophisticated enough that it accounts for all (or nearly all) the justifications and excuses that people might have for homicide. But that's also because there's a victim, so there's always something on the other side of the ledger—a reason not to kill—which wasn't true in the stop sign case.

When it is possible that an offense was committed but nothing wrong was done, the punishment ought to reflect that fact, and traffic fines typically do. They are small, relative to other punishment the state dispenses. And partly for that reason, they do not communicate the same sort of condemnation. Many states regard moving violations as criminal offenses, but few of us would brand a person a criminal simply on account of a speeding ticket. The word *criminal* works as an epithet because most criminal conduct is wrong, often seriously so. But the point of the criminal law is not to make conduct wrong. It is to provide the state the standing to punish. That's easier to do when the conduct proscribed is wrong, but as the stop sign case illustrates, the state might have standing even when it is not.

More Questions

This chapter has taken a winding path, but it ends with a plea to pay attention to the full range of moral consequences that our legal practices might have. Faced with that stop sign, you can ask lots of questions: Should I stop? Am I obligated to stop? Does the state have the standing to punish me if I don't stop? These are all different questions. And there are others that might be triggered by legal practices: Should I resist? Am I obligated to resist? Does the state have the standing to punish me if I resist? Those questions are the stock-in-trade of conversations about civil disobedience. I won't take them up here, partly because the philosophical conversation about them is in better shape than the conversation about whether, when, and why we are obligated to do what the law requires. But I do not mean to discount their importance. They are vital, as are other questions: Should I try to change the law? If so, how? What deference do I owe the law as I attempt to change it? Indeed, the main point I want to make is just this: our conversations about the moral consequences of legal practices need an awful lot more nuance than they have heretofore had.

CHAPTER SIX

Roy Moore and the Rule of Law

Chief Justice Fruit Salad

Roy Moore is one of America's least distinguished lawyers. His classmates at the University of Alabama Law School probably could have predicted as much. On the first day of his criminal law class, the professor called on Moore, and kept him on call—standing and answering questions—for the entire hour.[1] At the end of class, the professor pronounced his verdict: "Mr. Moore, I have been teaching in this school for thirty years, and in all of that time you're the most mixed-up person I've ever taught. I'm going to call you Fruit Salad." Two days later, the professor called on Moore again: "Fruit Salad, take this case." A puzzled Moore reminded the professor of his name. The professor told Moore to come to the front of the room, spun him around, and said: "Mr. Moore, you're all mixed up, like a fruit salad." And he called Moore Fruit Salad for the rest of law school.

I can't imagine treating a student so cruelly. And I can't fathom why some law professors mistake the Socratic method for a sadistic one. But the sympathy I feel for Moore is tempered because I know what comes next.[2] After graduation, Moore took a job as a deputy district attorney in Etowah County. Eventually, he ascended to the bench. To start, he was appointed presiding judge in Etowah County. Later, he was elected chief justice of the Alabama Supreme Court—not bad for Fruit Salad. But Moore's time on both courts was tumultuous. In Etowah County, Moore hung a plaque of the Ten Commandments behind his bench. Some litigants objected, kicking off a series of lawsuits that posed the question whether the plaque violated the Establishment Clause. A state judge held that it did and ordered Moore to take it down. But that ruling was set aside on technical grounds. The constitutionality of the plaque was never finally resolved, as the attention Moore received propelled him to higher office.

Shortly after he became chief justice, Moore placed a monument depicting the Ten Commandments in the court's rotunda. The monument (which came to be known as Roy's Rock, or just the Rock) weighed more than five thousand pounds. It was carved from some of the finest granite in the world. But the Rock wasn't in the rotunda long before a federal suit was filed, arguing again that a display of the Ten Commandments in a courthouse violated the Establishment Clause. A federal judge agreed and ordered it removed.[3] On appeal, Moore acknowledged that the First Amendment (which states that "Congress shall make no law respecting an establishment of religion") had long been held to constrain state governments too. But he contended that he hadn't made a law, since his display didn't prohibit or require any conduct.[4] Alas, that view had long been rejected too. The First Amendment has been held to restrict (though not entirely prohibit) religious displays on public property and prayers by public officials, even when they don't involve requirements or prohibitions.[5] The display of the Rock ran afoul of those restrictions, so Moore lost his appeal. Still, he refused to move the monument. And that cost Moore his job. The Alabama Judicial Inquiry Commission filed a complaint with the Alabama Court of the Judiciary, which suspended Moore from his post. The remaining justices of the Alabama Supreme Court removed the Rock from the rotunda and put it in storage, satisfying the federal court's order. Finally, the Alabama Court of the Judiciary permanently removed Moore from office.[6]

Or so it might have thought. After a failed gubernatorial bid, Moore recaptured his old job when he was reelected chief justice. He did not reinstall the Rock, which by then was something of a celebrity, touring the country, sometimes with Moore, sometimes without. But Moore's second tenure was every bit as rocky as his first. A federal district court declared Alabama's restrictions on same-sex marriage unconstitutional.[7] Moore responded with a memo instructing state probate judges that they were not bound by the federal court order and that they would violate the Alabama Constitution if they issued marriage licenses to same-sex couples. In the midst of that controversy, the Supreme Court of the United States settled the question, when it ruled, in *Obergefell v. Hodges,* that the Constitution guaranteed same-sex couples the right to marry.[8] But Moore still did not yield. Once again, he instructed state probate judges to refuse marriage licenses to same-sex couples. And once again, the Alabama Judicial Inquiry Commission filed a complaint with the Alabama Court of the Judiciary, and Moore was suspended from office for the remainder of his term.[9]

Had Moore stopped there, he might have slipped into obscurity, just another entry in the sordid history of Southern resistance to federal civil rights decisions. But he ran for the US Senate. And his candidacy failed amid credible allegations that he had dated—and sexually assaulted— several underage girls when he was a deputy district attorney in Etowah County.[10] Going forward, that should be the main source of Moore's disgrace. But I want to explore what his judicial career can teach us about the rule of law.

Law as a Source of Morality

Let's put Moore on hold for a moment, though. I want to start with an observation that Robert Nozick made about morality. It does not act on the world directly. Morality makes an impact on people's lives only to the extent that we recognize and respect its requirements.[11] In the first instance, we do that by doing what morality demands of us; we discharge obligations. But when we fail in that, we still have an opportunity to recognize and respect morality. When we appreciate our own wrongdoing, we can apologize and seek to set things right. And when we confront the wrongdoing of others, we can treat their wrongs as wrongs and respond to them appropriately. Legal practices can play a part in that. As I've argued elsewhere, both criminal law and tort law are (at least potentially, when they are well constructed) ways of recognizing and responding to the moral qualities of people's acts.[12] To differing degrees and in different ways, both institutions condemn wrongdoing and vindicate the social standing of victims.

But law, as we've seen, is not just a way of recognizing and responding to moral requirements. It is a way of adjusting them. Legal practices can create, extinguish, arrange, and rearrange our rights and obligations. So taking morality seriously means taking legal practices seriously as sources of moral requirements. Now, as I've said before and will say again, there's no guarantee that any particular legal practice will make a moral difference, let alone the moral difference the participants intend. But as we've seen, many legal practices do make a moral difference. And when they do, recognizing and responding to morality requires recognizing and responding to the difference that legal practices make.

What does all this have to do with Moore? Well, Moore is a man of many moral failings. The one I want to highlight is this: at two key moments in his career, he failed to recognize and respect the moral difference that the legal practices of his community made. Recall what we said way back at the start: we disagree about how we ought to live but nevertheless need to find ways to live together. This is true in at least two ways. First, we often need to coordinate our actions, so that we can solve problems we can't tackle on our own. Second—and more important here—we need peaceful ways to resolve conflicts, lest those conflicts shatter our lives. And that's what courts provide. Or, at least, that's what courts can provide—if people are willing to defer to their judgments.

Moore was twice barred from the Alabama Supreme Court because he failed to accord court orders the respect they deserved. Courts exist to resolve moral conflicts—conflicts about rights and obligations. Courts can do so only if the orders they issue are, by and large, followed. That makes those orders morally significant, even when they are morally regrettable. Every single one of Moore's colleagues on the Alabama Supreme Court recognized that. Some of them may have thought that the Supreme Court ought to be able to display the Ten Commandments. But all eight associate justices ordered the Rock removed as soon as Moore was suspended. And the Alabama Court of the Judiciary acted unanimously in removing Moore from office, even as it noted that it agreed with Moore that "acknowledgment of God is very much a vital part of the public and private fabric of our country."[13]

Why remove Moore from office? The official reason was that he had violated the Alabama Canon of Judicial Ethics, which among other things, requires a judge to "respect and comply with the law."[14] But in observing that Moore had run afoul of that provision, the Court of the Judiciary explained its significance: "Lawless judicial conduct—the administration, in disregard of the law, of a personal brand of justice in which the judge becomes a law unto himself—is as threatening to the concept of government under law as is the loss of judicial independence."[15] The court went on to explain:

> If a judge, or any other person, disagrees with a determination by a governmental body, that person has every right to seek legal redress. . . . Chief Justice Moore sought legal redress by appealing to the limit of judicial review; he was bound by, and had the duty to follow, the rulings of the federal courts.[16]

That last bit—that Moore had a duty to follow the rulings of the federal courts—is a moral claim every bit as much as it is a legal one. And it is a moral claim underwritten by (among other things) the court's observation that official defiance of the law threatens "the concept of government under law."

The court of appeals had sounded a similar theme when it ruled that display of the Rock violated the Establishment Clause. Moore had asserted that, as chief justice of the Alabama Supreme Court, he was obligated "to follow the state and federal constitutions 'as he best understands them, not as understood by others.'"[17] The court noted that Moore's view (that the highest officer of a branch of government is entitled "to determine whether a court order . . . is consistent with his oath of office to support the federal and state constitution") was previously embraced by Southern governors seeking to maintain segregation.[18] And the court categorically rejected the claim, insisting that the rule of law requires "that every person obey judicial orders when all available means of appealing them have been exhausted."[19]

Is that true? Does the rule of law require that everyone obey judicial orders? There's been a robust debate about that since the start of the republic. Moore was drawing on a tradition that Sanford Levinson calls Constitutional Protestantism, which holds that everyone is entitled to interpret the Constitution for themselves. He contrasts that with Constitutional Catholicism, which sees the Supreme Court as the ultimate arbiter of the Constitution's meaning.[20] There's a modest sense in which everyone endorses the Protestant position.[21] Congress can decline to enact a law it believes unconstitutional, even if it believes the Supreme Court would uphold the law. And the president may pardon people convicted under statutes whose constitutionality she doubts, even if the Supreme Court has upheld them.[22] In both cases, the Constitution commits the choice (to pass legislation, to issue pardons) to the actor's discretion. It would be odd if they did not act in ways consistent with their understanding of what the Constitution requires. But what happens when an official (like the president) is ordered by a court to take an action she regards as unlawful? By and large, officials follow those orders, and as I've already emphasized, many of the benefits that law can secure depend on their willingness to do so.

But there are surely occasions on which officials should refuse. Richard Fallon imagines the Supreme Court ordering the president to invade Iran, on the ground that the "security of the constitutional regime requires . . . preemptive action against a national enemy."[23] It's hard to imagine the Court issuing that order, since it's so obviously out of bounds for the Supreme Court to send us to war. But if the Court did attempt to do so, Fallon says he'd hope that Congress and the American people would back the president's refusal to follow the order.[24] And I agree. The rule of law requires constraints on courts too, so it may sometimes fall to other officials to assert that courts have overstepped their authority and decline to do as they've directed.

But that's not to be done lightly. If officials were in the habit of ignoring orders they disagreed with, we'd lose the ability to restrain them through peaceful means.[25] And that means we'd lose much of the benefit that law can provide. Happily, presidents have been reluctant to defy court orders. As Fallon observes, their actual or threatened defiance has, for the most part, "involved wartime or emergency."[26] In the most famous instance, President Lincoln declined to comply with a writ of habeas corpus, which he thought would undermine the Union's war effort.[27] He believed that the court was acting unconstitutionally. Indeed, he believed that he had the power to suspend the judiciary's authority to issue such writs, and he'd directed the army to do so whenever necessary. (In defending that choice to Congress, he famously asked: "Are all the laws but one to go unexecuted, and the Government itself go to pieces lest that one be violated?")[28] If Lincoln's case for ignoring the writ was compelling, that wasn't just because the court had issued it in error. It was because the stakes were high; the republic was at risk.

How high were the stakes in Moore's case? In his view, very high. Here's Moore, under cross-examination by Bill Pryor, the state attorney general, in the Ten Commandments case:

> PRYOR: And your understanding is that the federal court ordered that you could not acknowledge God; isn't that right?
>
> MOORE: Yes.
>
> PRYOR: And if you resume your duties as chief justice after this proceeding, you will continue to acknowledge God as you have testified that you would today?
>
> MOORE: That's right.
>
> PRYOR: No matter what any other official says?
>
> MOORE: Absolutely. . . .

Moore went on to explain that he regarded God as the "moral source" of the law.[29] No measly federal court could, in his view, displace God—or the Rock. He doubled down in the same-sex marriage case, claiming that he was not bound by *Obergefell* because it was "manifestly absurd and unjust and contrary to reason and divine law."[30]

I don't doubt that Moore was sincere or that, from his perspective, the moral stakes were high. But I think he made a moral mistake, and not just because I doubt the existence of divine law. Moore's entitlement to ignore court orders could not possibly be as broad as he claimed. Many (if not most) litigants who lose believe that their cases were wrongly decided—that the decisions were unjust and contrary to reason. If that was sufficient grounds for ignoring a judicial decision, we'd lose much of the benefit legal practices provide. Again, we disagree about how to live but must find ways to live together. That means that we must, most of the time, work through the institutions we establish to make decisions, not ignore or undermine them. Lincoln acted to save those institutions—to protect them from violent revolt. Moore could make no similar claim. He set his own view of how we ought to live above everyone else's. Alabamans were lucky that his colleagues were willing to constrain him.

There are no bright lines here. Lincoln's case was compelling in part because the survival of the institutions was at stake—but also because they were worth saving (especially when considered against the Confederate alternative). Some legal institutions aren't worth saving. Many states are brutal. They rule through violence and perpetrate or permit mass human rights violations. By and large, we should follow court orders because they provide peaceful means of conflict resolution. When courts fail at that—when they license slavery and other atrocities—they have less claim on our obedience. But they may still have some claim, some of the time. There are legal systems in which courts provide significant benefits, resolving run-of-the-mill tort claims, contracts suits, property disputes, actions for divorce, and so on, while at the same time sanctioning the oppression of some in society. Exactly what deference is owed court orders in such places, in exactly what contexts, is a question about which I can say nothing exact—or even inexact, without knowing an awful lot about the case.

But there is something worth saying: no community has ever had legal practices that were, in every way, morally satisfactory. When legal practices are bad, we have to decide how to reform them—both what reforms are warranted and how to go about getting them. When they are very bad, we have to decide how to resist or revolt. There is an obvious pragmatic dimension to these decisions: one has to ask what sort of resistance will yield the desired result. But there is an underappreciated moral dimension to them too. Legal institutions can do a lot that's good even as they do a lot that's bad. So there is, in some cases, moral pressure to respect them, even as one resists them. Civil disobedience is, among other things, a way of reconciling that tension. But I shall say no more about it here.

The Rule of Law

What is the rule of law? It's a complicated idea. In fact, it's a cluster of ideas. As Jeremy Waldron has explained, the central thought is that "people in positions of authority should exercise their power within a constraining framework of public norms, rather than on the basis of their own preferences, their own ideology, or their own individual sense of right and wrong."[31] It is easy to see how Moore ran afoul of that ideal. He would not yield when his moral views conflicted with the commands of courts. And as the Alabama Court of the Judiciary observed, his refusal was especially corrosive, since Moore himself held judicial office. Litigants in Moore's court had real reason to worry that the judge would ignore the law and dispense his own brand of justice.

But earlier, we learned that judges *must* rely on their own sense of right and wrong in deciding cases. The questions presented in court are questions about who has what rights—and who has committed what wrongs. They demand answers, and there is nothing a judge can do but call them as she sees them. Does that make the rule of law an empty ideal? No, not at all. As we saw in Chapter 1, the moral questions posed in court are narrowly drawn: typically, judges are asked to decide what the rights and responsibilities of the litigants are, not what they ought to be. So there is space for the ideal that Waldron articulates: judges should decide cases in accord with the rights the litigants have, even if they differ from the rights the judge thinks the litigants ought to have. *That* is the sense in which judges should set aside their own views about right and wrong.

But they cannot set them aside entirely, for their views about what rights and responsibilities litigants have will inevitably rest on their views about the moral significance of legal practices. We saw that back in Chapter 2, when we considered arguments for and against textualism in interpretation. Moore's problem was not that he had a moral view about the way in which the legal practices of his community affected his rights and obligations. Absolutely everyone involved in the litigation had views about that. Moore's problem was that he had the wrong view.

And therein lies the main lesson Moore has to teach us about the rule of law. The rule of law requires a shared moral outlook.[32] It requires that people in positions of authority, like Moore, view legal practices as sources of moral constraints—and treat them as such. Moore posed a danger to the rule of law because he was willing to defy a court order without adequate justification.[33] Now again: not all legal practices are sources of morality, and nearly none is the source of all the rights and responsibilities claimed by participants. But the court order Moore ignored in the Ten Commandments case had a strong claim to make the moral difference it purported to make. We disagree about the role religion should play in public life, so we've adopted a set of principles that protect religious freedom. The court order Moore defied applied those principles. Moore would prefer we live by others. But he's not entitled to make that decision on his own.

Happily, Moore's moral mistake did not pose much of a risk to the rule of law, as the moral outlook that underwrites it was widely shared in Alabama, at least among the relevant legal officials. Alabama also had procedures in place that made even the chief justice accountable to other judges. As Gerald Postema has argued, procedures of that sort are key to maintaining the rule of law. As he puts it, "law can rule only when those who are subject to it, the prince and officials of government and citizens alike, are bound together in a thick network of mutual accountability with respect to that law."[34] Absent practices of accountability, it's difficult to control people with power. That may not be a problem in the short term, if they see law as a source of morality and respect it as such. But in the long term, there are bound to be officials like Moore, so it's important that no one is free from accountability to others.

I said that the rule of law is a complicated idea—indeed, a cluster of ideas. How do the rest fit in? I won't attempt anything like a full account of the rule of law here. But I do want to suggest a way of thinking about it. One question worth asking is: What would legal institutions need to be like in order for their decisions to reliably make a moral difference (of the sort their participants intend)? The answer, I suspect, is that they would need to exhibit many of the virtues that we associate with the rule of law: governance by general norms, announced publicly, and applied prospectively; stability and consistency, at least over the short term; and congruence between the law as announced and the law as applied, among other things. These are the sorts of virtues Lon Fuller emphasized when he spoke about the "inner morality" of law.[35] But as Waldron observes, there's another tradition of thinking about the rule of law that focuses less on the norms and more on the procedures by which they are implemented. That tradition calls our attention to the value of impartial and independent decision makers, notice of charges, the opportunity to be heard and to examine evidence, and so on.[36] Though the procedural values are, for the most part, complementary to the Fullerian ones, they can come into conflict, in ways that Waldron has explored.[37] I won't address the conflicts here. I simply want to say that this list of rule-of-law virtues is not haphazard. What holds the items on it together is that they help make legal practices the sort of practices that can be sources of morality.

A legal practice that lacked every one of these virtues would almost surely not be a source of moral requirements (except in the perverse sense that people might be obligated to reform or resist the practice). But most cases are more mixed. It is common for a community's legal practices to have some of these virtues but not others, and to have them in different degrees, across the board or as to particular people or problems. That makes it difficult to do anything more than observe that the failure of legal institutions to fully manifest rule-of-law virtues is a source of disagreement about the moral difference their decisions make.

But I will venture just a bit more: in legal systems that provide an opportunity to be heard in court, to protest in public, to participate in politics, there are strong reasons to defer to final court orders, even if, in many ways, the legal process falls short of the ideal. This is because those systems hold out the prospect of reform through legal means. Think about Moore's case. As the Alabama Court of the Judiciary emphasized, Moore had his say in court, over and over again. (In the Ten Commandments case, thirty-four judges considered Moore's claims; every one ruled against him.) He also had his say out of court, and he could continue to do so as a participant in the political life of his community. Moreover, Moore was not in any way marginalized. He had the resources to exercise his legal and political rights, and he did so, repeatedly. The legal practices in Alabama—and in the United States more generally—leave an awful lot to be desired. But as to Moore, they were in good working order—good enough, at least, that he ought to have done as federal courts directed.

One last point about Roy Moore and the rule of law before we move on: I told you a story that had a happy ending. Moore was removed from office because he did not share the moral outlook that makes the rule of law possible. That moral outlook was widespread among judges in Alabama in 2016, when Moore was suspended from his post. Alas, that was the same year that Donald Trump was elected president of the United States. And the moral outlook seems less widely shared than it was before he came along. To a large extent, that's a reflection of Trump, who does not seem to recognize any constraints on his behavior, save what he can get away with. He lies with astounding frequency, about matters big and small.[38] He exploited his office for personal profit.[39] He fired the director of the FBI, in the midst of an investigation into his campaign's contacts with Russia.[40] He stonewalled congressional investigations.[41] He tried to shake down the Ukrainian president, Volodymyr Zelensky, seeking personal favors in return for aid money that Congress had appropriated.[42] And when he finally lost reelection, he refused to acknowledge the results, made baseless accusations of fraud, and encouraged violence, culminating in the January 6 insurrection.[43] Regular order prevailed, just barely. Congress completed its vote count and Joe Biden took office. But the transition of power was not peaceful.

These events are a reminder that the rule of law is fragile. The shared moral outlook on which it rests is hard won and easily lost. And the blame cannot be laid entirely at Trump's feet. In fact, the real danger was not Trump himself but the fact that so many people so quickly acquiesced. Postema's networks of accountability were in place. Trump was impeached twice. But Republican senators refused to remove him from office. Worse yet, many joined in his lies or stayed silent as he suggested abandoning our constitutional order.[44] There were many moral disgraces associated with the Trump administration, and the weakening of the commitment to the rule of law may seem slight in comparison with family separations at the border, relentless racism, and rampant self-dealing, among other sorts of awfulness. But it is not slight. And if the attitude of contempt toward law that Trump engendered persists, it may be a bigger disaster than all the rest, as many of our most serious moral problems can be solved only in a community that shares a commitment to seeing legal practices as sources of moral constraint.

What about the Rest of Us?

The Alabama Court of the Judiciary emphasized the risk that judicial defiance posed to the rule of law. And I have argued that the rule of law rests on a shared attitude among legal officials. What about the rest of us? Does the rule of law also rest on a shared moral outlook among those who are subject to it? The answer is yes, though in any given case, it's less important that laypeople see law as a source of morality than that officials do. The rule of law can survive recalcitrant litigants. Courts have lots of tools for ending obstinacy. They can garnish wages; attach property; hold parties in contempt; fine their failure to comply; and when all else fails, confine them. The criminal law can also respond to those who would disrupt the rule of law, as many of the January 6 insurrectionists have recently learned.

Putting things that way might make it sound like the rule of law rests on coercion. And perhaps, to some degree, it does. A state needs tools to coerce compliance; otherwise, people won't be willing to rely on it to resolve conflict. But if coercion is the primary way that a state secures compliance, it is doubtful that compliance is owed at all. Remember, a large part of the argument for legal practices is that they provide peaceful mechanisms for resolving moral conflicts. A state that rules through force and fear is not apt to provide that sort of peace. For legal practices to make a moral difference, they must be seen (at least by most) as making that sort of difference. Only then can law secure the peace that is part of its rationale.

It's important not to make too much of this point. There may well be pockets of law that people comply with for purely pragmatic reasons, or people who comply with law only because they are coerced to do so. But in well-functioning legal systems, people tend to see legal practices as sources of both rights and responsibilities. And the fact that they see them that way helps make them so.

You'll notice a bit of bootstrapping here. A practice makes a difference in part because it is seen to make a difference. But there is nothing odd in that. If no one took promising seriously as a source of obligations, then promises would not make the moral difference that they purport to make. In a world where no one took promises seriously, no expectations could be frustrated by the failure to keep one. And no one making a promise would see themselves as taking on an obligation. Promising is a serious affair in part because we take it seriously. So too with law. The fact that some set of people and practices could provide peaceful ways of resolving conflict is an argument for putting those people in power and deferring to the judgments that they make. But it is not an argument that the rest of us are already obligated to do as they decide. For that to be the case, the practice needs already to be in place.

The start of a new legal system is a speculative affair. If people think the new legal practices make a moral difference, they might well. (There is no guarantee; people make moral mistakes.) If people don't think so, then the practices won't. But this does not mean that people are free to free themselves from legal obligations simply by refusing to see legal practices as sources of them. As I've suggested, there are moral problems we can't solve except through law. Stronger still, I'm inclined to agree with Seana Shiffrin that democratic law, in particular, is morally mandatory.[45] I won't rehearse her arguments here. I'll simply observe that, if she is right, we all have an obligation to bring about the social conditions necessary to make democratic law possible. That means that we are obligated to see democratic legal practices as sources of morality, so that they can in fact be.

There's another reason that it's helpful for laypeople to see law as a source of moral constraint, at least in democracies. It's hard for officials to hold on to that attitude if the people who would put them in office don't hold it themselves. Few Republican officeholders were willing to hold Trump to account because many of their voters thrilled to Trump's transgressions and stood ready to punish anyone who stood in his way. Voters are vital participants in Postema's networks of accountability. Or at least they can be if they value the rule of law. Many Republican primary voters didn't make that a priority in the age of Trump. The electorate as a whole rose to the occasion and removed him from office. But the danger has not passed, in part because the contempt Trump cultivated for law seems likely to outlive him.

The Social and the Moral

There's a little bit more we can learn from Moore. In this chapter, I've argued that the rule of law requires a shared moral outlook—that officials and (to a lesser extent) laypeople must see legal practices as sources of morality. The emphasis I've put on moral agreement runs counter to much of recent jurisprudence, which has been dominated by discussion of disagreement. A standard story runs like this: We disagree about how we ought to act. We could keep arguing, endlessly. But endless arguments are a problem, especially if we are each going our own way while we argue—or, worse yet, coming to blows. What we need instead is some socially determined set of standards that can supplant our disagreements. Instead of arguing over what the right answer to any given controversy is, we can simply check to see what answer has been settled on.

In this story, law is a socially determined set of standards that allows us to set (some of our) disagreements aside. Different philosophers conceive of those standards in different ways. Joseph Raz, for instance, takes the law to be the directives of an authority (or something that could be presented as such).[46] Scott Shapiro takes the law to be a set of shared plans.[47] The differences are significant, but what they share in common is more so. Both Raz and Shapiro argue that the content of the law must be determined exclusively by social sources, lest people seeking to ascertain the law fall back into the moral conflicts that led them to law in the first place.[48]

I find this argument odd (and not only because it presents the law as a set of norms, a picture I've already suggested we reject). We can disagree about social facts, and often we do. So there is no guarantee that a set of norms whose content is socially determined will be, for that reason, uncontroversial. Two originalists might agree that the content of the right to bear arms found in the Second Amendment depends on the original public meaning of that text. But if they disagree about what that meaning was, they may still find themselves at an impasse over what gun regulations are permissible. These characters are in much the same position as people who agree that the content of the prohibition on cruel and unusual punishment depends on what, as a moral matter, counts as cruel, but disagree about which punishments those are. The first pair disputes a social fact; the second, a moral one. But both are stuck because they take the content of the law to depend on facts about which they disagree.[49]

Legal systems have tools for settling these sorts of disputes. They provide courts (and other adjudicative bodies) that resolve disputes about rights and obligations. And within courts, voting rules determine who decides cases when judges disagree. These procedures often help us to move past an impasse. But they don't have to resolve the original disagreement in order to do so. We can continue to disagree about what rights the Second Amendment protects, or what punishments the Eighth Amendment prohibits, and nevertheless coordinate our conduct *if* we agree that we ought to comply with court orders, even when we think them wrong. Legal systems do not supplant disagreement, so much as exploit moral agreement to move past it.

Think about Moore again. I do not doubt that, to this day, he continues to believe it legally permissible to display the Ten Commandments in a courthouse. And I don't doubt that, to this day, he continues to believe that the Constitution has nothing to say about same-sex marriage. Moore is mistaken on both counts. But he is not mistaken because he missed some social fact that would show him the error of his ways. He's not confused about the words in the Constitution or what the courts have said about what they mean. His mistake is a moral one; he fails to see the significance of those social facts. And he is not alone in that. Lots of people in our society persist in the errors that Moore makes, many influenced by Moore. And yet, on these questions, conduct in Alabama remains well coordinated. The Rock was removed from the courthouse. And state probate judges issue same-sex marriage licenses. All that happened because Moore's colleagues shared the moral view that they ought to respect the decisions of federal courts, even if they disagreed with them. Again, legal practices exploit moral agreement to help us move past moral disagreements. That is part of their genius.

CHAPTER SEVEN

Lawyers and Morality

How can you tell if a lawyer is lying?
His lips are moving.

LAWYER: Well, if you want my honest opinion—
CLIENT: *No, no. I want your professional advice.*

My uncle is a criminal lawyer.
Aren't they all?

A LAWYER to a prospective client:
If you want justice, it's two hundred dollars an hour.
Obstruction of justice runs a bit more.

No Joke

Lawyers are the butt of a lot of jokes. The ones that open this chapter are just a small sample of several hundred that Marc Galanter collected in *Lowering the Bar: Lawyer Jokes and Legal Culture.* Many portray lawyers as dishonest, self-interested, predatory, or just generally immoral. Against that backdrop, what I'm about to say might seem odd: lawyers are moral experts. No joke.

Without doubt, there are easier ways to end a book than defending the proposition that lawyers are moral experts. But, I promise, I'm not after degree-of-difficulty points. I think that proposition follows from the picture I've presented in this book. So I'm going to make my case, at the risk of supplying my own *reductio*—or, perhaps, becoming my own lawyer joke.

Are Moral Philosophers Moral Experts?

If anyone is a moral expert, you might think that the people who study morality seriously could make a good case. But many moral philosophers disclaim moral expertise. Bernard Williams pronounced that "there are, notoriously, no ethical experts."[1] He was echoing C. D. Broad, who insisted that "[i]t is no part of the professional business of moral philosophers to tell people what they ought or ought not to do."[2] Why not? "Moral philosophers," Broad explained, "have no special information, not available to the general public, about what is right and what is wrong."[3]

Some of the anxieties about seeing moral philosophers as moral experts stem from the first bit of what Broad said—that it is not a moral philosopher's business to tell people what they ought or ought not do. That's certainly not what they are paid to do. Most philosophers are paid to teach and write articles that hardly anyone reads. (That's the business I'm in.) And most people aren't in the habit of looking to moral philosophers for moral instruction, except in narrow domains. (Much of the discussion about whether moral philosophers are moral experts has taken place in bioethics journals, since moral philosophers are sometimes recruited to medical ethics boards.) People are more likely to look to religious leaders for moral instruction, if they seek it out at all. But not many people do. People with moral problems tend to puzzle them out themselves, seeking help, perhaps, from friends and family, a therapist, a pastor, an advice columnist, but nearly never from moral philosophers. If they did, this business might be a lot more lucrative than it is.

But Broad did not just mean to say that moral philosophers don't happen to be in the business of dispensing moral advice. Broad, and lots of others, think that philosophers shouldn't be in that business. Why not? Well, different philosophers have different reasons. Some point to autonomy and democracy. The idea is that individuals and groups ought to (at least sometimes) make moral decisions on their own, such that there's something unseemly (or worse) about a moral philosopher claiming expertise and dispensing advice. Others come at it the other way around. Sarah McGrath says that "there's something off-putting about the idea of arriving at one's moral views by simply deferring to an expert."[4] This was also Williams's worry:

> Anyone who is tempted to take up the idea of there being a theoretical science of ethics should be discouraged by reflecting on what would be involved in taking seriously the idea that there were experts in it. It would imply, for instance, that a student who had not followed the professor's reasoning but had understood his moral conclusion might have some reason, on the strength of his professorial authority, to accept it. . . . These Platonic implications are presumably not accepted by anyone.[5]

Williams was wrong about that last bit. David Enoch, among others, would accept that implication, or at least ones in the ballpark.[6] But I want to set aside all questions about advice (both whether philosophers should give it and whether others should take it), since they're separable from the question whether philosophers have moral expertise in the first place. Sometimes, there are reasons for people to figure things out for themselves—which means that, sometimes, people ought to keep what they know quiet, even when those around them are struggling for lack of knowledge. Teachers and parents frequently find themselves in that position. If philosophers are moral experts, perhaps they ought to keep their mouths shut, at least in lots of situations.

But are moral philosophers moral experts? Again, many philosophers say no, and their reasons are varied. Some point out that moral philosophers disagree about many moral questions. That's true, they do. But we should be careful not to exaggerate the extent of the disagreement. If you look to philosophy journals, you will find endless arguments. But that's a little like looking at appellate opinions and coming to the view that there are no noncontroversial propositions of law. There are, just not in the place you're looking, since people go to appellate courts to resolve contested questions of law. So too with philosophy journals; they are venues for philosophers to argue about contentious questions, not to co-sign consensus views.

But it's also important to remember that experts in other fields disagree with one another, and we do not doubt their expertise simply because they do so.[7] We seek second opinions from doctors because we know that two medical experts can come to different conclusions. Now, it might seem that disagreements among moral philosophers run deeper than differences in medical diagnosis. In addition to disagreeing about the answer to particular moral puzzles, philosophers disagree about the framework for answering them; some are consequentialist, some are Kantian, and so on. And moral philosophers hold different metaethical views too, so they disagree about just what it means to make a moral judgment. But there are disagreements that run just as deep in other fields. Doctors often disagree about the etiology of diseases, not just their diagnosis (and sometimes, they disagree about the diagnosis because they disagree about the etiology). And experts in some fields disagree about metaphysical questions that are similar to the metaethical questions that divide moral philosophers. Some physicists accept the many-worlds interpretation of quantum mechanics; others subscribe to the Copenhagen interpretation or Bohmian mechanics. These involve radically different pictures of reality, but the disagreements should not lead us to doubt that Hugh Everett, Niels Bohr, and David Bohm were all experts in quantum mechanics. So too, one might think, of the moral philosophers scattered across different metaethical positions.

The fact that moral philosophers disagree is not, on its own, a compelling reason to discount the possibility of moral expertise. But I suspect that, for some, there is something else lurking behind those arguments: skepticism about morality. We should, of course, concede that if there's no such thing as morality, there is nothing to be expert in. But all along, I've been proceeding on the assumption that morality does exist, and I don't plan to stop now. So let's set that possibility aside.

There are further arguments that lead some to doubt the possibility of moral expertise, but none, to be candid, that I find more impressive than the ones we've considered so far.[8] And rather than rattle them off and rebut them, I'd like to make an affirmative case for the moral expertise of at least some moral philosophers. Or rather, I'd like to borrow the case that Peter Singer made, because it strikes me as spot on. Singer observes that "thinking out" what one ought to do is often difficult.[9] He starts:

> I may, for instance, be wondering whether it is right to eat meat. I would have a better chance of reaching the right decision, or at least, a soundly based decision, if I knew a number of facts about the capacities of animals for suffering, and about the methods of rearing and slaughtering animals now being used. I might also want to know about the effect of a vegetarian diet on human health, and, considering the world food shortage, whether more or less food would be produced by giving up meat production.[10]

The point here is simple to see. To figure out what you ought to do, you need to know the facts that are relevant to the decision. A moral philosopher who, like Singer, spends a lot of time studying the morality of eating meat is likely to have gathered many facts that are morally relevant.

But there is more to the expertise of moral philosophers. Singer continues:

> Once I have got evidence on these questions, I must assess it and bring it together with whatever moral views I hold. Depending on what method of moral reasoning I use, this may involve a calculation of which course of action produces greater happiness and less suffering; or it may mean an attempt to place myself in the positions of those affected by my decision; or it may lead me to "weigh up" conflicting duties and interests.[11]

Again, we shouldn't be distracted by the fact that different philosophers hold different moral views and thus face different tasks when it comes time to crunch the facts. Singer's point is that someone practiced at crunching morally relevant facts is apt to do a better job of it, whatever moral views they happen to hold. Some of that comes down to experience, but not all of it. Singer adds: "Whatever method I employ, I must be aware of the possibility that my own desire to eat meat may lead to bias in my deliberations."[12] Amateurs may well be aware of this or that bias, but professionals are taught to attend to them and so might be expected to do so more consistently, if not effectively—but maybe more effectively too.

Add all that up, and we arrive at Singer's conclusion:

> None of this procedure is easy—neither the gathering of information, nor the selection of what information is relevant, nor its combination with a basic moral position, nor the elimination of bias. Someone who is familiar with moral concepts and with moral arguments, who has ample time to gather information and think about it, may reasonably be expected to reach a soundly based conclusion more often than someone who is unfamiliar with moral concepts and with moral arguments and has little time. So moral expertise would seem to be possible.[13]

All that strikes me as right—obviously so.

Here's a simple way to see the point. Suppose that you face a difficult moral decision. And then you learn that there is a moral philosopher who has spent her career thinking and writing about just that sort of decision. Would you be interested in talking to her, assuming that you had the time to do so? Or would you think, nope, there's nothing she could teach me? The latter view strikes me as arrogant. Chances are, she's familiar with a wide range of considerations that bear on both sides of the decision that you face. Chances are, she's worked through many of the most common arguments that people deploy and knows which ones won't work and how to put others in their strongest form. Chances are, she sees how your problem connects to others in ways that might not have occurred to you. And on and on.

Of course, none of this is to say you should defer to her judgment. As I said, the question what deference one owes the expertise of others is a different question from whether they have the expertise in the first place. Indeed, when the expertise is moral, it is a moral question whether one ought to defer. And that may not be a question that our expert philosopher is expert in, so perhaps she should be hesitant to offer her advice or to press it too strongly. But again, all of that is consistent with her having expertise. And if she has spent a substantial chunk of time studying an issue, she probably does.

But notice: her expertise depends on *that*—a substantial chunk of time studying the issue. So her expertise is issue-specific. Some of what Singer says suggests the possibility of a more general moral expertise. Whatever problems a moral philosopher studies, she is familiar with moral concepts and issues that crop up across moral problems. So it may be that our moral philosopher is, in some ways, better equipped than the average bear to handle most any moral problem we throw her way. But if that more general moral expertise exists (and I suspect it does), it is likely thinner than the expertise that is earned through sustained engagement with a single problem.

What a Lawyer Knows

If I am right about all that—that moral expertise exists, and for roughly the reasons that Singer sings—then it follows that lawyers are moral experts, at least for a narrow but important set of moral questions. They are the sorts of questions that lawyers study, in a sustained way, starting in law school and continuing through their careers. These questions differ a bit depending on the field in which the lawyer works. To make this concrete, let's think about tort law again.

As we saw in Chapter 1, a plaintiff in a tort suit asserts a right. The right has a nested structure. In the typical suit, the plaintiff claims a right to have the court enforce a right to compensation from the defendant. The question whether she has that right is a moral question, in the sense we outlined back at the start. That is, it is a question about who owes what to whom. And the answer to that question depends on an enormously complicated factual background, about which most laypeople know next to nothing—and about which lawyers know an awful lot. That is because the answer depends on the legal history of the community—what doctrines have been developed, what decisions have been made, what statutes have been adopted, and on and on.

Lawyers learn the basics of tort law as first-year students. The knowledge acquired then can carry them pretty far in assessing whether a plaintiff has the right she asserts. Lawyers will know that, in order for the answer to be yes, the plaintiff must have a cause of action. They are likely to know what the major causes of action are and perhaps, even, to remember the elements of the most common ones, like negligence. But lawyers also know where to look for what they have forgotten—or never learned in the first place—because even the best legal education only sketches the basics of any particular field. A major part of learning to be a lawyer is learning where one needs to look for the decisions that are relevant to determining just what people's rights are.

Those decisions, as we've seen, don't just determine people's rights according to some artificial normative system, separate from morality. The actions of legal institutions are (typically, though not necessarily) relevant to determining what people's moral rights are—to determining what they are genuinely owed by others. In virtue of her education, a lawyer knows an awful lot of facts that are morally relevant to assessing the sorts of claims that are asserted in court. She knows where to look to find relevant facts that she doesn't yet know. And if she's any good, she also has a sense of when there is something she needs to know but doesn't. The breadth and depth of this sort of knowledge varies by the lawyer. But good lawyers also know when they are out of their depth and how to find a lawyer that won't be.

But a lawyer's claim to moral expertise does not just rest on her knowledge of morally relevant facts. Much like a moral philosopher, she is familiar with concepts and arguments that play a key role in resolving certain sorts of moral questions. For instance, lawyers know the difference between objective and subjective standards; actual and proximate causation; compensatory and punitive damages; justifications and excuses; per capita and per stirpes distribution; and lots, lots else. Some of these concepts have lives outside the law. And sometimes, lawyers can learn from experts who work with these concepts in other domains. But lawyers' familiarity and facility with these concepts are a source of expertise in answering questions about the rights and duties asserted in court.

Similarly, lawyers are familiar with styles of argument that highlight facts that might be morally relevant in assessing people's rights. For instance, every lawyer is familiar with slippery slopes, floodgates, and forum shopping, among many other metaphors that call attention to problems that courts might face depending on the decisions they make. These arguments are not always good, and sometimes, they shouldn't carry the day even when they capture something significant. But they are important arguments to master precisely because they highlight facts that might be morally relevant to resolving contested claims of right. And I'll add:

it is no accident that the arguments just cited concern court dockets. The question whether a court should recognize a right depends, in part, on whether courts are in a position to enforce that right—effectively, efficiently, consistently, and so on. Remember, a plaintiff in a tort suit, and in lots of other domains too, asserts that she has a right that the court grant relief. The question whether she does depends on facts about courts that lawyers are in a good position to know and laypeople are not.

The story I just told was tailored to tort lawyers, but it is easily extended to all lawyers who litigate. Of course, not all lawyers do. Some work in transactional settings, merging corporations, transferring property, structuring financial relationships, and the like. These sorts of lawyers also have moral expertise, much of which is grounded in what they know. But it's also grounded in know-how. Transactional lawyers know how to help clients restructure their relationships with others, so that they can acquire new rights or, perhaps, transfer old ones. And again, the rights they know how to create are not just rights according to some artificial normative system. Lawyers know how to adjust what people actually owe each other (at least in places where the legal practices are capable of making a moral difference).

I do not want to oversell the moral expertise of lawyers. That expertise is, in some ways, quite narrow. As we saw in Chapter 1, the question whether a plaintiff has a right that a court enforce a right to compensation is different from the question whether the plaintiff has a right to compensation. And it is different yet again from the question whether the plaintiff has a right to an apology. Morality extends far beyond the legally enforceable bit of it. And lawyers may not have any expertise in judging the other bits. I suspect that, in some instances, they do, if only because some of the concepts that lawyers commonly employ—like justifications and excuses—are helpful for thinking about moral problems that arise independently of legal practices. But if lawyers have expertise in the nonlegal bits of morality, it is likely to be haphazard and patchy.

One last point about the moral expertise of lawyers: In Chapter 1, I observed that courts are in the business of deciding what rights litigants have, not what rights they ought to have. But as Justice Ginsburg's dissent in *Ledbetter* illustrated, judges are sometimes in a good position to judge what rights a litigant ought to have. Ginsburg came to *Ledbetter* with a wealth of experience with employment discrimination. She cofounded the Women's Rights Project of the American Civil Liberties Union, argued pathbreaking cases at the Supreme Court, and wrote significant decisions about women's equality as a member of the bench. She was better positioned than just about anyone to see the problem that the Court's cramped reading of Title VII created. So she spoke up about it. The question what the law ought to be is not itself a legal question. But it is a moral question—and it is one that lawyers are apt to have some expertise in.

That said, I sometimes worry that law schools (at least in the States) spend too much time trying to cultivate that knowledge. Many law school classes are less about lawyering and more about looking at the law critically. This is partly a consequence of the increasing interdisciplinarity of law schools. A student in an American law school is apt to learn what an economist sees when she looks at tort law, what a political scientist sees when she looks at administrative law, and what a sociologist sees when she looks at criminal law. Some of this is good. Lawyers should think about what the law should be, since they are stewards of its development. And these perspectives from other disciplines can aid in that. But sometimes, they push learning to be a lawyer aside. And that is not good. A law student should learn the legal history of her community. She should master the concepts that the law uses to carve moral problems. And she should hone her ability to craft arguments and draft legal documents. If she does these things—if she comes to know what she ought to know— then she will be a lawyer *and* a moral expert.

Asshole Lawyers

But, wait. What about the lawyer jokes? If lawyers are moral experts, why do so many people see them as morally repugnant? The answers are complicated, and I won't develop anything like a comprehensive account here. Some of the answers are sociological. In many institutions, the lawyer is the person that says no, slows things down, or just generally gets in the way of fun and profit. In all that, the lawyer may be acting well, or she may be absurdly risk averse, but many people experience lawyers as limitations, and it would be surprising if that was not the source of some hostility. More important, perhaps, in places that have adversarial legal systems, many people will come to know lawyers as adversaries. And those adversaries often have the power to disrupt people's lives. Again, it would be a surprise if that was not a source of hostility.

Other answers are historical. As Galanter observes, lawyers have been a subject of scorn for thousands of years,[14] but antilawyer sentiment waxes and wanes with social developments. He suggests that an explosion in late twentieth-century litigation and regulation fueled antilawyer sentiment in recent decades. But he also observes that pop culture lawyers have an outsize influence on the way that people perceive the profession. *L.A. Law* paints a different picture than *Better Call Saul*. So whatever story we might tell about the sources of lawyer jokes—and the attitudes they represent—would be complicated, if we could see our way through to a story at all.

In any event, I'm not interested in the origins of antilawyer sentiment. What interests me is the fact that some of it seems warranted. Lots of lawyers are assholes. That's obvious to anyone who spends even a little bit of time around them. Why is that? And how could it be, if lawyers are moral experts? The second question is easier to answer than the first. Moral expertise is no guarantee of good behavior. Any expertise can be put to bad use, and a lawyer's knowledge is no different. For instance, lawyers can use their expertise to help their clients avoid accountability, making it easier for them to misbehave. Just when that is out of bounds is a difficult question; defense attorneys are, after all, in the accountability avoidance business. But ultimately, I don't think that lawyers are reviled because they abuse their moral expertise. I think that they are reviled for reasons that have little to do with it. And that should not be a surprise. The moral expertise that lawyers have is quite narrow. As to other bits of morality, they might be morally obtuse. And more generally, knowing a bit about morality does not guarantee that one aims to act well. Lawyers often don't. A lot of them, as I said, are assholes.

Before I carry on, let me warn you: I'm going to keep using that word, which I know many find abrasive. I'm not doing it to shock or scandalize. I'm doing it because I've been persuaded by Aaron James that the word names a kind of character who warrants serious study. Why? Assholes disrupt our lives. They treat us poorly and too often get away with it. They're frustrating. And infuriating. And it's hard to figure out how to handle them. They're also more common in some spaces than others. So it's worth attending to that fact and asking what we might do about it. To start, though, we need to know what an asshole is. And James has a theory. An asshole, he says, is a person who

(1) allows himself to enjoy special advantages and does so systematically;
(2) does this out of an entrenched sense of entitlement; and
(3) is immunized by his sense of entitlement against the complaints of other people.[15]

In everyday life, James says, the asshole is the person who "habitually cuts in line," "frequently interrupts in conversation," or "persistently emphasizes another person's faults."[16] Or perhaps he's the person who "is extremely sensitive to perceived slights while being oblivious to his crassness with others."[17] Or, well . . . there are endless ways to be an asshole. But what makes someone an asshole, James explains, is not just what he does. A person who claims special advantages for himself might just be a jerk. What makes an asshole a distinct character, James says, is that he claims special advantages out of "a firm sense that *he is special,* that the normal rules of conduct do not apply to him."[18] The sense that he is special makes an asshole "entirely comfortable flouting accepted social conventions."[19] He simply does not care about the complaints of others.

   That sense of specialness—the sense that one is entitled to ignore the normal rules of conduct—can have lots of sources. And James distinguishes many different sorts of assholes. The smug one sees himself as intellectually superior and thus entitled to demean those he deems dumb.[20] The asshole boss thinks that his position of power permits him privileges that do not come with the job.[21] The boorish asshole believes he is entitled to act rudely, either because he's up to something important or just because he's entertaining.[22] Those who think they're up to something important share something in common with a character James calls the "self-aggrandizing asshole with thin moral pretext," who takes the righteousness of his cause, real or perceived, to justify his bombastic behavior.[23]

And neither last nor least, there's the character James really can't stand: the "delusional asshole banker," who thinks that bankers are so important to society that they are entitled to live the high life, even as their firms are bailed out in the wake of a financial crisis they caused.[24] (OK, that one's tailored to the time and place that James wrote.) I mention the bankers because they reveal something important for our inquiry. An asshole does not necessarily think that *he alone* is special. He might allow that others are too, if they share membership in some group that he sees as special.

James did not put asshole lawyers on his list, but they more than merit an entry. In fact, they might merit more than one. Why do lawyers think themselves special? Some are just standard-issue self-aggrandizing assholes with thin moral pretexts. They fight for causes—free speech, gun rights, victims' rights. It doesn't matter what the cause is. What matters is that there is a cause, which is seen (by the asshole) to be so important that, so long he is acting in pursuit of it, normal standards of decency need not be observed. No one typifies this character better than Nancy Grace (who also qualifies as a "cable news asshole" in James's taxonomy).[25] For more than a decade, Grace, a former prosecutor (who was repeatedly reprimanded for misconduct), held court on CNN's Headline News network, sensationalizing the most sensational cases of the day.[26] David Carr, then the *New York Times* media critic, described the show best: "Working with a contingent of experts who have all the independence of a crew of trained seals, Ms. Grace races toward judgment, heedlessly ignoring nuance and evidence on her way to finding guilt."[27] The results were worse than you might guess.

> Ms. Grace knows what she knows with a great deal of certainty, but she was wrong about the now debunked rape charges against the Duke lacrosse team, she was wrong about who kidnapped Elizabeth Smart. She taped a corrosive interview in 2006 with Melinda Duckett, whose 2-year-old son had gone missing, and Ms. Duckett killed herself the next day. Ms. Grace broadcast the interview anyway.[28]

And that barely scratches the surface of Grace's sins. Perhaps the most telling bit: she fabricated details about the murder of her fiancé to give herself a better backstory.[29] But it was all OK, in Grace's eyes, because she was an advocate for the unheard voices of victims. "All I could think of was putting violent offenders behind bars. To this day, I feel like it's my duty to keep going forward and trying to fight the good fight."[30] I'm sure it didn't hurt that fighting the "good" fight was good for Grace's ratings.

Nancy Grace is a self-aggrandizing asshole on a grand scale. There aren't many of those in the legal profession. But self-aggrandizing lawyers exist on smaller scales too. There are lawyers who inflate their importance within their firms, among their friends, within their families—all in pursuit of a noble cause, which they see as somehow releasing them from the norms of good behavior. But though these characters are infuriating, they aren't distinctively legal. They populate many professions. I'm more interested in a character that I think is distinctively legal. We can call him the zealous advocate asshole. The name says it all, but if we need to spell it out, we can't do better than this story, told by Jeena Cho:

> When I was a young lawyer, I was invited to sit in on a deposition with one of the managing partners at the firm. This was my first deposition, and one of my first experiences coming face to face with an adversary. When I got to the conference room, I asked opposing counsel and his client if they wanted anything to drink and if they were comfortable. I don't recall if they asked for anything, but what I do remember is what happened after the deposition. The managing lawyer pulled me aside and told me never to do that again. It was not my job to offer water or make the opposing side comfortable and in fact, it was my job to do the opposite. To make them as uncomfortable as possible.[31]

Cho extended the simplest of human courtesies: water, for someone who might be thirsty. But even that kindness was too much for her managing partner. Why? Because the people to whom she was kind were on the other side. And a lawyer is supposed to be a zealous advocate for her client. Maybe, just maybe, a dry mouth would make opposing counsel lose his nerve or wit. That is amazing assholery, in part because it has so little chance of achieving anything. The point is to be petty. And the point of reprimanding Cho was to communicate just how thoroughly petty the partner expected her to be.

And let's be clear, there's nothing aberrational about that story. That is how many lawyers do their job. And it is how many lawyers think they are ethically obligated to do their job. A legal columnist named Keith Lee acknowledged that Cho's managing partner was an asshole, but nevertheless thought it important to warn against allowing the "pendulum" to "swing too far toward kindness and civility."[32] In bold letters, he declared: **"[U]ltimately, the practice of law is not about you or your feelings. The practice of law is about what's best for your client.** And there will be times where what is best for your client is to be the biggest jerk possible to people on the other side of a case or deal from you."[33] As it happens, I've read the American Bar Association's Model Rules of Professional Conduct, and nowhere do they say or even suggest that "the practice of law is about what's best for your client." They require competent[34] and diligent[35] representation, the avoidance of conflicts of interest,[36] and deference to some decisions that clients make.[37] They also expressly limit the extent of a lawyer's advocacy, prohibiting frivolous claims,[38] requiring candor with courts,[39] and proscribing activities that would prejudice judicial proceedings.[40] The comments on the rules do say that a lawyer must "act with commitment and dedication to the interests of the client and with zeal in advocacy upon the client's behalf."[41] But they make clear that a lawyer is *not* bound to "press for every advantage that might be realized for a client."[42] And they specifically say that a lawyer's duty "does not require the use of offensive tactics or preclude the treating of all persons involved in the legal process with courtesy and respect."[43] Still, the myth that lawyers are to put their clients' interests above all else is so firmly fixed in legal culture that the misbehavior of Cho's managing partner and the justification he offered for it are completely unremarkable. Lawyers are assholes. Get your own.

Or grow your own. Some friends of mine worked at a firm where the partners passed around a story about a lawyer they'd once hired from another firm. They checked references, and they checked out. The lawyers at the old firm loved the guy and were sad to see him go. As it turns out, they were passing the trash. The guy was a full-fledged asshole, rude to the staff, rude to his colleagues, rude to everyone. So the new firm fired the guy and adopted a rule prohibiting lateral hires, which the partners put this way: "From now on, we grow our own assholes." That was a joke. Sort of. Because the problem was not that the lawyer was an asshole. The problem was that he was an indiscriminate asshole. If you're rude to the staff, you're an asshole boss. If you're rude to your colleagues, you're a smug asshole or, maybe, a self-aggrandizing one. And the firm didn't want any of *those* assholes around. But a zealous advocate asshole? That's a credential, not a criticism.

I've lingered on this because zealous advocate assholes are one of the worst parts of American legal culture (though I doubt the species is distinctively American). And if we're thinking about lawyers and morality, it's worth seeing the stories that lawyers tell to justify their bad behavior. But actually, there's another kind of asshole lawyer that is even more important in the context of the picture I've painted in this book. We could call him the ludic asshole lawyer, since he seems to think law is just a game. But I'd rather call him the not-my-job-to-do-justice asshole, since this character likes to make that clear. We might have met him back in Chapter 3. In Ronald Dworkin's rendition of the Hand-Holmes story, Justice Holmes indignantly insisted that it was not his job to do justice. I suggested a sympathetic reading of Holmes's remark: Judges do not have a roving mandate to pursue justice in all the cases that come before them. Their job is to answer the moral question put to them, which is typically about the rights that the parties hold, not what a just resolution of their dispute would be. But there are repugnant ways to read Holmes's remark—ways that place justice, and the rest of morality, beyond the responsibility of lawyers. And the not-my-job-to-do-justice asshole is all too happy to accept that picture—to treat the practice of law as a morality-free zone.

You can find these characters in every corner of legal practice. They are the lawyers who press every advantage, push every boundary, and cross them too, if they think they won't get caught or the consequences won't be bad. And they don't think of themselves as behaving badly, because, hey, it's not their job to do justice. They are the defense attorneys who drown plaintiffs in paper, filing frivolous motions to raise their rival's costs (as well as their own billable hours). They are the plaintiffs' attorneys who file strike suits, seeking settlements for claims they know lack merit. They are the prosecutors who refuse to reopen cases where there's compelling evidence of innocence. They are the divorce attorneys who use children as leverage to extract unfair settlements. "Do you feel bad about what you do?" you might ask, hoping for a hint of humanity. But the answer will be no. It's not their job to do justice. They are just playing the game. Someone else wrote the rules. Someone else could change them. They are right, in a way. It's not their job to do justice. But they make that an all-purpose excuse for bad behavior. And that makes them assholes, of a particularly pernicious sort.

These assholes may not see themselves as special among lawyers. They might allow that it's OK for opposing counsel to act the same way. They might even respect it. But make no mistake, they are assholes in James's sense, because they see themselves as entitled to special privileges on account of the fact that they are lawyers. Most laypeople would hesitate to threaten people with financial ruin. They'd never dream of depriving someone of their children undeservingly. They'd go to great lengths to keep someone innocent out of prison, not keep them there. Lots of lawyers would too. But the not-my-job-to-do-justice asshole is willing to do all these things and more. And he thinks he's entitled to do them, because he's a lawyer, and it's not his job to do justice.

Law Is a Moral Practice

What should we do about asshole lawyers? That is a hard question. James wrote eloquently about asshole management. If you find yourself persistently frustrated with particular assholes, it's worth a read.[44] The key challenge, I think, is to avoid responding in kind—to avoid being an asshole back. I worked with a judge who summed up his approach to asshole management with a slogan: "Kill them with kindness." He meant: Be tough, don't back down. Beat them if you can. But do it kindly. I think that's the best you can do. It won't help the asshole see the error of his ways; assholes nearly never do. But it keeps you from becoming an asshole. And it shows others, who are not yet assholes, that there are better ways to be.

We could make more progress, I think, at a systemic level. To start, we ought to stop teaching lawyers that their client's interest trumps all else. And we ought to invite lawyers to think of what they do differently. We ought to invite lawyers to see law as a moral practice—to see themselves as part of a moral endeavor. We ought to teach them that the questions posed in court are moral questions—questions about who owes what to whom. We ought to teach them that their job, as advocates, is to help the court reach the right answer. Their role may be to represent a client—to help her vindicate her rights. But we ought to make clear that that's all a lawyer owes a client. Every new lawyer should learn David Luban's distinction between what the law provides and what it can be made to give.[45] And they should learn their obligation extends only to the former. It may be naive to think that a shift in perspective could stem the tide of asshole lawyers. The incentives to be an asshole are so great. But the alternative is acquiescence. And then the fight is lost.

The suggestion that we link law and morality runs counter to a long tradition in jurisprudence that counsels just the opposite. As Liam Murphy has observed, legal positivists—including Jeremy Bentham, Hans Kelsen, and at times, H. L. A. Hart—offered instrumental arguments for seeing law and morality as separate normative systems.[46] They worried that too close an identification between law and morality would lead people to think about law uncritically, to lapse into obedience too easily. I am sympathetic to those arguments. I have insisted on a distinction between the rights people have and the rights they ought to have, which makes space for thinking about our legal practices critically. And I have repeated almost ad nauseam that, though law is a moral practice, there is no guarantee that any particular legal practice makes a moral difference, let alone the difference intended. I have stressed that many legal practices are morally corrupt, and I've acknowledged that most need some sort of reform. But for all that, I think there is a risk in seeing law and morality as separate normative systems. The risk is that lawyers will cease to see themselves as part of a moral enterprise—and then cease to see themselves as subject to moral constraint. Law is a moral practice. The point is to make a moral difference: to create, extinguish, arrange, rearrange, articulate—and sometimes vindicate—our rights and responsibilities. And we would do well to teach lawyers that.

Conclusion

Law Is a Moral Practice

———◆·◆·◆———

In 1985, an employee of the Zapata Corporation started to pass forged checks, drawing on Zapata's accounts with the Rhode Island Hospital Trust National Bank.[1] She started in March, writing checks for small amounts—never more than $800. So it took Zapata a while to catch on. By July, when it finally found the fraud, the employee had drained more than $100,000 from its accounts.

Who's responsible for that loss? The employee, obviously. But assume (as was likely the case) that the employee couldn't make good the loss. Must Zapata absorb it? Or does the bank have any responsibility? You won't be surprised to learn that Zapata believed that the bank was responsible for the loss, while the bank believed that it was (mostly) Zapata's problem. Indeed, the bank sued, seeking to limit its liability for the forged checks. The case was governed by a complicated statutory scheme, set out in § 4-406 of the Uniform Commercial Code, which Rhode Island had enacted into law. The bank agreed that, under those provisions, it was liable for honoring some of the early forged checks. They hadn't been signed by an authorized representative of Zapata, so the bank shouldn't have paid them out.

But the bank believed that its liability was limited to checks cleared on or before April 24. Why? It turns out that there's an exception to the rule that a bank must reimburse a customer's losses when they honor forged checks. I'll explain how it works in a moment, but I'd like you to see the statute:

(1) When a bank sends to its customer a statement of account accompanied by items paid in good faith in support of the debit entries or holds the statement and items pursuant to a request or instructions of its customer or otherwise in a reasonable manner makes the statement and items available to the customer, the customer must exercise reasonable care and promptness to examine the statement and items to discover his unauthorized signature or any alteration on an item and must notify the bank promptly after discovery thereof.

(2) If the bank establishes that the customer failed with respect to an item to comply with the duties imposed on the customer by subsection (1) the customer is precluded from asserting against the bank

   (a) His unauthorized signature or any alteration on the item if the bank also establishes that it suffered a loss by reason of such failure;

   (b) An unauthorized signature or alteration by the same wrong-doer on any other item paid in good faith by the bank after the first item and statement was available to the customer for a reasonable period not exceeding fourteen (14) calendar days and before the bank receives notification from the customer of any such unauthorized signature or alteration.[2]

Wow, that's wordy. If you read it slowly, you've probably got the basics down. But I'm here to help if you skipped or skimmed. Once Zapata received its statement, it was supposed to review it, reasonably and promptly, and notify the bank of any unauthorized signatures. If it didn't do so, then Zapata was barred from asserting an "unauthorized signature . . . by the same wrongdoer on any other item paid in good faith," starting two weeks after the statement was made available to Zapata. That was April 25.

But as Zapata pointed out, there's an exception to the exception. The next section of the statute states that "[t]he preclusion under subsection

(2) does not apply if the customer establishes lack of ordinary care on the part of the bank in paying the item(s)."[3] And the bank, Zapata said, didn't take ordinary care, since it didn't examine the signature on most checks under $1,000. In fact, it examined only 1 percent of such checks, chosen randomly, unless there was a specific reason to suspect fraud.

Was Zapata right? Did the bank fail to take ordinary care in processing the checks? Well, they took care that was ordinary in at least one sense. Most banks don't check signatures on every small check; they randomly sample, as recommended by industry experts. But as then-judge Stephen Breyer explained (when Zapata appealed an adverse ruling to the First Circuit), industry standards and practice don't fully determine what counts as ordinary care.[4] ("Ordinary care" is a term of art; it's most often defined as the care that a reasonably prudent person would take.) Zapata could try to show that the entire industry was being unreasonable—that banks should check more checks. Unfortunately for Zapata, the evidence suggested that the juice wasn't worth the squeeze. It's expensive to check checks, and boring too, so the costs are high. And it's not an effective way of finding fraud, or so the evidence suggested. Judge Breyer concluded that the bank had taken ordinary care.[5] So the exception to the exception didn't apply, and Zapata couldn't shift its loss to the bank.

I teach this case in torts, mostly because it provides an opportunity to think through what counts as ordinary care—a common phrase in the common law. But I also want my students to get practice working through wordy statutes. That's what a lot of lawyering is like. And when you slog through statutes and cases, like the court did, it hardly seems like you're engaged in a moral inquiry. It feels like a technical exercise. The question isn't what's fair or just. It's how does this statutory scheme work, and how does it apply to the case at hand. And if the scheme were to change, as they sometimes do, then all the lawyers who specialize in commercial transactions would master the new one, without regard to whether it was fair or just or even in any way better than the one that came before it. And every one of them would know that they couldn't come to court and say that their client ought to win because that was the fair or just result. The court wouldn't care. It would simply want to know how the statute worked.

It's easy to get lost in law, especially when you specialize, as most lawyers do. You master some bit of doctrine that is useful to your clients, or some skill, like litigation. Your day-to-day work will be deep in the weeds—sorting through statutes, regulations, and cases, alongside documents, like deeds and contracts, and evidence, like bank statements and phone records. And when you show up in court—if you're that sort of lawyer—you won't talk about Aristotle or Kant, or anyone else who's made a mark on moral philosophy. Chances are you'll talk about U.C.C. § 4-406 or something similarly arcane. But even if the argument takes on a more explicitly moral cast (perhaps you're debating whether a particular punishment counts as cruel, for purposes of the Eighth Amendment), the conversation won't approach the question directly, as a moral philosopher might. It will do so through the lens provided by prior decisions.

All that makes it easy to think that law is something other than morality—that it's a separate normative system. But that thought rests on a mistaken picture of morality. Morality is not insulated from the messy details of our lives. It cares about them. Indeed, it tells us what we owe each other in light of them. That's what the bank and Zapata were arguing about. And there's every reason to believe that, as a moral matter, their rights and responsibilities depended on the details of § 4-406. Why? For many reasons, which you can probably fill in by now. We need to find ways to live together, even when we disagree about how to live. The Rhode Island Constitution provides a partial solution to that problem by establishing a democratic process through which decisions can be made collectively. The Rhode Island legislature adopted § 4-406 to specify the responsibilities of banks and their customers. And commerce is conducted in Rhode Island on the assumption that the scheme it establishes will be enforced. What are the rights and responsibilities of banks in Rhode Island in respect of forged checks? You won't find the answer in Kant or Aristotle. You'll find it in § 4-406.[6]

• • •

Laws like § 4-406 serve important moral functions. Thomas Aquinas famously argued that human laws are needed to make the demands of natural law more determinate. Indeed, he argued that human law was derived from natural law through a process he called *determinatio*. He likened it to a craftsman taking the idea of a house and giving it concrete shape.[7] Morality might, in absence of our practices, require that we relate on fair terms. But it takes laws like § 4-406 to put flesh on the idea of fairness, to give it life in a world that contains corporations and banks.

I don't think Aquinas is right to say that human law is derived from natural law. I don't think that every law is (or even should be) a working out of some abstract idea in morality. But I do think that morality demands that we establish legal practices so that we can make its requirements concrete—and enforceable too. And that's not the only reason to think legal practices morally mandatory. Kant emphasized that law (and only law, in his view) can make it possible for us to relate to one another as equals.[8] And earlier, we saw Seana Shiffrin's argument that only democratic law can do that.[9] I think she's right. But we don't need to revisit Shiffrin's arguments or work through Kant's. Because it's clear that legal practices play a major part in our moral lives—that they figure, prominently and perhaps indispensably—in determining what we owe each other across a wide range of contexts.

And not just what we owe each other "according to law." Law isn't a game that we play when we wish, or a story that we take off the shelf when we want to hear what it has to say. It's not a perspective on how we should act. Law is deeply embedded in our lives. Our legal practices structure almost every relationship we have—as parents, as partners, as landlords, as lessees, as employees, as citizens, and on and on. Many of these relationships wouldn't exist absent law, and the ones we might have anyway would have a different character. Indeed, it's hard to conceive of what we owe each other without taking account of our legal practices, since law shapes almost all that we do.

If law is deeply embedded in our lives, shaping what we owe each other, why would we conceive it as something separate from morality? A standard answer, embraced by positivists like Jeremy Bentham, John Austin, and H. L. A. Hart, is that distinguishing law and morality helps us remember that law can be criticized, and might not deserve our deference. Hans Kelsen put the point this way:

[A] terminological tendency to identify law and justice, to use the term law in the sense of just law . . . has the effect that any positive law . . . is to be considered at first sight as just, since it presents itself as law and is generally called law. It may be doubtful whether it deserves to be termed law, but it has the benefit of the doubt. He who denies the justice of such "law" and asserts that the so-called law is no "true" law has to prove it. . . . Hence the real effect of the terminological identification of law and justice is an illicit justification of any positive law.[10]

That sentiment is often summed up in slogans. Bentham and Hart cautioned against confusing "law as it is and law as it ought to be,"[11] while Austin insisted that the "existence of law is one thing; its merit or demerit is another."[12]

Those are good slogans. We should distinguish the law as it is from the law as it ought to be. And we should remember that the existence of law is one thing, its merit or demerit another. More than that, we should maintain a healthy skepticism toward our legal practices. We should worry that they aren't what they ought to be. In fact, we should worry that many of them are immoral.

But as we've seen, we can do all that *and* recognize that law is a moral practice. Indeed, we can do all that *and* recognize that legal rights and responsibilities are moral rights and responsibilities. As we saw in Chapter 1, morality often assigns us rights and responsibilities that we ought not have. It does this because it's sensitive to the way we've arranged our affairs, even when we should have arranged them differently. So seeing law as a moral practice doesn't preclude us from distinguishing law as it is from law as it ought to be. We can recognize that legal rights are moral rights, while also acknowledging that some of them should be abrogated— or others added.

For the same reason, we can agree that the existence of law is one thing, its merit or demerit another. Indeed, we can agree in several different senses. We can see the slogan as an iteration of the point just made— that sometimes we have rights and responsibilities, but there's little to recommend our having them and maybe even much to recommend against. But we can also see it as a reminder that we talk about law in lots of senses, some of which are sociological. As we've seen throughout, our legal practices are often awful. When they are, they might not generate any rights or responsibilities, save a duty to resist or reform them. But still, they'll shape our lives, especially if the rights and responsibilities the practices purport to assign are enforced.

Positivism derives much of its attraction from the ambiguity latent in our talk about law. When people say "law is a social fact,"[13] the claim rings true, precisely because legal practices affect our lives regardless of whether they have any moral merit—or succeed in creating any genuine rights and obligations. The practices themselves are social facts. And it's guaranteed that people with power take the practices seriously; otherwise, they wouldn't exist. So we're apt to be treated as if we have the rights and responsibilities the practice purports to assign, even if we don't. That's another social fact. And that fact looms large in our lives, especially (but not only) when the legal practices are oppressive.

All this, though, is consistent with the idea that law is a moral practice. Indeed, it's consistent with the idea that legal rights and responsibilities are moral rights and responsibilities. Bentham, Austin, Hart, and Kelsen set themselves in opposition to a straw man—a simpleminded reading of the natural law slogan "an unjust law is not a law" (or *lex iniusta non est lex,* if you like your Latin). They took that phrase to blur the distinction between law as it is and law as it ought to be. But the phrase actually exploits that distinction.[14] It trades on two ways we use the word *law.* It tells us that a law that exists in one sense (because it's expressed or enforced) doesn't exist in another sense (because it's not authoritative or binding). Even so, the phrase is false. As we've seen, laws that are unjust are often binding. (Recall the tax law that demands too little from the wealthy; still, they must pay what they owe.) But in extreme cases, the slogan captures something important. Laws that purport to enslave people or permit genocide do not bind us. So there's a sense in which they're not law: no one ought to take seriously claims that are grounded in them, except perhaps on prudential grounds. But there's also lots of senses in which they are law. And I don't buy Kelsen's suggestion that we'll get confused if we try to hold both thoughts in our head at once.[15] The distinction is simple to spell out; indeed, it's apparent on the surface of the slogan.

Positivism doesn't help us to talk more clearly about law. Indeed, it obscures important aspects of it. It invites us to focus on social facts. That's good. They matter. But it paints an impoverished picture of the role morality plays within our legal practices. Positivists would have us believe that law demands whatever it does—and then we assess its demands to see if they're legitimate. The truth is that moral assessment is internal to legal judgment.[16] We disagree about what law demands because we disagree about the moral significance of our legal practices. We contest their significance when we argue about what the law is—in court and out.

• • •

Does it matter whether we see law as a moral practice? I just offered one reason for thinking it does. It helps us appreciate the character of legal conflicts. They are moral conflicts—conflicts about who owes what to whom. It's puzzling, on a positivist picture, that we can disagree about law, even when no social facts are in dispute.[17] The fact that morality plays a part in determining what the law demands makes sense of those disagreements. It also provides a partial explanation for their persistence; there are no simple procedures for settling moral disputes.

The moral practice picture can also improve our understanding of the ways in which legal practices shape our rights and responsibilities. As we saw in Chapter 5, many conversations about the moral significance of legal practices are misguided, since they tend to assume that moral assessment is external to legal judgment. We take the law for granted and ask whether we're obligated to obey it, rather than recognizing that legal conclusions are reached by nuanced consideration of competing moral arguments. Seeing law as a moral practice encourages us to attend to the wide variety of ways law shapes what we owe each other.

Finally, the moral practice picture sheds light on morality. As we've learned, morality isn't insulated from our activities. It's sensitive to social facts. And we can do a lot to shape its demands. Moreover, morality isn't perfect. If our social practices aren't what they ought to be, then our moral rights and responsibilities won't be either. We've developed these ideas by thinking about law. But they can help us think about the moral significance of many other social practices—sports, games, codes for clubs, and so on. The moral practice picture provides a road map for thinking through how social practices affect what we owe each other, why we often disagree about that, and how we should relate to practices that aren't what they should be.

I told you up front that I don't have a knockdown argument against other ways of looking at law. I don't trust those sorts of arguments anyway.[18] Instead, I issued an invitation: take up the idea that law is a moral practice, see how it works, see where it leads, and see how it accommodates the fact that so many legal practices are morally objectionable. I hope you see the appeal of the moral practice picture. I hope you see that it isn't easy to dismiss. And I hope you're thinking through the questions I said I'd ask at the end: Are there any reasons to suppose that law and morality are separate normative systems? What does that view allow us to appreciate about law that we can't see if we suppose it's a moral practice? I don't think this book contains the last word on these questions. But I think law is a moral practice.

APPENDIX: FAQS

NOTES

ACKNOWLEDGMENTS

INDEX

Frequently Asked Questions

As I said at the start, my aim in writing this book was to provide a concise account of the idea that law is a moral practice. I said I'd engage other views only as necessary to move the main idea of this book forward. Here, I've collected questions that readers commonly ask. Some of them pose challenges to the view I presented, others highlight alternatives, and some seek clarification about the relationship between the idea that law is a moral practice and other prominent positions in the field.

Aren't you just a positivist?

At some point, every antipositivist is accused of being a secret positivist. But I'm happy to accept the label, at least in some contexts. As we saw in Chapter 3, there are many sets of norms associated with any community's legal practices, among them the norms that are expressed in legal texts, the norms that are accepted by legal officials, the norms that are enforced, and the norms that are authoritative or binding. Moreover, talk about the law of a community could, depending on the context, refer to any of these sets, or several others.

Legal positivism is the thesis that the existence and content of the law are determined by social facts (either exclusively or ultimately). And that thesis is true of several of these sets (the norms that are expressed, the norms that are accepted, and the norms that are enforced). So I am, indeed, a positivist about those sets. But positivism is not true of the last entry on our list from Chapter 3:

the norms that are authoritative—that is, the ones that we have reason to apply or follow. And it's those norms that are contested in court.

Ronald Dworkin held a similar view, but he expressed it differently. In *Justice in Robes,* he drew a distinction between different concepts of law: doctrinal, taxonomic, sociological, and aspirational.[1] Two are relevant here: the doctrinal concept (which we use "in stating what the law of some jurisdiction requires or forbids or permits"); and the taxonomic concept (which we use to "classify a particular rule or principle as a legal principle rather than a principle of some other kind.").[2]

Dworkin was concerned with the doctrinal concept. He aimed to show that the truth conditions of propositions about what the law permits or requires encompass moral facts, not just social facts. He was right about that.

When it came to taxonomic questions, Dworkin said he might be a positivist—if he could be moved to care about them. *Is this a legal principle or merely a moral one? Is this a principle of Polish law, or merely a principle of Greek law that Polish courts are obligated to apply?* It's tempting, Dworkin said, to say that a principle becomes part of the law only if it's been "cited and relied on often in a particular legal jurisdiction."[3] But he didn't think claims of that sort significant: "It is of course important what we take to be relevant to deciding what legal rights and duties people and officials have. But nothing important turns on which part of what is relevant we describe as 'the law.'"[4]

I've come at the same point a different way, since I find talk about concepts in this context more confusing than illuminating. (For instance, I don't think Dworkin's four concepts cover the field if we're trying to capture all the ways that we talk about law.) I find it more helpful to focus on sets of norms—the norms that are expressed, the norms that are enforced, and so on. Separating out those sets of norms helps us to see which ones we should be positivists about.

But I also find it helpful to remember another point that Dworkin made: it's misleading to suppose "that the 'law' of a community consists of a finite body of rules, principles, and other standards that might in theory all be listed or counted."[5] Many different sets of norms might count as the law depending on what we want to emphasize. (And on top of that, there's no canonical way to individuate norms, once we know what we want to emphasize.) So the taxonomic question whether a principle is part of the law in a given jurisdiction admits of many answers, some of which might track positivist pictures and some of which might not. The upshot is that we should be positivists in some senses but not others. But we shouldn't let the possibility that we should be positivists in some senses obscure the fact that the legal rights and obligations we contest in court are moral rights and obligations.

Aren't you just a natural lawyer?

As I said earlier, this label has been used to refer to lots of different ideas, so it's not a helpful way of characterizing positions in jurisprudence.[6]

On some renderings, a natural lawyer holds that morality is a source of law, independent of a community's legal practices.[7] That is not my view. In fact, I mean to say just the opposite. A community's legal practices are (at least potentially) sources of morality.

But I have also emphasized that a community's legal practices will succeed in adjusting moral requirements only if moral principles that exist independently of them endow them with that significance. On some renderings, that is the central commitment of the natural lawyer.[8] So on that score, I am a natural lawyer. But so are most positivists.

In any event, I don't endorse the slogan often associated with natural law—*lex iniusta non est lex* (an unjust law is not a law). The saying plays off the fact that we use the word *law* in different ways. The idea is that an unjust (posited) law is not a (morally binding) law. But though the slogan makes sense when spelled out that way, it's false. Lots of unjust laws are morally binding. The tax law that demands too little of wealthy people is an easy illustration. But even laws that demand too much, or frustrate important aims, may be morally binding if the practices through which they were adopted are, say, suitably democratic or play an important role in peaceful dispute resolution—and the laws themselves aren't too awful.

The upshot is that I'm a natural lawyer in some senses, but not others—just as I am a positivist in some senses, but not others. That's why I'd prefer we leave these labels behind.

How does your view relate to Ronald Dworkin's?

My view is very close to the view that Dworkin first articulated in "Model of Rules II" and "Hard Cases."[9] In those papers, Dworkin made clear that legal practices are sources of moral requirements and that legal claims are best understood as moral claims.

Dworkin's view may have shifted in *Law's Empire*. There, he seemed to accept that law was a separate normative system from morality. But he argued that morality played a part in determining the content of the law. At least, that's how Dworkin was read by many, including (perhaps) Dworkin himself. Steve Schaus and I wrote a paper tracing the development of Dworkin's views across time.[10] We argue that *Law's Empire* is ambiguous, but we think it's best read as a refinement of the view presented in "Model of Rules II" and "Hard Cases," not as a departure from it.

Regardless, in his later books (*Justice in Robes* and *Justice for Hedgehogs*), Dworkin explicitly embraced the idea that law is a part of morality, not a separate normative system. I think it's more helpful to say that law is a moral practice. That is, I think it more helpful to highlight the fact that the activities we associate with law (legislation, adjudication, regulation, contracting, and so on) are oriented toward rearranging our rights and responsibilities in the ordinary moral sense. But that reflects the fact that I'd frame the issues differently than Dworkin does. We both believe that the legal claims contested in court are moral claims, that legal rights are moral rights, and that legal obligations are moral obligations. So the views are substantially similar. Indeed, I see myself as trying to further develop and explain the view I take Dworkin to have held.

How does your view relate to Mark Greenberg's Moral Impact Theory?

My view is quite close to Greenberg's too, and I owe a large debt to his work.[11]

Here are some ideas we hold in common. Both of us think that legal practices can be sources of moral requirements. And both of us think that the legal claims contested in court are moral claims. We also think that legal rights are moral rights, and that legal obligations are moral obligations. Those are the most important parts of my view. So I see Greenberg as a fellow traveler.

That said, I have some reservations about the Moral Impact Theory, as Greenberg has developed it. The reason is that Greenberg construes the task of jurisprudence differently than I do. He thinks our legal practices create something ("the law") about which we should do metaphysics. The Moral Impact Theory is a thesis about how the content of the law is constituted. According to Greenberg, "the content of the law is that part of the moral profile created by the actions of legal institutions in the legally proper way."[12]

Elsewhere, I've expressed doubts that this view can be made to work, even on its own terms, mostly because I'm skeptical about the notion of "legally proper" that it employs.[13] I suggested that, if I had to choose, I preferred Dworkin's suggestion that legal rights and obligations are moral rights and obligations that people are entitled to enforce in court (or other adjudicative institutions). That way of characterizing the domain of the legal has practical import; we need to know which of our rights we can enforce and how. Greenberg calls this the Judicial Enforcement Theory, and he conceives of it as a rival to the Moral Impact Theory, alongside other candidate theories that are all part of a family of views (called Dependence

Theories) that hold "that legal obligations constitutively depend on moral obligations."[14] Greenberg argues against the Judicial Enforcement Theory; he aims to show that the Moral Impact Theory provides the correct characterization of the content of the law.

As I indicated in Chapter 1, I'm not moved by the arguments Greenberg offers against the Judicial Enforcement Theory.[15] But my more fundamental objection is that there is no need to settle on a single characterization of what constitutes "the law." As I've said repeatedly, we can and do draw the boundaries of the law differently depending on what we want to emphasize (the sources of a requirement, its mechanism of enforcement, and so on). That makes both the Moral Impact Theory and the Judicial Enforcement Theory answers to a question I don't think we should ask. I think we should instead acknowledge that our talk about "the law" is flexible—that the phrase takes on different referents in different conversations. And that's true even when talk about "the law" refers to a subset of our moral obligations. The members of that subset shift, depending on what's being discussed or emphasized.

There's one more aspect of Greenberg's presentation I find puzzling. The main lesson of the Moral Impact Theory is that the law is a part of morality—that our legal obligations are a subset of our moral obligations. That makes it odd to say that "legal obligations constitutively depend on moral obligations," since that way of putting things makes it sound as if they are separate entities, one whose existence and content depends on the other.[16] One reason I'm resistant to putting "the law" at the center of jurisprudence is that it invites people to think that there's something separate from morality that needs explaining. My aim is to get people to stop thinking of "the law" as a distinct entity—and to start seeing legal claims as moral claims.[17]

But in the big picture, these are small differences. And I think Greenberg would agree. He acknowledges that, on his view, the distinction "between legal and non-legal obligations" is "less important than on many other theories," since it "has no effect on what we take our genuine obligations to be."[18] I think the distinction even less important than Greenberg does. But the differences between us are mostly matters of emphasis, presentation, and argumentative path, not substance.

So what should we call your view?

Let's call it the Moral Practice Picture.

One attraction of that label is that it shifts our attention away from "the law"—the mythical entity that sits at the center of lots of misguided jurisprudence—and toward the impact our legal practices have on our rights and obligations.

How does your view relate to Joseph Raz's?

As I suggested in Chapter 3, Raz's view shares a lot in common with the picture I've presented, even though he's regarded as a leading proponent of positivism.

To start, Raz thinks that law is a moral practice, in the relevant sense. He says that law claims authority over its subjects, and by *authority* he means, among other things, the power to confer rights and impose obligations.[19] So Raz thinks that law is a moral practice, in the relevant sense.

Raz also agrees that judges are moral actors, making moral decisions.[20] And he agrees that the norms that courts apply are binding, if they are, only in virtue of moral principles that make them so.[21] Indeed, Raz says that we can't "conceive of the law as a normatively valid point of view contrasting with morality" because "it is not . . . possible to think of the law as a ground of reasons independently of morality."[22] Why not? Because the principles that "endow governments with legitimacy are . . . moral principles. . . . They are principles that allow, perhaps even require, some people to interfere in important ways in the lives of others. Valid principles that have such content are moral principles, or nothing is."[23]

I agree with all that. And there is further overlap between Raz's view and mine. Raz has long held that a person has a normative power (that is, a power to bring about a normative change by a certain act) if, all things considered, it is desirable that she have the power to bring about that change by that act.[24] We have the power to obligate ourselves by making a promise, on Raz's view, because, all things considered, it is desirable that we have that power (at least in a range of cases). In a recent paper, Raz added a new wrinkle to his picture of normative powers. It's possible, he said, for a person to have a normative power that she shouldn't have.[25] How could that be, if the test for whether we have a normative power is whether it's desirable that we do? The answer is that normative powers can be chained. It may be desirable that one person has a normative power to confer normative powers on others. And it may further be desirable that they have that power even in cases where they might use it poorly, conferring normative powers on others that they ought not have.[26] Raz calls the resulting powers "chained" or "non-basic." And he says that they "belong with a class of normative conditions that can be both normatively binding and yet normatively defective to the degree that it would have been better had they not existed."[27] In conversation, Raz has also allowed that the opposite might be true—that a person might lack a normative power he ought to have, because it has not been conferred on him by someone who has the power to decide whether it will be.

In saying all that, Raz recognizes that morality can fall short of what it ought to be. And once you allow that, it's easy to get the moral practice picture of law up and running. As I've said throughout, courts are called on to decide what people's rights and responsibilities are, given the history and practices that we have. Those rights and responsibilities may differ from the ones people ought to have. Raz's recent essay explores one way in which that might come to be. And indeed, he offers many legal examples: "wills, gifts, marriages, agreements, patent rights, laws, administrative regulations, as well as customary rules whose existence is not owed to the use of normative powers, could all be valid and binding yet so defective that it would have been better if they had not been created, and sometimes, it would be better to terminate them."[28]

So again, I find myself in agreement with Raz. That said, there are points of disagreement. The central one is this: Raz insists that when the law is legitimate, judges (who are moral actors, making moral decisions) are required to leave morality behind and make decisions according to law.[29] The law, he insists, is a set of directives whose content is determined solely by social facts. He allows that it's possible that the law might direct a judge to apply a moral principle, but he insists that the moral principle is not thereby rendered part of the law. In that way, he accepts that morality can be relevant to judicial reasoning, but nevertheless denies that it contributes to the content of the law.

This is not the place to explore the arguments in favor of Raz's view or the problems with it. I've done that elsewhere, and so have others.[30] I'll just say that I don't find the arguments in favor of the view persuasive. Indeed, I think Raz gerrymanders the boundaries of law for little purpose other than preserving a place for positivism. He's picked out a set of social facts that are relevant in answering the questions that courts ask, and he insists that we call those (and only those) law, though he allows that other facts (including moral facts) are relevant to deciding whether people have the rights they claim. That said, I think it worth appreciating how close Raz's view is to the moral practice picture.

Surely there are some artificial normative systems. What about games? Or fashion? And if you accept that those are artificial normative systems, why not law?

"At least on the surface of things," Mitch Berman says, "we inhabit a multiplicity of normative systems—law and morality, of course, but also sports and games, prescriptive grammar and fashion, etiquette, religious ritual, families, militaries, corporations, and so on. The multiplicity of normative systems seems a plain fact of our lives."[31] Moreover, Berman adds, many of these systems are "artificial," in that they are "normative systems of human construction."[32]

Is it a "plain fact" about our lives that we inhabit many different normative systems? It's plain that we engage in lots of different activities (sports, games, and so on) and that we are members of many different communities (families, militaries, and so on). It's also plain that there are norms associated with these activities and communities. And it's further plain that many such norms are artificial, in the sense that they're crafted or chosen to suit these activities and communities. But Berman's assertion—that the norms associated with different activities and communities constitute their own "normative systems"—is a theory-laden claim, not a plain fact about our lives.

All along, I've been urging the opposite view, at least as to law and morality. Instead of seeing them as separate normative systems, I've suggested that we see our legal practices as (in part) efforts to adjust what we owe each other—as a matter of morality. I've tried to show that this is not just a coherent but attractive way to think about law.

Is my argument specific to law? In some ways, it is. Legal practices affect almost every aspect of our lives, and they're often intrusive. They are practices of punishment and accountability. They constrain where we live, with whom, and how. They demand sacrifices and impose burdens. Legal practices instruct some people to lay down their lives and take others. And they don't limit their impositions to people who have chosen to participate in the practices. I agree with Raz: any principles that would warrant these sorts of interferences "are moral principles, or nothing is."[33]

So here's a possibility: you could accept that the social world is, as Berman says, "densely populated by countless normative systems of human construction."[34] But you could nevertheless see law as part of the moral normative system.

That's not how I see it, though, since I don't think our normative lives are fractured in the way that Berman does. I don't think, for instance, that games (like baseball, backgammon, chess, and checkers) are their own separate normative systems.[35] I'd say instead that games are moral practices (though the stakes are often lower than they are with law). Games are built up out of rights and responsibilities, privileges and powers, immunities and liabilities. The people who design them aim to structure relationships between participants in ways that make new activities possible—activities that they hope will be challenging, fun, or in some other way rewarding.

Now, I've just acknowledged that people design games. Doesn't that indicate that games are, after all, artificial normative systems, separate from morality? They are artificial. But that doesn't mark them off from morality. We design many of our moral relationships. We make promises and reach agreements. We waive claims and give consent. As I've emphasized throughout, we have a lot of control over what we owe each other. And creating and playing games are ways in which we exercise that control. C. Thi Nguyen describes games as "morally transformative technologies" that temporarily "reconfigure their players' social relationships," often in profound ways.[36] Among other things, Nguyen observes, games can "take an action that is normally negatively valenced—brutal competition—and turn it into something good."[37] And not just good from the perspective of the game, but good in the lives of the players. "Games," Nguyen says, "are morally active, and game designers are thereby partially morally implicated, for good or ill, in the moral functioning of their designs."[38]

In saying that, Nguyen is resisting the idea that games are played in a "magic circle" that is "morally separated from normal life."[39] Games have spillover effects. Sometimes money is at stake. Sometimes fame is. Sometimes bragging rights are. All that makes games morally meaningful. But there's moral meaning even when we just play for fun. Bragging in those circumstances might breach the terms on which we played.

These sorts of spillover effects make the moral significance of games stark. But games would matter morally even absent them. It can be wrong to interfere with others' fun or to deprive them of a challenge by failing to compete—or to compete too hard, as parents of young kids learn. Games aren't insulated from our moral lives.

But it's easy to understand why people might think they are. The way we relate to each other in games can be radically different from the way we relate outside them. In a game, I can have rights and responsibilities that are wholly different from the rights and responsibilities that I have in everyday life. For instance, I can have a right to take a base when a fielder throws the ball in the stands, or an obligation to move a chess piece once I've touched it. I couldn't have those sorts of rights and obligations unless someone imagined—and conveyed to others—new ways in which we could relate to each other. But I don't have them just because someone imagined the ways in which we might relate when we play baseball or chess. I have them (when I do) because the norms that structure those relationships have become (at least for a little while) norms that govern us, norms that are authoritative, norms that bear on how we ought to act, norms that we have reasons to follow (at least until it's time for lunch).

Typically, the norms govern us because we're playing the game. Sometimes we agree to do so. Other times, we just start to play, creating in each other the expectation that we'll continue—and not just carry on, but carry on as we might reasonably expect of each other (moving the knight, say, in that L-shaped way, rather than dipping it in salsa). But the point is the same as it was with law:

the norms associated with games create reasons for action only when there are moral principles that bring them to bear on how we ought to act.

Berman might agree. But he would insist that the norms of baseball and chess can exist independently of any reason we might have to apply them. They exist as part of an artificial normative system.

I agree with the first bit, but not the second. Of course, there are norms associated with activities like playing chess. In fact, there are many sets of norms associated with that activity. To start, there are the norms expressed in texts. These might include official rule books, like the ones promulgated by chess governing bodies, or informal rules, like the ones printed inside a boxed chess set. There are also rules that are expressed but not in writing, like the ones announced at the start of your family chess tournament.

But as we saw with law, there are lots of norms floating around chess beyond the ones that have been expressed. There are the norms that the authors of the various texts intended to express, which might come apart from the norms that they did express. And there are norms that participants observe, which might be a different set yet again—and different in different ways depending on the occasion. And there are norms that are enforced, which again might differ from the rules expressed, or intended, or observed—and on and on, until you arrive at the set of norms that are, on this particular occasion of play, the ones that are authoritative for us, if any are. It's that last set, of course, that tells us what to do, how to act, what we owe each other on this occasion. And it's morality that determines which norms those are. It could direct us to the norms that were expressed, the ones intended, the ones observed, or a mishmash of those sets, or even some slightly different norms nearby. But if we want to know what we owe to others, on this occasion of play, it's morality that tells us which norms to apply.

That sounds odd to some ears. And the owners of those ears might say that I'm overmoralizing. Games aren't serious affairs. It's not a moral question whether I may take a base or capture your pawn. (But what if there's money at stake? Or your kid's emotions?) As I said way back in Chapter 1, we use the word *moral* in many ways. On some renderings, calling a question *moral* signals that we're dealing with something serious, something that calls into question people's character. If you use the word that way, then it might seem that I'm wrong to treat the question how I may move a knight as a moral question, at least much of the time. But I haven't been using the word that way. I've said that morality is the domain of rights, wrongs, and the reasons that relate to them. And the question how I must move a chess piece is absolutely a moral question in that sense.

And we treat it like one. We assert rights when we play games. We make demands. We blame each other for misdeeds. We get angry. And that anger doesn't always dissipate when the game ends. It can rupture relationships that exist outside the game—because the rights and responsibilities involved in games are real. Often, the damage can be contained. "It's just a game," we say, "let it go." And sometimes, that's the right thing to do. The relationships we have outside games generally matter more than the relations we have within them. But sometimes, it's hard to let it go—because we take games seriously, some of the time, and we can be disrespected or even injured in the course of play.

To be clear, Berman could accommodate these insights. He acknowledges that there are many rules for playing chess.[40] There are official rules from FIDE (the International Chess Federation) and other chess governing bodies. There are rules that govern casual, friendly games. At my house. Maybe they differ at your house. And then there are the rules of the school chess club. And the high school chess association. In Montana. And Nebraska. And on and on. These are all different normative systems, according to Berman—they are members of a chess family of normative systems.[41]

Berman also acknowledges that there are many different norms associated with each of these variants of chess.[42] There are the rules in the rule book (if there is one). But there are many other rules associated with these activities, like the ones that the authors of the rule book intended to express, the ones that are observed (which might differ from place to place), the ones that are enforced (ditto), and so on. And he further acknowledges that the rules expressed in rule books, where they exist, don't fix the content of these different normative systems.[43] Other norms might supplement or supplant them.

How? And how do we know which ones? Berman doesn't have an answer. "It remains to discover," he says, "what determinants *do* give the norms of artificial normative systems the contents that they have."[44] Indeed, he says that it's a "principal task of general jurisprudence" to make that discovery.[45] And many people would agree. The recent history of jurisprudence (at least on the positivist side) consists, in large part, of attempts to explain how law gets its content.

The problem is that none of those attempts has been successful (as even Berman seems to recognize).[46] We could, of course, continue the search. We could look for better theories of law. And chess. And baseball. And on and on, because we shouldn't assume that there's a general answer to the question how artificial normative systems get their content.

Or we could drop the idea that different activities and communities each have their own separate normative systems—and with it, the need to say how any of them are constituted. We could instead see games as moral practices, which aim to structure what we owe each other when we play. And we could recognize that the question what we owe each other when we play is a moral question, whose answer will be heavily influenced by social facts (like what the rule book says, or what expectations people have, or what our past practice has been, or what would make the game go well) but won't be fully determined by them. That's not (as Berman seems to think that I think) an abandonment of the idea that there are rules for playing chess and baseball.[47] There are so many rules for playing chess and baseball! And they exist in all sorts of ways. It's just a recognition that those rules affect what we ought to do only when morality makes it so—and that morality tells us which norms matter when we play.[48]

Can I prove that my way of looking at the world is better than Berman's? No. I told you up front that I don't have a knockdown argument that other ways of thinking about law (or games) are wrong. But I can report that I don't see any benefit to thinking Berman's way.[49] I don't think he can explain anything that I can't. And his way of thinking comes with the burden of explaining how artificial normative systems get their content—not just generally, but one by one, for an endless series of them.

You might be tempted to think that I've got an equivalent burden. I have to explain how morality picks out the norms that people have reason to follow on any particular occasion. That's a big task. But Berman has it too. Because morality governs how we should act—even when we are in court, even when we are playing games.

That said, neither Berman nor I need to carry out this task, because the people who participate in these practices do it every day. They argue in court, at ballparks, and over chess sets, debating what we owe each other in light of the social practices and histories we have. To be sure, philosophers can help, at the retail and wholesale levels. We've got relevant expertise. And sometimes, we use it for good. But for the most part, people do fine without us, and the jurisprudential theories Berman imagines wouldn't be any assistance at all.

What about fashion?

Fashion is not a moral practice. People do not design clothes, buy clothes, or decide what to wear for the purpose of adjusting their moral relationships with others (at least not in the normal case). But some people take facts about fashion to affect what we ought to do and maybe even what we owe each other. They make claims like: "You cannot wear *that* to a party after Labor Day." Or "Are you really going to wear *that* to a job interview?," where the implication is definitely, no, you should not. Some of those claims are moral claims. Some are not. Let's work it through to see which are which.

The first thing to note is that there are many sets of norms associated with fashion. There are the norms that are followed, which differ widely among communities and across time. There are the norms that people articulate to one another, which again, vary widely, across communities and across time. There are norms printed in various texts—fashion magazines, advice columns, and so on. There are the norms that are accepted, even if they are sometimes flouted. There are the norms whose flouting will draw rebuke. There are norms whose flouting is routinely ignored, or even celebrated. And so on.

Are there authoritative norms of fashion—norms that we have reason to follow? In some contexts, yes. (Remember, Dworkin's case of the baby and the bonnet was a case about which norms of fashion, if any, are authoritative for babies, or rather, the people who dress them.) There are occasions for which people ought to dress respectfully—at funerals, in church, on job interviews, and so on. Since what counts as respectful is largely a matter of social signaling, the norms that are accepted will loom large in determining which norms are authoritative. But they will not settle the matter, as those norms might be racist, sexist, or otherwise morally defective.

For many years, the Clerk at the Supreme Court advised female attorneys to wear skirt suits, not pantsuits. He gave them this advice because he knew that Justice O'Connor thought it disrespectful for a woman to wear a pantsuit. She grew up in a time when formal dress for a woman meant a skirt, and the Court is a formal place if any place is. (The solicitor general argues in a morning coat.) But O'Connor was wrong to be offended. The norm that sets a skirt as the only appropriate formal wear for women is sexist. A pantsuit is plenty respectful enough, and indeed, no less respectful than a skirt suit.

So was the Clerk wrong to advise women to wear skirt suits? Yes, to the extent that he thought it required as a matter of respect for the Court. But perhaps he had a different argument in mind. Suppose that you are heading to the Supreme Court to argue a case for your client, and you learn about Justice O'Connor's view. You had planned to wear a pantsuit. Should you switch to a skirt suit? You certainly don't owe it to Justice O'Connor or the Court. But you might owe it to your client. If you anticipate that Justice O'Connor will be distracted or annoyed, such that she won't give your arguments the attention or weight that they deserve, you might think that you owe it to your client to wear a skirt suit. I'm not saying that you do. There are cross-cutting considerations. Your client's interests are not all that matters. Your comfort does, as does the small blow you might strike for sex equality by insisting that a pantsuit is as appropriate for women as it is for men. But there's an argument to be made. And regardless of whether it wins out, it's clear that fashion can matter morally.

But most of the time, it doesn't. When someone says you shouldn't wear white after Labor Day, she's probably not making a moral claim. That is, she's probably not saying that you owe it to her—or to anyone else—to avoid it. Rather, she's reminding you of a norm that is accepted, at least in some communities, and thus drawing your attention to the reactions others are likely to have if you flout it. You might care. You might not. But most often, there's no moral decision to be made, as no rights or responsibilities are in play.

You didn't offer an argument for your central claim. Why should I think that the legal claims advanced in court are moral claims?

The legal claims advanced in court are claims about who owes what to whom—they are (depending on the case) claims about what defendants owe plaintiffs, what courts owe plaintiffs, what defendants owe the state, and so on. Moreover, the rights claimed in courts are claimed as genuine—they are meant to move the court to action. Indeed, they are frequently intended to warrant significant interference in others' lives. That makes them moral claims, given the way I'm using the term. Remember, morality, as I've construed it here, is the domain of rights, wrongs, and the reasons that relate to them.

So you just defined morality so as to make the moral practice picture true?

There's a bit of truth in this. I did define morality in a way that makes the moral practice picture true. But I did not render it that way for that reason. I defined it that way because it seems to me a reasonable way to define it. But remember, also, that I don't mean to put much weight on the word. We use *morality* in lots of ways, and that's fine with me. I'm using it to pick out the domain of rights, wrongs, and the reasons that relate to them.

I think there are many ways in which we might owe each other something, some of which are moral and some of which are not. But I don't think legal rights are moral rights. What's wrong with that view?

This is, I think, the most plausible alternative to the picture I've presented. The suggestion is that the domain of what we owe each other is not unified. On this alternative picture, if I say that you owe me $500, you won't know whether that's true until you know what sort of owing is in question: owing (morally), owing (legally), owing (in the way associated with a homeowner's association), owing (in the way associated with the baseball league), and so on endlessly. On this picture, we don't have a unified category of rights or obligations. Rather, we have a hodge-podge of related ideas: rights$_{morality}$, rights$_{law}$, rights$_{baseball}$, and so on, endlessly.

There are two ways to fill out this view. On the first, moral rights are the only genuine ones. The others are as if, pretend, or perspectival. (For instance, some read the claim that you have a legal right to $500 to mean that you have a moral right to $500 from the law's point of view.)[50] On the second, the legal rights (and all the rest) are genuine rights. It just turns out that genuine rights come in different flavors. For that reason, I call this the Baskin-Robbins view (though there might be more than thirty-one flavors of rights).[51]

I have not argued against either of these views in this book, at least not directly.[52] What I hope to have shown is that both are needlessly complicated. We can make sense of all of our talk about rights and obligations—in morality, law, and other moral practices—without the apparatus employed by the perspectival view, and without supposing that rights come in different flavors. And the fact that we can *is* an argument for looking at law and morality in the way that I've suggested.

But I'll say a bit more about the Baskin-Robbins view, since I think it has some intuitive appeal. It's important not to adopt it for the wrong reasons. I've argued for a unified picture of rights and obligations. They're the same sort of relationships, wherever we find them. They differ in lots of ways—in their sources, content, significance. And because they differ, we're apt to group them together in ways that are helpful. We distinguish our family obligations from our work obligations. We distinguish the obligations of friendship from the obligations of fatherhood. And we distinguish legal obligations and moral obligations—from each other and from others as well.

Those categorizations can, as I said, be helpful. They highlight commonalities, draw our attention to differences, and help us ensure that we're considering all that's relevant. They also help us see conflicts among our obligations—and explain them to others: "Sorry I can't make the party; I know I said I'd come, but I have a work obligation that weekend." There's nothing deep about these distinctions, though. We draw them in different ways at different times for different purposes. Earlier we explored some of the ways we use the word *legal*—to highlight sources, modes of enforcement, and so on. And we explored some of the ways in which we use the word *moral*. The fact that these labels are so flexible is what allows me to say that (conceived one way) legal obligations are moral obligations, but (conceived differently) there's a distinction to draw between the two (relating, say, to modes of enforcement).[53]

The Baskin-Robbins view purports to say more than that we group rights together in different ways depending on what we want to emphasize. What more does it say? It's hard to say. The idea is that there's some deep metaphysical divide between rights$_{\text{morality}}$, rights$_{\text{law}}$, and rights$_{\text{baseball}}$. It isn't the divide between rights that are genuine and rights that are not, since the Baskin-Robbins view holds that all these rights can be genuine. It's also not a divide grounded in sources or content or significance. Or at least it's not just that, since those distinctions fit within the unified picture I've presented. I'm not sure what's left. And I'm not sure that proponents of the Baskin-Robbins view have it sorted out either. But I will say this: they're multiplying metaphysical problems.[54] In addition to explaining what rights and obligations are, they need to explain how they differ across different domains—and how those domains work. (How many domains are there? How are they constituted? How do they interact?) And I don't see any payoff whatsoever, as I don't yet see what features of rights and obligations we can't explain from within a unified picture.

I am skeptical about morality. Why should I accept the moral practice picture?

Really? You don't act like it. I don't even know you, and I know you don't act like it. As I said in Chapter 1, I have met people who acted as if they did not owe anything to others. But I have never met anyone who acted as if she wasn't owed anything by others. And I doubt there are such people.

But, I know, that's not your point. You might *act* as if people owe you things. But at the end of the day (or in the middle of the day, if you find yourself in philosophy class), you are an error theorist about morality. There are no such things as rights or obligations. They are mass delusions—helpful ones, perhaps, but delusions nonetheless.

I won't try to talk you out of your skepticism here. What I will say is that, if you are skeptical about moral claims, you should be skeptical about legal claims too. A plaintiff in a tort suit asserts a right that the court enforce a right to compensation. If no one owes anyone anything, because no one can, then she doesn't have the right that she asserts. But she *is* making a moral claim—or so I want you to think.

Some people are skeptical about moral rights, but not legal rights. Nothing in nature, they think, grounds moral rights. But legal practices ground legal rights. The perspectival version of this view still leads to the conclusion that people engaged in legal practices are massively deluded. They are attempting to adjust moral rights and duties, when there are no such things to adjust.

The Baskin-Robbins view might fare better. But to make it work, someone would have to explain what legal rights are, if not moral rights or perspectival claims about them. Perhaps that can be done. But no one has done it yet.

Are you an eliminativist about law?

In "The End of Jurisprudence," I described my view as "a kind of eliminativism."[55] Some people think that legal practices generate a new, distinctively legal kind of normativity; that's the Baskin-Robbins view. Others think that legal practices generate a new kind of quasi-normativity, composed of entities (like legal rights and obligations) that look normative, but aren't really. My eliminativism was aimed at those ideas. I said that we could get along just fine without supposing that our legal practices generate "a distinctively legal domain of normativity, or quasi-normativity."

I didn't mean to suggest that we stop talking about law or asking what it requires of us. Hillary Nye, Liam Murphy, and Lewis Kornhauser have wondered whether we could do without Dworkin's doctrinal concept of law (the one we use when we make claims about what the law requires).[56] The thought is that, instead of asking what the law requires, we could just ask what we should do (as judges, as legislators, as lawyers giving advice, and so on). To the extent that our legal practices affect what we ought to do, we'll take account of them, and there's no need to worry about what the law is separate from that.

Nye and Kornhauser are sympathetic to this sort of eliminativism. Murphy is opposed. I think Murphy is right to say that talk about what the law requires has practical significance, such that it's nearly impossible to imagine abandoning it.[57] And I never meant to suggest that we should. I just think we have to be careful in the way we interpret such talk. I don't think our legal practices generate something called "the law," understood as a separate normative system. Instead, I think they adjust our moral relationships. Talk about what "the law" requires often refers to moral obligations that are enforceable in court. But it can refer to lots of other things—some moral, some sociological. (Recall the analogy with the rules of the house.) I don't think we should eliminate such talk. But we should notice how flexible it is, so that we aren't misled into thinking that "the law" is something about which we must do metaphysics.[58]

I'm an act utilitarian. I don't believe in rights and obligations.
So why should I accept this view?

Again, you can accept the view as an account of what people in the practice are doing and see them as confused. That's fine with me, so far as the argument in this book goes. I happen to think that act utilitarianism is misguided, but I won't make that case here.

But I'll add: on all but the strictest of act-utilitarian views, there are ways to get rights and obligations up and running within utilitarianism. So most utilitarians can sign on to the picture I've presented, though they might want to revise some of what I say to characterize morality.

How does morality fit into the rest of reality?
What's your metaethics?

I've tried to explain how law fits into the rest of reality; it's part of the moral part of our lives. Legal rights and obligations are moral rights and obligations. Legal claims are moral claims. But how does morality fit into the rest of reality?

That's an important question for philosophy, but not for this book. The claims I've advanced about law don't depend on any particular metaethics. You might be a realist about morality, a quietist, a noncognitivist. And all that (and more) is fine with me so far as my claims about law are concerned. It's even fine with me if you're skeptical of metaethical claims, as Dworkin was. For purposes of this project, I'm neutral on the question how morality fits into the rest of reality. I just want to say that law is a moral practice.

Notes

Introduction

1. For what it is worth, some experts say that we are doing it wrong. When we pressure Hank to try new foods, we're making those foods a source of stress. So we should just relax and let him live off yogurt, cheese, and chocolate, while presenting a wider set of options. Or so they say. We've seen parents succeed (and fail) with a wide range of approaches, so I'm skeptical that the research translates into practical parenting advice. For a short overview of the literature, see Melinda Wenner Moyer, "Why Is My Kid Such a Picky Eater?," *Slate* (December 19, 2012), http://www.slate.com/articles/double_x/the_kids/2012/12/picky_eater_kids_their_eating_habits_might_be_your_fault_but_they_ll_survive.html.

2. In case you are wondering, Hank is not confused about what rules are. If you ask him what the rules are at school, he can tell you several. If you ask him to make up a rule, he can do so on the spot. What he's noticed is that we claim the power to establish rules simply by our say-so. He's asserting the opposite power for himself. I've asked him who can make rules for our house, and he says, "Mommy, Daddy, Rex, and Hank," but he does not recognize any hierarchy of authority among us, at least not at the moments he tilts towards defiance.

3. See H. L. A. Hart, *The Concept of Law,* 2nd ed. (Oxford: Oxford University Press, 1994), 84 ("Where rules exist, deviations from them are not merely grounds for a prediction that hostile reactions will follow or that a court will apply sanctions to those who break them, but are also a reason or justification for such reaction and for applying the sanction.").

4. See Verizon v. FCC, 740 F.3d 623 (D.C. Cir. 2014); Comcast Corp. v. FCC, 600 F.3d 642 (D.C. Cir. 2010).

5. United States Telecom Association v. FCC, 825 F.3d 674 (D.C. Cir. 2016). Alas, the rule did not last long, as a subsequent administration repealed it. See Keith Collins, "Net Neutrality Has Officially Been Appealed. Here's How That Could Affect You," *New York Times,* June 6, 2018, https://www.nytimes.com/2018/06/11/technology/net-neutrality-repeal.html.

6. National Federation of Independent Business v. Sebelius, 567 U.S. 519, 530 (2012).

7. U.S. Const. pmbl.

8. See Richard Primus, "Unbundling Constitutionality," *University of Chicago Law Review* 80 (2013): 1133 ("[T]he First Amendment gives freedom of speech a place in the constitutional text, but the constitutional law of free speech goes far beyond the text of the First Amendment. Constitutional protection of free speech runs against all government actors, even though the First Amendment's guarantee is textually addressed only to Congress.").

9. Primus, "Unbundling," 1130–1131 and 1130n137, citing Department of Revenue of Kentucky v. Davis, 553 U.S. 328, 361 (2008) (Thomas, J., concurring, observing that the Dormant Commerce Clause has no basis in the text of the Constitution).

10. Hart, *The Concept of Law,* chapter 6.

11. Hart, *The Concept of Law,* chapter 6.

12. The actual rule would have to be much more complicated than this, and for lots of reasons. First, there are rules that my wife and I would not recognize our authority to establish (e.g., everyone must sprinkle arsenic on their eggs). Second, we have to account for the fact that we share authority, but often act on our own. (Our standard practice is to defer to the rules that one of us hands down unilaterally, at least until there is opportunity for joint reconsideration. But we are not completely consistent about that and do not think that we should be.) Third, we often take the rules that we establish to be slightly different from what we said. (We tell Rex, "You may not play in the street," but the rule that establishes is that he needs permission—and supervision—by an adult whom he knows. If he has that, he has not broken the rule.) And . . . well, you get the point. The fact that our rule of recognition would turn out to be so complicated casts doubt on whether any practice that my wife and I have could fix its content. Ronald Dworkin pressed this concern in his first reply to Hart. See Ronald Dworkin, "The Model of Rules I," in *Taking Rights Seriously* (Cambridge, MA: Harvard University Press, 1977), 45. And of course, there is a more general worry that finite social facts are not capable of fixing a rule with infinite extension. See Saul A. Kripke, *Wittgenstein on Rules and Private Language: An Elementary Exposition* (Cambridge, MA: Harvard University Press, 1982). (On the relevance of Kripke's argument to law, see my "Wittgenstein on Rules and Private Language," *Oxford Journal of Legal Studies* 22 (2002): 619.) See also Mark Greenberg, "How Facts Make Law," in *Exploring Law's Empire: The Jurisprudence of Ronald Dworkin,* ed. Scott Hershovitz (Oxford: Oxford University Press, 2006) (arguing that social facts cannot, on their own, fix the content of the law). I will not take up these worries here, even though I think they raise serious—indeed, insurmountable—problems for Hart's view.

13. Sometimes, conflict that appears to be about one thing is really about something else. And it's tempting to think that's what's going on here. I say there's a rule in our house that requires Hank to try everything on his plate; Hanks says there's not. But you might want to say that what we are *really* contesting is whether the rule will be followed or enforced. There is something to this, since we are, of course, contesting that. But that contest has been going on ever since Hank first refused to follow the rule. The first stage of his resistance was simply an assertion of will: "I won't do this." But every subsequent stage has been marked by the assertion of a reason, which he regards as sufficient to rebut the requirement. It would sell Hank short to think that we are engaged only in a contest of wills. We are having an argument, not just a standoff.

14. Dworkin articulated a view like the one I will develop in "The Model of Rules II" and "Hard Cases," both of which are reprinted in *Taking Rights Seriously.* The view came to the fore again in the concluding chapter of *Justice for Hedgehogs* (Cambridge, MA: Harvard University Press, 2011). In *Law's Empire* (Cambridge, MA: Harvard University Press, 1986), however, Dworkin seemed to embrace the dominant view that *law* and *morality* name separate sets of norms. Or maybe he didn't? The book wasn't clear. For more on the development of Dworkin's views across time, see Scott Hershovitz and Steven Schaus, "Dworkin in His Best Light," forthcoming in *Interpretivism and Its Critics,* ed. Nicos Stavropoulos (manuscript on file with author); and my "The End of Jurisprudence," *Yale Law Journal* 124 (2015): 1195–1198.

15. See Mark Greenberg, "The Moral Impact Theory of Law," *Yale Law Journal* 123 (2014): 1288–1342; Steven Schaus, "How to Think about Law as Morality: A Comment on Greenberg and Hershovitz," *Yale Law Journal Forum* 124 (2015): 224–245; Nicos Stavropoulos, "Legal Interpretivism," *The Stanford Encyclopedia of Philosophy* (Spring 2021), ed. Edward N. Zalta, https://plato.stanford.edu/archives/spr2021/entries/law-interpretivist/; Jeremy Waldron, "Jurisprudence for Hedgehogs" (New York University School of Law Public Law & Legal Theory Research Paper Series, Working Paper No. 13-45, 2013), http://ssrn.com/abstract =2290309.

1. A Moral Practice

1. See Ronald Dworkin, *Law's Empire* (Cambridge, MA: Harvard University Press, 1986), 191 ("[T]hough obligation is not a sufficient condition for coercion, it is close to a necessary one. A state may have good grounds in some special circumstances for coercing those who have no duty to obey. But no general policy of upholding the law with steel could be justified if the law were not, in general, a source of genuine obligations."). I suspect Dworkin is right: obligation is not a necessary condition for coercion. But I think it is a necessary condition for condemnation, in which case it's also a necessary condition for punishment.

2. Absent these institutions, we would still be accountable in the sense that we would have rights to redress in respect of wrongdoing. But the institutions make our accountability

more robust, by giving us the power to enforce these rights. They also help render rights concrete where they would otherwise be inchoate (by, for instance, settling on what will count as satisfactory redress from a range of possible options).

3. Here, I am tracking Judith Jarvis Thomson's account of the moral significance of rights and obligations, which is, I think, roughly right:

> [I]t does seem right to think that X's having a claim against Y is at least equivalent to, and perhaps just *is*, Y's behavior being constrained in a certain way. We have taken note of two things included in that constraint, namely the need to seek a release in advance if the claim will otherwise have to be infringed, and the need to compensate later for harms or losses caused by the infringement if a release was unobtainable. But it is only in special circumstances that Y may permissibly fail to accord the claim; other things being equal, Y ought to accord it.

Judith Jarvis Thomson, *The Realm of Rights* (Cambridge, MA: Harvard University Press, 1990), 123.

4. I do not mean that it is a promise that ought to be kept come what may. If the only way for the mobster to care for the thug's family is to continue his campaign of violence, then he ought not keep the promise. Very few obligations are absolute, in the sense that they ought to be discharged come what may. Rather, obligations ought to be discharged unless there is sufficient reason not to discharge them. The best discussion of what counts as a sufficient reason is in Thomson, *The Realm of Rights,* 149–202.

5. H. L. A. Hart, *The Concept of Law,* 2nd ed. (Oxford: Oxford University Press, 1994), chapters 5–6.

6. Here, I am following T. M. Scanlon, *What We Owe to Each Other* (Cambridge, MA: Harvard University Press, 1998), 6–7, 171–177; and R. Jay Wallace, *The Moral Nexus* (Princeton, NJ: Princeton University Press, 2019), 1: "[O]n the relational interpretation, morality could be said to be fundamentally a matter of what we owe *to* each other." Both note that there are broader ways to construe morality. I say a bit more about that later.

7. See Scott J. Shapiro, *Legality* (Cambridge, MA: Harvard University Press, 2011), 58–59.

8. See Mark Greenberg, "The Moral Impact Theory, the Dependence View, and Natural Law," in *The Cambridge Companion to Natural Law Jurisprudence,* ed. George Duke and Robert P. George (Cambridge: Cambridge University Press 2017), 277.

9. There are certainly differences between our genuine obligations and those of the ancient Israelites. But that's because our circumstances are different, not (just) because our beliefs are. (The parenthetical *just* is important because our beliefs are among the circumstances that might affect our genuine obligations. But the question what obligations we have is not just a function of our beliefs.)

10. In his early work, Ronald Dworkin advanced a thesis similar to the one I'm defending here by insisting that legal rights are genuine rights. He wrote:

I argue that legal rights are genuine rights: they supply what might be called a moral kind of reason for a judicial decision. I use the awkward construction "a moral kind of reason" rather than "a moral reason" to avoid confusion. We sometimes use the word "moral" to contrast what we call moral rights with legal rights: we say (for example) that though someone has a moral right to the aid of his neighbors in certain circumstances, he has no legal right to it. I have tried, on various occasions, to explain the force of this contrast; in particular I have tried to show that it is a distinction between rights of different kinds, from different sources, both of which are nevertheless genuine rights because they both provide reasons for action that rest, in the end, on moral considerations. Legal rights are different from the rights we call moral, when we have that distinction in mind, because legal rights are rights based in the political history and decisions of the community and have special institutional force against judges in litigation. But legal and "moral" rights are nevertheless species of a common genus: they are both, in the broader sense I described, creatures of morality.

Ronald Dworkin, "A Reply by Ronald Dworkin," in *Ronald Dworkin and Contemporary Jurisprudence,* ed. Marshall Cohen (Totowa, NJ: Rowman & Allanheld, 1983), 256. See also Greenberg, "The Dependence View," 278 ("I understand the moral domain broadly, with the consequence that, on my view, genuine practical obligations and moral obligations are roughly interchangeable. . . . Readers who take genuine obligations to be importantly different from moral obligations can substitute the former for the latter throughout.").

11. Some people like to subdivide our genuine obligations. Some of them, they'd say, are moral. But others are religious, or familial, or work-related—or legal. As you'll see, I think these sorts of subdivisions can be helpful. They help us highlight the sources of our obligations, their content, or perhaps their modes of enforcement. But I don't think there's anything deep about these divisions. We could draw the boundaries of the categories differently, depending on what we wanted to emphasize. And in the broad sense I'm using the term, all genuine obligations are moral—even if they are also religious, familial, work-related—or legal. In the appendix, I say a bit more about these sorts of subdivisions and why I think it's implausible that legal obligations are genuine but not in any sense moral.

12. Again, here I am tracking the analysis Thomson offers in *The Realm of Rights,* beginning at 123.

13. For a lengthy discussion, see Thomson, *The Realm of Rights,* 149–202.

14. Again, Thomson is spot on. See *The Realm of Rights,* 118–122. If you're more attracted to these phrases than I am, it should be little trouble to reframe the arguments to follow in your preferred terminology.

15. For more on justified wrongs, see Jules Coleman, *Risks and Wrongs* (Oxford: Oxford University Press, 2002), esp. chapter 15.

16. Nico Cornell thinks it's a mistake to equate wrongs with breaches of rights. See Nicolas Cornell, "Rights, Wrongs, and Third Parties," *Philosophy and Public Affairs* 43, no. 2 (2015): 109–143. I have misgivings about his argument. See my "Wrongs without

Rights," *Jotwell Torts,* January 2017, https://torts.jotwell.com/wrongs-without-rights/. But if you are attracted to it, you can amend the sentence in the text to say "Morality is the domain of rights and wrongs; rights and wrongs are relationships." The difference does not affect the argument that follows.

17. John Rawls, "Two Concepts of Rules," *Philosophical Review* 64, no. 1 (1955): 3n1.

18. See *Merriam-Webster,* s.v. "Practice," accessed March 18, 2023, https://www.merriam-webster.com/dictionary/practices.

19. See, e.g., Mark Greenberg, "The Moral Impact Theory of Law," *Yale Law Journal* 123 (2014): 1341 ("On the face of it, law-creating institutions try to create binding obligations."). In an earlier essay, Greenberg argued in favor of what he called the *bindingness hypothesis:* "[A] legal system is supposed to operate by arranging matters in such a way as to reliably ensure that, for every legal obligation, there is an all things considered moral obligation with the same content." Mark Greenberg, "The Standard Picture and Its Discontents," in *Oxford Studies in Philosophy of Law,* ed. Leslie Green and Brian Leiter, vol. 1 (Oxford: Oxford University Press, 2011), 84. This is a stronger claim than the one I advance here, since it implies that law is defective if it does not generate binding obligations. See "The Standard Picture," 90–93. I think that something like this strong claim is probably true, though I would not frame it the way Greenberg did, since his hypothesis presupposes that legal obligations are not themselves moral obligations. (For what it's worth, I suspect Greenberg would revise the hypothesis too, since he argues in "The Moral Impact Theory of Law" that legal obligations just are a species of moral obligation.) In any event, though I suspect something like the stronger claim is true, the argument advanced in this chapter depends only on the weaker claim that our legal practices aim at adjusting our moral relationships.

20. Joseph Raz, "Authority, Law, and Morality," in *Ethics in the Public Domain,* rev. ed. (Oxford: Oxford University Press, 1995), 215–217.

21. Raz, "Authority, Law, and Morality," 215–216:

> The claims the law makes for itself are evident from the language it adopts and from the opinions expressed by its spokesmen, i.e. by the institutions of the law. The law's claim to authority is manifested by the fact that legal institutions are officially designated as "authorities," by the fact that they regard themselves as having the right to impose obligations on their subjects, by their claims that their subjects owe them allegiance, and that their subjects ought to obey the law as it requires to be obeyed (i.e. in all cases except those in which some legal doctrine justifies breach of duty).

22. Joseph Raz, "Incorporation by Law," *Legal Theory* 10 (2004): 6.

23. When people don't defer, then many of the benefits that legal practices can secure are lost.

24. I say that court is *a* place we go to contest what we owe each other because courts are not the only institutions that aim to resolve such conflicts. Increasingly, questions about our rights are resolved through administrative proceedings, which might or might

not be reviewable in court. And private arbitration plays a similar role (also increasingly). I focus on courts both because they are the paradigmatic legal institution through which we contest what we owe each other (what happens in administrative adjudication and arbitration is often a stripped-down version of what happens in court) and because courts often (though not always) have the final say on what our rights are. The claim I am pressing—that litigation poses moral questions—holds in arbitration and administrative proceedings every bit as much as it holds in courts.

25. This is true whenever the plaintiff asserts that she is entitled to relief as a matter of right. Some remedies, however, are discretionary—punitive damages, for instance, or equitable remedies, like injunctions. In those cases, the plaintiff requests a remedy from a court, rather than asserting a right to it. She also asserts that she is qualified to make the request—sometimes, in virtue of having suffered the right sort of wrong; other times, in anticipation that she will suffer one.

26. The decision in *Aikens v. Debow,* 541 S.E.2d 486 (W. Va. 2000), illustrates the application of the rule to a fairly standard set of facts: the defendant damaged an overpass on the highway, and the plaintiff—who owned a hotel and restaurant nearby—lost income while the overpass was closed for repairs. The decision also explores the rule's historical roots, as well as some of the exceptions that have been carved out.

27. Aikens v. Debow, 493–497.

28. Aikens v. Debow, 496 ("The recognized necessity of imposing a line of demarcation on actionable theories of recovery serves as another rationale for the denial of purely economic damages.").

29. When I say that this feature of morality is entrenched, I mean that we have built so many practices around it that it would be difficult to flip. To do so, we would have to restructure a lot about our lives. Maybe we should do that, but until we do, we are not obligated to watch out for each other's economic interests, except in special cases.

If the idea that we might flip what morality requires sounds odd, remember that morality is sensitive to social facts. Before you promised to meet me for lunch, you were not obligated to do so. After you promised, you were obligated. That's an easy flip to execute, since not much depends on your lacking an obligation to have lunch with me. Around here, however, a lot depends on our freedom to act adverse—or simply indifferent—to the economic interests of others, at least within limits.

30. I do not mean to suggest that all markets are moral. Modern societies have a tendency to employ markets—and market-oriented ethics—in areas of life that ought to be organized differently, and the results are often regrettable.

31. At least, insofar as we are concerned with interpersonal morality. We surely do have collective obligations to take care of each other's economic interests; those are among the obligations that we aim to discharge when we create job-training programs or establish social welfare schemes.

32. This might not be a realistic assumption, as a jurisdiction that recognized a general duty to protect against purely economic losses would likely have to find ways to limit

liability, lest it run amok. When courts recognize duties that are too broad, they often press proximate cause into service to limit the consequences. That sort of shell game has led to lots of confusion about the nature of duties and causation. But we will not worry about that here. We will assume that the plaintiff's claim fits within her jurisdiction's conception of causation.

33. On integrity and the role it plays in underwriting a practice of precedent, see my "Integrity and Stare Decisis," in *Exploring Law's Empire: The Jurisprudence of Ronald Dworkin,* ed. Scott Hershovitz (Oxford: Oxford University Press, 2006), as well as Dworkin's original statement of the idea in *Law's Empire,* chapters 5–7.

34. Ledbetter v. Goodyear Tire & Rubber Co. 550 U.S. 618 (2007).

35. Ledbetter v. Goodyear, 642–643.

36. See 42 U.S.C. § 2000e-5(e)(1) (2017) ("A charge under this section shall be filed within one hundred and eighty days after the alleged unlawful employment practice occurred. . . .").

37. She won a jury verdict at trial. See Ledbetter v. Goodyear, 622.

38. Ledbetter v. Goodyear, 624–625.

39. Ledbetter v. Goodyear, 646 (Ginsburg, J., dissenting).

40. Ledbetter v. Goodyear, 654.

41. Ledbetter v. Goodyear, 644–645.

42. Ledbetter v. Goodyear, 661.

43. Ledbetter v. Goodyear, 661.

44. Lilly Ledbetter Fair Pay Act of 2009, 123 Stat. 5 (2009).

45. See Sheryl Gay Stolberg, "Obama Signs Equal Pay Legislation," *New York Times,* January 29, 2009, http://www.nytimes.com/2009/01/30/us/politics/30ledbetter-web .html.

46. See Lily Ledbetter Fair Pay Act, 123 Stat. 5 § 2000e-5(e)(3A).

47. The Lily Ledbetter Fair Pay Act did not revive Ledbetter's claim; the Act applied only prospectively. See 123 Stat. 5, at § 6. Though Goodyear was encouraged to compensate Ledbetter (see, e.g., Joanne Bamberger, "Goodyear, Can You Spare $360K for Lily Ledbetter?" *Huffington Post,* March 11, 2009, http://www.huffingtonpost.com /joanne-bamberger/goodyear-you-can-spare-36_b_164726.html), I can't find any evidence that the company did so.

48. Ronald Dworkin, *Justice for Hedgehogs* (Cambridge, MA: Harvard University Press, 2011), 406 ("Legal rights are those that people are entitled to enforce on demand, without further legislative intervention, in adjudicative institutions that direct the executive power of sheriff or police.").

49. Mark Greenberg develops a suggestion along these lines in Greenberg, "The Moral Impact Theory of Law," 1321–1323. He argues that legal rights are the rights that are generated by legal practices in what he calls "legally proper" ways.

50. Steven Schaus develops a suggestion along these lines in his dissertation "Law as Morality" (PhD diss., University of Michigan, 2019), Deep Blue Repositories, https:// deepblue.lib.umich.edu/bitstream/handle/2027.42/151416/srschaus_1.pdf?sequence=1.

51. See Greenberg, "The Moral Impact Theory of Law," 1300n28: "[I]t is a familiar idea that the President and Congress may have legal duties that the courts should not enforce" (citing Lawrence Gene Sager, "Fair Measure: The Legal Status of Underenforced Constitutional Norms," *Harvard Law Review* 91 (1978): 1212).

52. Greenberg objects to Dworkin's way of distinguishing legal rights from the rest. He finds it inadequate partly because he thinks that there are legal rights that are not enforceable in court. I have answered that objection, but Greenberg has another one. He says: "Another problem with the appeal to what courts should enforce is that an account of law should help us to *explain* why courts should enforce some rights and not others; we therefore cannot appeal to what courts should enforce in order to explain what is law." Greenberg, "The Moral Impact Theory of Law," 1300n28. I do not find this persuasive. The idea is that we must preserve the possibility for courts to say that they are not enforcing a right because it is not a legal right. But courts don't refuse to hear claims because the right asserted is not a legal right; they refuse because there is no cause of action in respect of that right, or because the defendant is immune, or the statute of limitations has expired, or . . . well, you get the picture. They may sum up by saying that the right asserted is not a legal right, but that is only a way of summing up; the reason for nonenforcement is always something more substantive.

53. See Charles E. Wyzanski, "Nuremberg: A Fair Trial? A Dangerous Precedent," *Atlantic,* April 1946, 66–70 (arguing that some of the charges considered by the tribunal did not have any basis in domestic or international law, even though they covered acts that were atrocious).

54. See, e.g., Brian Leiter's "Legal Positivism about the Artifact Law: A Retrospective Assessment" and the other papers collected in *Law as an Artifact,* ed. Luka Burzain, Kenneth Einar Himma, and Corrado Roversi (Oxford: Oxford University Press, 2017).

55. I've borrowed this example from Steven Schaus, "How to Think about Law as Morality: A Comment on Greenberg and Hershovitz," *Yale Law Journal Forum* 124 (2015): 226–227.

2. A Tale of Two Textualists

1. See H. L. A. Hart, *The Concept of Law,* 2nd ed. (Oxford: Oxford University Press, 1994), 147–154.

2. Antonin Scalia, *A Matter of Interpretation* (Princeton, NJ: Princeton University Press, 1997).

3. Scalia, *A Matter of Interpretation,* 22.

4. Scalia, *A Matter of Interpretation,* 22–23, citing Felix Frankfurter, "Some Reflections on the Reading of Statutes," *Columbia Law Review* 47 (1947): 527, 538.

5. Henry M. Hart Jr. and Albert M. Sacks, *The Legal Process,* ed. William N. Eskridge Jr. and Phillip P. Frickey (Westbury, NY: Foundation Press, 1994), 1169 (quoted in Scalia, *A Matter of Interpretation,* 14).

6. That is, it would not have caused H. L. A. Hart to doubt his jurisprudence. He might, however, have thought it bad for Americans that so much law in the United States was (at least by his lights) indeterminate.

7. For a detailed explanation of why Hart would be committed to seeing indeterminacy here, see Mark Greenberg, "What Makes a Method of Legal Interpretation Correct? Legal Standards vs. Fundamental Determinants," *Harvard Law Review Forum* 130 (2017): 114–117.

8. Scalia, *A Matter of Interpretation,* 22.

9. Scalia, *A Matter of Interpretation,* 22.

10. See Scott J. Shapiro, "The 'Hart-Dworkin' Debate: A Short Guide for the Perplexed," in *Ronald Dworkin,* ed. Arthur Ripstein (Cambridge: Cambridge University Press, 2007), 42–43.

11. Brief for Petitioner at 21, Jett v. Dallas Indep. School District, 491 U.S. 701 (1989), quoted in Green v. Bock Laundry Machine Co., 490 U.S. 504, 530 (1989) (Scalia, J., concurring) (quoted in Scalia, *A Matter of Interpretation,* 31).

12. An anonymous reader worried that this chapter does not engage the latest and greatest arguments for textualism or originalism. That's true, but the point here is not to settle debates about statutory interpretation. It's to display something about the character of those debates—to show that they are disputes about the moral significance of acts of legislation. Scalia's candor helps make that clear.

13. A quick reminder (or primer for those new to law): the common law is developed through decisions in particular cases, rather than through acts of legislation.

14. Scalia, *A Matter of Interpretation,* 7.

15. Scalia, *A Matter of Interpretation,* 9.

16. It is also, perhaps, a projection, given the tendentious way Scalia deployed history in constitutional cases. For a quick review of Scalia's textualism, see Richard A. Posner, "The Incoherence of Antonin Scalia," *New Republic,* August 24, 2012.

17. A reminder (or primer): For the most part, there is no federal common law. When federal courts hear common-law cases (as opposed to, say, cases that arise under a federal statute), they apply state law to the dispute.

18. Scalia, *A Matter of Interpretation,* 14.

19. Scalia, *A Matter of Interpretation,* 16.

20. Scalia, *A Matter of Interpretation,* 17.

21. Scalia, *A Matter of Interpretation,* 16–17.

22. Scalia, *A Matter of Interpretation,* 17.

23. Scalia, *A Matter of Interpretation,* 24.

24. Scalia, *A Matter of Interpretation,* 17-18.

25. Scalia, *A Matter of Interpretation,* 18.

26. Church of the Holy Trinity v. United States, 143 U.S. 457 (1892).

27. Church of the Holy Trinity v. United States, at 458.

28. See Adrian Vermeule, "Legislative History and the Limits of Judicial Competence: The Untold Story of Holy Trinity Church," *Stanford Law Review* 50 (1998): 1833. But it is controversial just what the legislature intended. See generally Carol Chomsky, "Unlocking

the Mysteries of Holy Trinity: Spirit, Letter, and History in Statutory Interpretation," *Columbia Law Review* 100 (2000): 901.

29. Scalia, *A Matter of Interpretation*, 22.

30. Herein, I demonstrate that you can figure out what someone meant without falling into the trap of thinking that they meant what you think they should have meant. I don't think Scalia should have said any of this, let alone meant it.

31. Scalia, *A Matter of Interpretation*, 22. Scalia seems also to think that the Constitution's Presentment Clause settles the question (see p. 75). But it doesn't. The Presentment Clause (i.e., U.S. Const. art. I, § 7, cl. 2), sets out the rules for making *a law*. It says nothing about how laws should be read. In particular, it says nothing about whether the rule generated by an act of legislation is the rule Congress intended to adopt when it made the law, or whether it is the rule expressed in the text, whether or not it was intended.

32. The *sometimes* is doing some work here. In conversation, Chris Essert suggested that a soldier is insubordinate if he doesn't do as directed, even when he thinks (with good reason) that the directive issued was not the one intended. Perhaps. I don't doubt that there are instances in which one ought to defer to the words said even if they were not the words intended. Sometimes we should be fussy about language, and perhaps the military context is one in which we should be. But I'm also confident there are occasions for implementing the order intended rather than the order issued.

33. If he didn't realize that she meant recycling, then it would not be defiant to put out the trash. (Deference requires implementing the order as best you understand it.) But it would also not be true that he ought to put out the trash. He ought to put out the recycling, and he ought to do so because of the order his mother issued, even though she said "trash" and not "recycling." (It is also possible that he ought to do so independently of the order; the recycling truck is, after all, on its way, and he's able to help. But there's no guarantee that this is so; perhaps it is his sister's job to put out the trash, such that he has no reason to do so until his mother issues her order.)

34. Conduct is malum prohibitum if it is wrong in virtue of the fact that it is prohibited. In contrast, conduct is malum in se if it is wrong independent of the prohibition. Parking violations fit in the first category, murder in the second.

35. See Seana Valentine Shiffrin, "Inducing Moral Deliberation: On the Occasional Virtues of Fog," *Harvard Law Review* 123 (2010): 1214. Jeremy Waldron, "Torture and Positive Law: Jurisprudence for the White House," *Columbia Law Review* 105 (2005): 1695–1703.

36. Ronald Dworkin, "Comment," in Antonin Scalia, *A Matter of Interpretation* (1998), 117.

37. Dworkin, "Comment," 117.

38. I suspect Dworkin was quick to concede the irrelevance of intended consequences because he wanted to exploit a tension in Scalia's argument for textualism. In the second part of his reply to Scalia, Dworkin points out that Scalia is happy to consider the Framers' hopes and expectations about how provisions in the Constitution would be applied, notwithstanding his insistence that the text—and nothing but the text—is the law.

39. For a similar argument and a deeper dive on some of the problem with textualism, see Mark Greenberg, "Legal Interpretation and Natural Law," *Fordham Law Review* 89 (2020): 109–144.

40. Dworkin tried to capture the difference between courts and legislatures by saying that courts are forums of principle, whereas it is open to legislatures to consider arguments of policy as well as principle. In calling courts forums of principle, he meant to indicate that they should decide what rights the parties have, not what rights it would be good for them to have. See Ronald Dworkin, *Taking Rights Seriously* (Cambridge, MA: Harvard University Press, 1978), 82–86.

41. King v. Burwell, 576 U.S. 473 (2015).

42. More precisely, the plaintiffs came to court seeking to invalidate an Internal Revenue Service (IRS) rule that would have made them eligible for the subsidies. They argued that the rule was inconsistent with the statute. King v. Burwell, at 484.

43. King v. Burwell, 484.

44. I do not just mean that it is prudent for the plaintiffs to purchase health insurance, though it is. I mean that they have a moral obligation to do so, unless they plan to decline life-saving care in the event that they cannot afford to pay for it out of pocket. Even then, they may wrong those who care about them—or who are dependent on them— by deciding in advance to die rather than purchase insurance.

45. For a subtle and sophisticated account, see Seana Valentine Shiffrin, *Democratic Law* (New York: Oxford University Press, 2021).

46. 124 Stat. 119 §1311(b) (2010).

47. 124 Stat. 119, at §1321(c)(1).

48. 124 Stat. 119, at §1401(b)–(c).

49. King v. Burwell, at 499 (Scalia, J., dissenting).

50. King v. Burwell, at 499.

51. King v. Burwell, at 486.

52. King v. Burwell, at 486.

53. King v. Burwell, at 486.

54. In fact, I'm skipping over lots of details, including the fact that the IRS had issued a regulation interpreting the Act to make subsidies available on federally established exchanges. King v. Burwell, at 483. Roberts saw no reason to defer to the IRS's interpretation, *King v. Burwell,* at 485–86, so I have passed it by. But notice how that adds another layer of complication to the case. The IRS had said that the plaintiffs had the right they disclaimed, so the Court had to determine the significance of that pronouncement, in addition to the statute.

55. King v. Burwell, at 489–492.

56. King v. Burwell, at 490.

57. King v. Burwell, at 493.

58. King v. Burwell, at 493.

59. King v. Burwell, at 494.

60. King v. Burwell, at 494.

61. King v. Burwell, at 494.

62. King v. Burwell, at 494.

63. King v. Burwell, at 497.

64. King v. Burwell, at 497–498.

65. King v. Burwell, at 498.

66. King v. Burwell, at 498.

67. King v. Burwell, at 498.

68. King v. Burwell, 576 U.S., at 506 (Scalia, J., dissenting).

69. King v. Burwell, at 510–511.

70. King v. Burwell, at 516.

71. King v. Burwell, at 516.

72. King v. Burwell, at 516.

73. King v. Burwell, at 516.

74. Again, I'll reiterate what I said in note 12. The point here is not to settle debates about statutory interpretation—either generally, or in the context of this case. It's to see that they are moral disagreements.

75. For detailed discussion of statutory interpretation from a jurisprudential perspective, see Nicos Stavropoulos, "Words and Obligations," in *Reading HLA Hart's The Concept of Law,* ed. Luis Duarte d'Almedia, James Edwards, and Andrea Dolcetti (Portland, OR: Hart Publishing, 2013).

76. At least, when they are deeply contested; not all of them are.

3. Not a Set of Norms

1. Michael Herz wrote a fun essay detailing the diversity in the ways the story is told. See his "'Do Justice!': Variations of a Thrice-Told Tale," *Virginia Law Review* 112 (1996): 111–161. As he notes, the facts often shift to suit the purpose of the person telling the story.

2. Ronald Dworkin, *Justice in Robes* (Cambridge, MA: Harvard University Press, 2006), 1.

3. Learned Hand, "A Personal Confession," in *The Spirit of Liberty: Papers and Addresses of Learned Hand,* ed. Irving Dillard, 3rd ed. (New York: Knopf, 1960), 306–307.

4. Herz reads Holmes's remark in Hand's version of the story the same way. See Herz, "Do Justice!," 113–114, 129, 134.

5. Giving people what they are owed is a kind of justice, but it does not exhaust the field. That is evident from the fact that we can and do worry about justice in the distribution of rights.

6. See Sheryl Gay Stolberg and Brian M. Rosenthal, "Man Charged after White Nationalist Rally in Charlottesville Ends in Deadly Violence," *New York Times,* August 12, 2017, https://www.nytimes.com/2017/08/12/us/charlottesville-protest-white-nationalist .html.

7. Leslie Kendrick, "How to Defend the Constitution when the KKK Comes to Town," *CNN,* July 12, 2017, http://www.cnn.com/2017/07/12/opinions/free-speech-isnt -free-kendrick-opinion/index.html.

8. Kendrick, "How to Defend the Constitution." For more on the idea that there's something unjust in the way free speech doctrine allocates the costs of harmful speech and what we might do about it, see Fred Schauer, "Uncoupling Free Speech," *Columbia Law Review* 92 (1992): 1322 ("It ought to be troubling whenever the cost of some general societal benefit must be borne exclusively or disproportionately by a small subset of the beneficiaries. And when in some situations those who bear the cost are those who are least able to afford it, there is even greater cause for concern. If free speech benefits us all, then ideally we all ought to pay for it, not only those who are the victims of harmful speech.").

9. Kessler v. City of Charlottesville, No. 3:17CV00056 (W.D. Va., August 11, 2017), 2.

10. Kessler v. City of Charlottesville, at 1.

11. See, for example, National Socialist Party of America v. Village of Skokie, 432 U.S. 43 (1977).

12. Kessler v. City of Charlottesville, at 3–5.

13. The court said that the city's concern about the number of attendees expected at the rally was "purely speculative," *Kessler* at 4, so if there was a failure here, it may be the city's fault for not supplying an adequate record. That said, the hearing was held the day before the march, so there may not have been much time to develop a record.

14. Herz highlights sources suggesting this reading. See Herz, "Do Justice!," 113–114, 129–134.

15. See H. L. A. Hart, *The Concept of Law,* 2nd ed. (Oxford: Oxford University Press, 1994), 8 (quoting O. W. Holmes, "The Path of the Law," in *Collected Papers* (1920), 173: "The prophecies of what courts will do in fact, and nothing more pretentious, are what I mean by the law.").

16. Ronald Dworkin, *Freedom's Law: The Moral Reading of the American Constitution* (Cambridge, MA: Harvard University Press, 1996), 334. I've spliced the Hand quote into my own sentence, but reproduced it as Dworkin did.

17. See Mark Greenberg, "How Facts Make Law," in *Exploring Law's Empire,* ed. Scott Hershovitz (Oxford: Oxford University Press, 2008), 241 ("In legal discourse, both ordinary and academic, constitutional or statutory provisions and judicial decisions are often conflated with rules or legal propositions. For example, lawyers will sometimes talk interchangeably of a statutory provision and a statutory rule, or of a judicial decision and the rule of that case.").

18. There's a longer list in Scott J. Shapiro, *Legality* (Cambridge, MA: Harvard University Press, 2011), 41.

19. Hart, *The Concept of Law,* chapter 5.

20. Shapiro, *Legality,* chapter 7.

21. In *Law's Empire,* Dworkin suggested that the law is a set of principles. See Ronald Dworkin, *Law's Empire* (Cambridge, MA: Harvard University Press, 1986), 400 ("The actual, present law, for Hercules, consists in the principles that provide the best

justification available for the doctrine and devices of law as a whole."). Or perhaps the principles plus the propositions that follow from them. See Dworkin, *Law's Empire*, 225 ("According to law as integrity, propositions of law are true if they figure in or follow from the principles of justice, fairness, and procedural due process that provide the best constructive interpretation of the community's legal practice."). When he first challenged Hart, however, Dworkin seemed to allow that the law contained rules. He simply insisted that it contained principles too. And he argued that the rules and principles that constituted the law were not picked out by a master rule, like Hart's rule of recognition. See Ronald Dworkin, "The Model of Rules I," in *Taking Rights Seriously* (Cambridge, MA: Harvard University Press, 1977), 43–45.

22. Responding to criticism of "The Model of Rules I," Dworkin wrote: "My point was not that 'the law' contains a fixed number of standards, some of which are rules and some of which are principles. Indeed, I want to oppose the idea that 'the law' is a fixed set of standards of any sort." Ronald Dworkin, "The Model of Rules II," in *Taking Rights Seriously*, 76. He invoked this passage again in *Justice in Robes*, 234.

23. Mark Greenberg was the first to frame the issue this way. See Greenberg, "How Facts Make Law," 225 ("In fact, a central—perhaps the central—debate in the philosophy of law is a debate over whether value facts are among the determinants of the content of the law (though the debate is not usually characterized in this way).").

24. Or at least it is according to an influential way of characterizing the view. See Shapiro, *Legality*, 27; Greenberg, "How Facts Make Law," 225. As I said in the Introduction, the label has been attached to lots of different views, some of which are captured by this thesis, and some of which aren't.

25. See Shapiro, *Legality*, 27; Greenberg, "How Facts Make Law," 226.

26. Do we exist in the most robust way possible? The possibility that we do not is part of what is disorienting about the prospect that we live in a simulated world. It would be disturbing to learn that there are people for whom we seem less than fully real in something like the way Potter—or the characters in a video game—seem to us.

27. Can you print rules? Nicos Stavropoulos tells me that you can't. Rules, he says, are abstract objects. They stand to written expressions of them as numbers stand to numerals. There's something to that, but our language is flexible. We write down phone numbers, not phone numerals. And we can write down rules too. It's just important to remember that the rule on the page is a symbolic representation of the rule itself, which is an abstract object.

28. Some philosophers think that some social facts, including facts about meaning, might depend on moral facts. But for purposes of jurisprudential debates, philosophers tend to ignore metaphysical questions about the constitution of nonlegal social facts, like what a text says. See Shapiro, *Legality*, 44. I'm following that custom here, as it helps keep our focus in the proper place.

29. As Steve Schaus pointed out, moral facts might have played a causal role in determining the content of the Rules of This Book, since I set out to pick rules that were so ridiculous no one would think they were binding. But they don't play a constitutive role

in determining why the Rules of This Book are what they are. They are what they are, in that sense, because I wrote them down.

30. As should be clear by now, I'm using the words *authoritative* and *binding* synonymously. On this usage, a rule can be authoritative even if it was not promulgated by an authority, legitimate or otherwise. It's authoritative (if it is) simply in virtue of the reasons to follow it, which may or may not relate to someone's having authority to impose the rule. This implies that authoritativeness can come apart from authority, which is true, I think. But if this usage bothers you, you can substitute *binding* for *authoritative* wherever it appears, without disrupting the argument.

31. This is a little too loose, since, as Joseph Raz once observed, "[a]n act is an exercise of a normative power only if it affects a norm normatively and not causally." See Joseph Raz, "Voluntary Obligations and Normative Powers," *Proceedings of the Aristotelian Society* 46 (1972): 94. Raz explained, "An act affects a norm causally if its consequences regulate the application of the norm. It affects a norm normatively if the act itself or its result affects the existence or application of the norm." Raz, "Voluntary Obligations and Normative Powers," 94.

32. On the idea of triggering reasons, see David Enoch, "Giving Practical Reasons," *Philosophers' Imprint* 11, no. 4 (2011): 1–22.

33. On duties of fair play, see John Rawls, *Collected Papers,* ed. Samuel Freeman (Cambridge, MA: Harvard University Press, 1999), 122.

34. Hart, *The Concept of Law,* 55–57.

35. Hart, *The Concept of Law,* 55.

36. Hart, *The Concept of Law,* 55–57.

37. Hart, *The Concept of Law,* 94–95, 100–103.

38. Dworkin, *Taking Rights Seriously,* 54.

39. Hart allowed that a group might have a rule despite "the existence of a minority who not only break the rule but refuse to look upon it as a standard for either themselves or others." Hart, *The Concept of Law,* 56. But he resisted saying just how large that minority could be, suggesting that asking that was like asking "the number of hairs a man may have and still be bald." Hart, *The Concept of Law,* 56. But even if the threshold is vague, there must be points past which a group cannot be said to have a rule in Hart's sense, and an even split seems solidly in that terrain. See also Dworkin, *Taking Rights Seriously,* 54–55.

40. Dworkin, *Taking Rights Seriously,* 57–58.

41. Hart, *The Concept of Law,* 55.

42. For instance, just two paragraphs after Hart poses the question "What is the acceptance of a rule?" he says this: "But such general convergence or even identity of behavior is not enough to constitute *the existence of a rule* requiring the behavior: where *there is such a rule,* deviations are generally regarded as lapses or faults open to criticism and threatened deviations meet with pressure for conformity, though the forms of criticism and pressure differ with different types of rules." Hart, *The Concept of Law,* 55 (emphasis added).

43. Nicos Stavropoulos helpfully pressed me on this point. For an explanation of the qualifier *may*, see note 45 below.

44. At least at the time he wrote *The Concept of Law*, 167–180. There, he delineates differences between moral and legal rules, but he seems to think that his analysis applies to both. See Kevin Toh, "Hart's Expressivism and His Benthamite Project," *Legal Theory* 11 (2005): 88–89. By the time he wrote *Essays on Bentham: Jurisprudence and Political Theory* (Oxford: Oxford University Press, 1982), he may have changed his views about morality, but I won't pursue the possibility here.

45. I say Hart *may* have meant to offer an account of morally binding rules, because while it's clear that he meant to offer an account of moral rules, I'm not sure he thought moral rules binding (at least, as of the time he wrote *The Concept of Law*). Arguably, he was offering an account of mores, not morality. Or rather, he might not have seen any difference between the two. David Plunkett helped me appreciate the ambiguity.

46. Dworkin called cases like this instances of "conventional morality." See Dworkin, *Taking Rights Seriously*, 53–58.

47. Dworkin, *Taking Rights Seriously*, 57 ("The fact that a practice of removing hats in church exists justifies asserting a normative rule to that effect—not because the practice constitutes a rule which the normative judgment describes and endorses, but because the practice creates ways of giving offense and gives rise to expectations of the sort that are good grounds for asserting a duty to take off one's hat in church or for asserting a normative rule that one must.").

48. See Dworkin, *Taking Rights Seriously*, 58.

49. For a similar set of observations, see David Plunkett and Daniel Wodak, "The Disunity of Legal Reality," *Legal Theory* 28 (2022): 235–267; and Hillary Nye, "Does Law 'Exist'? Eliminativism in Legal Philosophy," *Washington University Jurisprudence Review* 15, no. 1 (2022): 29–78, 61–62.

50. 5 U.S. 137, 177 (1803).

51. Of course, the *this* and the *that* vary with the philosopher who does the insisting.

52. This is a simpleminded realism, only loosely related to the views of more sophisticated realists like Karl Llewellyn and Alf Ross. But it's a distressingly common view, at least among American lawyers.

53. Hart, *The Concept of Law*, 84 ("The fundamental objection is that the predictive interpretation obscures the fact that, where rules exist, deviations from them are not merely grounds for a prediction that hostile reactions will follow or that a court will apply sanctions to those who break them, but are also a reason or justification for such reaction and for applying the sanction.").

54. See Plunkett and Wodak, "The Disunity of Legal Reality," 265.

55. And not just as a group. If she is arguing before one judge, she'll be interested in the rules that judge accepts. And if she is arguing before a multimember court, she'll focus her attention on the median member of the panel. (Before his retirement, you'd often hear people say that "the law is whatever Justice Kennedy thinks it is." And for at least some issues, there was a sense in which that was true, as Kennedy often cast the deciding vote.

But there were also senses in which the claim was false: Justice Kennedy—like any other justice—could get the law wrong, and often he did. Happily, context usually makes clear which sense is in play.)

56. See Plunkett and Wodak, "The Disunity of Legal Reality," 236.

57. Could morality play a role in determining what materials are legal materials, if not what norms are expressed in those materials? Perhaps, but it depends what legal materials are, and that's not an easy question to answer. For instance, it would be a mistake to say that legal materials are the materials that are issued by authoritative institutions, since such institutions routinely produce texts that are not authoritative (e.g., the Supreme Court issues press releases). It would also be a mistake to say that legal materials are materials that express authoritative norms. Those norms could be expressed in a newspaper op-ed, as well as in a judicial opinion. And dissenting opinions are legal materials even though the norms articulated in them are not authoritative (or, at least, their authority does not rest on their being articulated in a dissent). It would also be a mistake to say that legal materials are those records that are relevant to answering legal questions, since that definition could encompass evidence, such as phone records or blood test results. I'm happy to settle for a loose characterization of legal materials—the sorts of documents that are characteristically produced in the course of legal practices. I don't think we need anything sharper than that. See Dworkin, *Justice in Robes,* 238 ("It is of course important what we take to be relevant to deciding what legal rights and duties people and officials have. But nothing important turns on which part of what is relevant we describe as 'the law.'"). This is why Dworkin once allowed that if the question was what counts as a law of Massachusetts or New York, he would be a positivist, though his "heart [wouldn't be] in it," since it doesn't matter how we answer taxonomic questions of that sort. Dworkin, *Justice in Robes,* 239.

A related point: One of the most persistent confusions among philosophers of law—and lawyers more generally—runs like this. Dworkin, they say, allowed that you could identify legal materials without recourse to morality, so he was just a positivist. That's a fair charge only if positivism is best read as a thesis about what determines the existence and content of legal materials. But if, instead, it is read as a thesis about what determines the existence and content of legal rights and obligations, then the charge is false. I don't know that Hart ever sharply distinguished these questions, but he did make claims about the existence and content of legal rights and obligations, and those were the claims to which Dworkin objected.

58. The seminal papers include Jules Coleman, "Negative and Positive Positivism," *Journal of Legal Studies* 11, no. 1 (1982): article 8; Philip Soper, "Legal Theory and the Obligation of a Judge: The Hart / Dworkin Dispute," *Michigan Law Review* 75, no. 3 (1977): 473–519; and David Lyons, "Principles, Positivism and Legal Theory," *Yale Law Journal* 87, no. 2 (1977): 415–435. In his posthumously published postscript to *The Concept of Law,* Hart embraced inclusive legal positivism (though he called it "soft positivism"). See Hart, *The Concept of Law,* 250. For more on the development of inclusive legal positivism, see Scott J. Shapiro, "The 'Hart-Dworkin' Debate: A Short Guide for the Perplexed," in

Ronald Dworkin, ed. Arthur Ripstein (Cambridge: Cambridge University Press, 2007), 33–35. See also W. J. Waluchow, *Inclusive Legal Positivism* (Oxford: Oxford University Press, 1994).

59. Shapiro, *Legality,* 269–271.

60. See Shapiro, "The 'Hart-Dworkin' Debate," 31–33.

61. Shapiro, *Legality,* 225.

62. Shapiro, *Legality,* 127–129.

63. See Hart, *The Concept of Law,* 147–154.

64. An analogy: my children should insist that my decisions are justified, full stop—not just by my own lights. And I should see my task that way too.

65. See Joseph Raz, "Incorporation by Law," *Legal Theory* 10 (2004): 6–7.

66. Raz, "Incorporation by Law," 7–17.

67. Or at least they can; as I've said before, sometimes legal practices misfire and don't have the moral significance intended or, perhaps, any at all.

68. See Raz, "Incorporation by Law," 2–7.

69. Raz, "Incorporation by Law," 7 ("[W]here the law is normatively valid, it is so in virtue of a moral principle.").

70. For what it's worth, I don't think Raz's argument is sound. But I won't pursue the point here, since I think the picture underlying Raz's argument misleading. For problems with Raz's argument, see Scott Hershovitz, "The Authority of Law," in *The Routledge Companion to Philosophy of Law,* ed. Andrei Marmor (New York: Routledge, 2014), 65–75. See also Scott Hershovitz, "The Model of Plans and the Prospects for Positivism," *Ethics* 125 (2014): 152–181.

71. Dworkin, *Taking Rights Seriously,* 292–293.

72. See H. L. A. Hart, "American Jurisprudence through English Eyes: The Nightmare and the Noble Dream," *Georgia Law Review* 11, no. 5 (1977): 969–989.

73. See Hart, "American Jurisprudence through English Eyes," 972–978.

74. See Hart, "American Jurisprudence through English Eyes," 983.

75. Hart, "American Jurisprudence through English Eyes," 989.

76. Dworkin, *Taking Rights Seriously,* 293.

77. See Wayne LaFave, *Criminal Law,* 5th ed. (Saint Paul, MN: West Academic Publishing, 2010), 11 ("The final basic principle of criminal law is that conduct is not criminal unless forbidden by law providing advance warning that such conduct is criminal. This idea, sometimes termed 'the principle of legality,' is often expressed by the Latin phrase *nullim crimin sine lege, nulla poena sine lege* ['no crime or punishment without law'].").

78. See LaFave, *Criminal Law,* 308 ("[T]he doctrine [that ignorance of the law is not an excuse] has long been applied even when the defendant establishes beyond question that he had a good reason for not knowing the applicable law."). LaFave illustrates the point with *Rex v. Bailey,* 168 Eng. Rep. 651 (1800), in which the defendant was convicted under a statute passed while he was at sea for an act committed before any word of the statute could have reached him.

79. See John Gardner, "Legal Positivism: 5 ½ Myths," *American Journal of Jurisprudence* 46, no. 1 (2001): 200 (suggesting that the central thesis of legal positivism is that "in any legal system, a norm is valid as a norm of that system solely in virtue of the fact that at some relevant time and place some relevant agent or agents announced it, practiced it, invoked it, enforced it, endorsed it, or otherwise engaged with it.").

80. A clear statement rule is a guide to statutory interpretation. It holds that a statute won't be read to work certain changes in the law (say, the abrogation of sovereign immunity or derogation of the common law) unless it is clear from the text that such a change was intended.

81. Dworkin, *Taking Rights Seriously,* 293.

82. U.S. Const., art. 2, § 2, cl. 2.

83. This assumes that no state would have jurisdiction over these offenses. But if they were committed at the White House, there's a strong chance that none would.

84. And the relevance of the inference depends on the view that what was said—or meant—is what matters, which is often contestable.

4. An Immoral Practice?

1. Susan Dach, *Donkeys Can't Sleep in Bathtubs and Other Crazy Laws* (Mahwah, NJ: Watermill Press, 1993).

2. Dach, *Donkeys,* 94.

3. Dach, *Donkeys,* 11.

4. Dach, *Donkeys,* 68.

5. Dach, *Donkeys,* 27.

6. Miss. Const. art. 4, § 106 (1890).

7. See Louisville, N. O. & T. Ry. Co. v. State of Mississippi, 133 U.S. 587 (1890).

8. An aside, left over from Chapter 3: The phrase *on the books* is an illustration of the suppleness of our talk about law. There's a sense in which the provision I'm about to describe is part of Mississippi law. And there's a sense in which it's not. And any account that insists that it's either in or out misses the rich and varied ways we talk about law. (For the statute, see Miss. Code Ann. § 37-113-31 (2017).)

9. Ratliff v. Beale, 20 So. 865, 868 (Miss. 1896). See also Williams v. Mississippi, 170 U.S. 213, 219–223 (1898) (detailing the provisions in the Mississippi Constitution that were adopted with the aim of disenfranchising Black voters).

10. "Revealed: The Ten Commandments of the Mafia," *Telegraph,* November 7, 2007.

11. The bit about availability would seem to undercut the requirement to respect wives. But that is not what these rules are actually after—it's respect for men's proprietary control of women.

12. I include the parenthetical qualification because you can issue an edict requiring someone to do something they are already required to do. This is not pointless, since the edict rearranges the relationship between you and the recipient, even if it does not shift

what the recipient is required to do. Failure to do what was ordered becomes an act of defiance and (perhaps) wrong for that reason, in addition to whatever other reasons would have been in play absent the edict.

13. Authority, as we have seen, is not the only way that a set of rules might make a moral difference. Rules can become binding because they help solve coordination problems, create reliance interests, facilitate morally worthy goals, and so on. But it's hard to see how any explanations of this sort would make the rules in the Lo Piccolo list authoritative.

14. The standard wording is this: "I swear to be faithful to Cosa Nostra. If I should betray it my flesh must burn, just as this image burns." See "Police Find Ten Commandments for Mafiosi," *Italy Magazine,* November 8, 2007.

15. Well, in a limited way, they might be. Soccer involves competition, and losing a competition can be painful, in a way. But that pain makes possible goods that can be realized only through competition, and the pains are not so significant that they undermine that value. Moreover, the pain generally falls on people who have consented to participate in the practice.

16. That is, they might offer an argument similar to Dworkin's famous argument about associative obligations. See Ronald Dworkin, *Law's Empire* (Cambridge, MA: Harvard University Press, 1986), 206–215.

17. Upton Sinclair, *I, Candidate for Governor: And How I Got Licked* (Berkeley: University of California Press, 1995), 109.

18. We also disagree about the boundaries of this category, which gives us reason to defer to the Constitution's rules regarding the scope of legislative authority.

19. Seana Valentine Shiffrin, *Democratic Law,* ed. Hannah Ginsborg (New York: Oxford University Press, 2021), 156.

20. Shiffrin describes democracy as "a political system that treats all its members with equal concern, regards their lives as of equal importance, and treats all competent members of the community (by which I mean those having reached the age of majority and without profound intellectual disabilities) as, by right and by conception, the equal and exclusive co-authors of and co-contributors to the system, its rules, its actions, its directives, its communications, and its other outputs." Shiffrin, *Democratic Law,* 20. She adds: "A healthy democracy is one in which the members have regular opportunities to exercise these rights and do so with some frequency." Shiffrin, *Democratic Law,* 20–21. And she observes that this "characterization of democracy lends little support to the view that elections, in particular, are the defining characteristic of democracy. A free speech regime including the legal right to petition government (and to expect consideration and a reasoned response) and a robust, vibrant free speech culture are equally essential components." Shiffrin, *Democratic Law,* 21.

21. Shiffrin, *Democratic Law,* 53–54.

22. Jeremy Waldron, *Law and Disagreement* (Oxford: Clarendon Press, 1999), 100.

23. Shiffrin, *Democratic Law,* 55.

24. Shiffrin, *Democratic Law,* 55.

25. Though, as Richard Primus has argued, the fact that the Constitution enumerates legislative powers does not entail that the powers enumerated are limited. See his "The Limits of Enumeration," *Yale Law Journal* 125 (2014): 576–642.

26. See NFIB v. Sebelius, 567 U.S. 519 (2012).

27. Ratliff v. Beale, 20 So. 865, 868 (Miss. 1896). I almost called the acknowledgment an admission, but we admit things we'd rather keep quiet, and the court was not concerned to do that.

28. The classic study is Robert Cover's *Justice Accused: Antislavery and the Judicial Process* (New Haven, CT: Yale University Press, 1975).

29. In fact, judges routinely do so even when they aren't faced with starkly immoral laws. A judge who sits on a multimember court will find it helpful to pay close attention to what her colleagues think. Sometimes, she'll need to shade her views, or qualify her arguments, in order to assemble a majority. And even trial court judges who work alone often have reason to adopt a sociological stance, since they know that their decisions can be appealed to other judges. If trial court judges care to protect their decisions from reversal, then they will attempt to account for the views appellate judges are likely to hold as they craft their opinions.

30. Shiffrin, *Democratic Law*, 19.

5. Stop! In the Name of Law

1. For a similar lamentation, see Ronald Dworkin, "Hart's Postscript and the Character of Political Philosophy," *Oxford Journal of Legal Studies* 24 (2005): 35–37.

2. John Tasioulas, Twitter, July 11, 2017, 9:23 a.m., https://twitter.com/JTasioulas /status/884765033166757888.

3. The maybes were broken down into two categories—those who thought you might be obligated if you had consented (about 8 percent) and those who thought you might be obligated even if you hadn't (about 9 percent). See Tasioulas, Twitter, July 11, 2017.

4. I say you are "probably" obligated to pay, to paper over the fact that we'd need to know a lot more about the law in order to decide whether you were obligated to pay. At the least, we'd need to know whether it was adopted pursuant to the proper procedures. We'd also need to know more about the law's substance. For instance, we would need to know whether it conflicted with the Constitution or some other more fundamental law. And we might need to know something about its uptake too; if no one pays, then perhaps you are not obligated to pay either. So there are lots of reasons you might not be obligated to pay. The point is simply this: the mere injustice of a law is not, on its own, reason to conclude that one is not obligated to do as it directs. The nature of the injustice matters, as do many other facts.

5. M. B. E. Smith, "Is There a Prima Facie Obligation to Obey the Law?," *Yale Law Journal* 82 (1973): 950–976.

6. Smith, "Is There a Prima Facie Obligation to Obey the Law?," 951.

7. Smith distinguishes this sense of *prima facie* from what he calls the "lawyer's sense." Smith, "Is There a Prima Facie Obligation to Obey the Law?," 952. In legal writing, he says, to ask whether someone has a prima facie obligation to obey the law is to ask whether illegality is evidence that an act is wrong, absent evidence that shows it right. My sense is that philosophers also employ this sense of *prima facie;* nowadays, I think, they would be more likely to use the term *pro tanto* for what Smith means by *prima facie.* But I don't want to get bogged down by the terminology. As I said in Chapter 1, I agree with Judith Jarvis Thomson that talk of pro tanto or prima facie obligations tends to be misleading. For now, however, I'll talk as Smith does.

8. Smith, "Is There a Prima Facie Obligation to Obey the Law?," 951. This passage has a problem, as it is not clear that an obligation not to violate a prohibition amounts to an obligation to obey it. It depends on what obedience consists in. See Scott Hershovitz, "The Authority of Law," in *The Routledge Companion to Legal Philosophy,* ed. Andrei Marmor (New York: Routledge, 2012), 65–75. For our purposes, however, we can pass this problem by.

9. Smith, "Is There a Prima Facie Obligation to Obey the Law?," 951.

10. Smith, "Is There a Prima Facie Obligation to Obey the Law?," 952.

11. Ronald Dworkin makes a similar point in criticizing Hart's practice theory of rules. See Ronald Dworkin, *Taking Rights Seriously* (Cambridge, MA: Harvard University Press, 1978), 57 ("But the social rule theory misconceives the connection. It believes that the social practice *constitutes* a rule which the normative judgment accepts; in fact the social practice helps to *justify* a rule which the normative judgment states.").

12. Morality may not always condemn breach of contract, but Smith's observation seems oriented toward occasions on which it does.

13. An exception is Mark Greenberg, "The Moral Impact Theory of Law," *Yale Law Journal* 123 (2014): 1310–1317, which catalogs lots of ways legal practices affect our moral rights and obligations.

14. See Greenberg, "The Moral Impact Theory of Law," 1316–1317; Mark Greenberg, "The Standard Picture and Its Discontents," in *Oxford Studies in Philosophy of Law,* ed. Leslie Green and Brian Leiter, vol. 1 (Oxford: Oxford University Press, 2011), 99–100.

15. On integrity and the role it plays in underwriting a practice of precedent, see my "Integrity and Stare Decisis," in *Exploring Law's Empire: The Jurisprudence of Ronald Dworkin,* ed. Scott Hershovitz (Oxford: Oxford University Press, 2006), as well as Dworkin's original statement of the idea in Ronald Dworkin, *Law's Empire* (Cambridge, MA: Harvard University Press, 1986), chapters 5–7.

16. See A. John Simmons, *Moral Principles and Political Obligation* (Princeton, NJ: Princeton University Press, 1979).

17. For a fair-minded review, see William A. Edmundson, "State of the Art: The Duty to Obey the Law," *Legal Theory* 10 (2004): 215–259.

18. Smith suggests that Rawls's duty to support just institutions might do the work. But it doesn't. See Dworkin, *Law's Empire,* 193. Another candidate worth considering is Kit Wellman's samaritan solution. See his contribution to Christopher Heath Wellman

and A. John Simmons, *Is There a Duty to Obey the Law?* (Cambridge: Cambridge University Press, 2005).

19. Smith, "Is There a Prima Facie Obligation to Obey the Law?," 971.

20. Smith, "Is There a Prima Facie Obligation to Obey the Law?," 970.

21. Smith, "Is There a Prima Facie Obligation to Obey the Law?," 971.

22. Smith, "Is There a Prima Facie Obligation to Obey the Law?," 971.

23. Smith, "Is There a Prima Facie Obligation to Obey the Law?," 971.

24. Smith, "Is There a Prima Facie Obligation to Obey the Law?," 971.

25. Smith might try to avoid this conclusion by decomposing the obligation. He might say that the obligation not to cheat by a lot, for instance, is serious by his test, even if the obligation not to cheat by a little is not. I'm not sympathetic to this sort of gerrymander since it serves no purpose beyond salvaging Smith's test. Most of us, at least, think that we are obligated not to cheat, full stop, and noticing that some cases of cheating are worse than others does not warrant abandoning that judgment; all it suggests is that we should calibrate our response in particular cases. (Andy Lieberman helped me to see this problem with Smith's argument.)

26. Smith is live to this sort of worry. He writes:

> The second principle may be thought objectionable on the ground that it trivializes obviously weighty prima facie obligations. It may perhaps be held that, were a man to kill a thousand persons, his act would not have been much worse had he killed but one more. The principle therefore seems to imply that the prima facie obligation not to kill a person is trivial. The objection is plausible but misguided. Surely there is a substantial moral difference between killing a thousand persons and killing a thousand-and-one—exactly the difference killing one person and killing none. To deny this is to imply that the thousand-and-first person's life has little moral significance. At first glance, we might be inclined to take the difference to be trivial, because both acts are so monstrous that we should rarely see any point in distinguishing between them.

Smith, "Is There a Prima Facie Obligation to Obey the Law?," 970n37.

I am not sure this response is adequate, since what is at issue is the badness of the act, rather than the value of the people affected, and it does not seem implausible that at some point—perhaps the point at which we judge the act monstrous—each additional victim makes only a minor marginal contribution to the badness of the act. Discovering that the mass murderer's tally was actually 999—one less than originally thought—might make us glad for the life saved, but it hardly registers when we consider the monstrousness of the murderer or his murder spree. In any event, even if you are with Smith in the mass murder case, the Manafort case seems relevantly different. When an extra victim has been spared, we do indeed have reason to rejoice: at least Bloggs survived. But if Manafort colluded to tip the election without committing tax evasion, it would seem awfully odd to say, "Well, at least he didn't cheat on his taxes." To put the point another way, it is not clear to me that the badness of any particular act is the sum of the badness of its component parts. (Stealing two cookies is not always twice as bad as stealing one cookie.) The moral calculus seems to me more complicated, though I won't pursue it further here.

27. I am skeptical, but several sources suggest as much. See, e.g., "Weird Laws: Tea Cups, Hopscotch, and Cigarette Butts," *LawInfo Blog,* August 5, 2011, https://web.archive .org/web/20171017112458/http://blog.lawinfo.com/2011/08/05/weird-laws-teacups -hopscotch-and-cigarette-butts/.

28. To be clear, what the law says matters. If it declared a different set of places off-limits in a snowstorm, then the locations where it would be wrong to park would likely shift. But that's because a lot of social facts are likely to shift alongside the law. The plows will clear different paths, people will adjust their expectations, and so on.

29. Also recall: we shouldn't make the mistake of supposing that you don't, after all, have a right to the money, on account of the fact that my kid needs it more than you do. I should apologize for failing to pay you. And you should forgive me, since my breach suggests no hostility toward you. Both the apology and forgiveness are intelligible only as responses to the wrong that I committed, as are further remedies, like paying as soon as I'm able.

30. For what it's worth, I don't think Plato was simply employing a dramatic device when he had Socrates imagine a dialogue with the laws of Athens in the *Crito.* The laws assert that Socrates would wrong them by fleeing, not just that Socrates would act wrongly. *Crito,* 50b.

31. State v. R.Z.M., Summary Opinion, No. JS-2015–1076 (Okla. Crim. App. March 24, 2016).

32. 21 Okla. Stat. Ann. § 1111 (2018).

33. 21 Okla. Stat. Ann. § 888 (2016).

34. See Clayton v. State, 695 P.2d 3, 6 (Okla. Crim. App. 1984).

35. 21 Okla. Stat. Ann. § 888 (2016).

36. 21 Okla. Stat. Ann. § 1111(A)(4) (2018).

37. 21 Okla. Stat. Ann. § 1111(A)(5) (2018).

38. Molly Redden, "Oklahoma Court: Oral Sex Is Not Rape if Victim Is Unconscious from Drinking," *Guardian,* April 27, 2016.

39. Beyond due process, it's worth flagging that there are substantive limits on the state's standing to punish, too. The criminal law is a blunt tool, which tends to wreak havoc in people's lives. It should be used only when it's a proportional response to the wrong.

40. Joseph Raz, *The Authority of Law* (Oxford: Oxford University Press, 1979), 25.

41. On the difference between first-order and second-order reasons, see Raz, *The Authority of Law,* 22–23.

42. For those unfamiliar with trusts, when you create one, you give property to a trustee, who is required to manage it for the benefit of a third party—the trust's beneficiary. For instance, you might set up a trust to manage property for a minor child. The trustee will hold title to the property, but she must manage the property in a way that advances the child's interests, not her own. The child is called the "beneficial owner" of the property, since the benefits of ownership accrue to the child, even though the trustee holds title.

6. Roy Moore and the Rule of Law

1. The story in this paragraph is drawn from Charles Bethea, "Why Roy Moore's Law School Professor Nicknamed Him Fruit Salad," *New Yorker,* October 26, 2017, https://www.newyorker.com/news/news-desk/why-roy-moores-law-school-professor -nicknamed-him-fruit-salad.

2. The basics of Moore's biography are set out in Joshua Green, "Roy and His Rock," *Atlantic,* October 2005, https://www.theatlantic.com/magazine/archive/2005/10/roy -and-his-rock/304264/. Unless otherwise noted, the details of the account below are drawn from Green's reporting.

3. Glassroth v. Moore, 229 F. Supp. 2d. 1290 (M.D. Ala. 2002).

4. Glassroth v. Moore, 335 F.3d 1282, 1293–94 (11th Cir. 2003).

5. Glassroth v. Moore, 335 F.3d 1282, at 1294 (collecting cases).

6. In the Matter of: Roy S. Moore Chief Justice of the Supreme Court of Alabama, Court of the Judiciary, Case No. 33, Final Judgment 13 (November 13, 2003).

7. Searcy v. Strange, 81 F. Supp. 3d 1285 (S.D. Ala. 2015).

8. Obergefell v. Hodges, 576 U.S. 644 (2015).

9. In the Matter of: Roy S. Moore Chief Justice of the Supreme Court of Alabama, Court of the Judiciary, Case No. 46, Final Judgment (September 30, 2016). A majority of the court wanted to remove Moore again, but that required unanimity, so they settled on suspension. Moore did not seek reelection, choosing to run for the Senate instead.

10. See Stephanie McCrummen, Beth Reinhard, and Alice Crites, "Woman Says Moore Initiated Sexual Encounter When She Was 14, He Was 32," *Washington Post,* November 9, 2017.

11. See Robert Nozick, *Philosophical Explanations* (Cambridge, MA: Harvard University Press, 1983), 369 ("Since an act's moral qualities, qua moral qualities, seem to lack causal power, if something is to happen to someone because of the moral quality of his act, this must occur through another's recognition of that moral quality and response to it."); Peter French, *The Virtues of Vengeance* (Lawrence: University of Kansas Press, 2001), 80 ("The only power that morality has to affect human affairs resides in the response of moral people, members of the moral community, to the recognition of the moral quality of actions and characters.").

12. See Scott Hershovitz, "Treating Wrongs as Wrongs: An Expressive Argument for Tort Law," *Journal of Tort Law* 10, no. 2 (2017): 1–43.

13. In the Matter of: Roy S. Moore Chief Justice of the Supreme Court of Alabama, Court of the Judiciary, Case No. 33, Final Judgment 1 (November 13, 2003).

14. In the Matter of: Roy S. Moore (2003), at 4.

15. In the Matter of: Roy S. Moore (2003), at 10 (quoting In re Ross, 428 A.2d 858, 861 (Me. 1981).

16. In the Matter of: Roy S. Moore (2003), at 10–11.

17. Glassroth v. Moore, 335 F.3d 1282, 1301 (11th Cir. 2003).

18. Glassroth v. Moore, 1302.

19. Glassroth v. Moore, 1303.

20. See Sanford Levinson, *Constitutional Faith* (Princeton, NJ: Princeton University Press, 1988), 27–30, 37–50.

21. Within the federal government, the Protestant position is known as departmentalism. It holds that each branch of government is entitled to interpret the Constitution for itself. For careful evaluation of different sorts of departmentalist claims, see Richard H. Fallon Jr., "Judicial Supremacy, Departmentalism, and the Rule of Law in a Populist Age," *Texas Law Review* 96 (2018): 487–553.

22. On pardons, see Fallon, "Judicial Supremacy," 499–500.

23. Fallon, "Judicial Supremacy," 494.

24. Fallon, "Judicial Supremacy," 494.

25. Elections could continue to constrain, but a president who routinely ignored court orders might not honor them either.

26. Fallon, "Judicial Supremacy," 504.

27. The case was *Ex parte Merryman,* 17 F. Cas. 144 (C.C.D. 1861). For background and analysis, see Dan Farber, *Lincoln's Constitution* (Chicago: University of Chicago Press, 2003), 157–163, 188–195.

28. Abraham Lincoln, "July 4th Message to Congress," 1861, available at https://millercenter.org/the-presidency/presidential-speeches/july-4-1861-july-4th-message-congress.

29. Green, "Roy and His Rock."

30. Ex parte State ex rel. Alabama Policy Institute, 200 So. 3d 495, 589 (2015) (Moore, C.J,, concurring). ("The *Obergefell* opinion, being manifestly absurd and unjust and contrary to reason and divine law, is *not* entitled to precedential value.")

31. Jeremy Waldron, "The Concept and the Rule of Law," *Georgia Law Review* 43 (2008): 6.

32. Gerald Postema says the rule of law requires an *"ethos* of law." Gerald Postema, "Law's Rule," in *Bentham's Theory of Law and Public Opinion,* ed. Xiaobo Zhai and Michael Quinn (New York: Cambridge University Press, 2014), 8. Brian Tamanaha says that the rule of law requires "a shared cultural belief." See Brian Tamanaha, "The History and Elements of the Rule of Law," *Singapore Journal of Legal Studies* (December 2012): 246. Both believe that the outlook must be shared by more than just officials. More on that later.

33. Moore, no doubt, would see the situation differently. As I said, in his view the stakes were high; better to breach the law than dishonor God. I won't contest Moore's judgment that he'd dishonor God here. But I will say that it's reasonable for the law to make demands on Moore nonetheless, since it can hardly to defer to every individual's judgment of what God (or morality for that matter) requires. It's also worth noting that Moore could have resigned his office if he wasn't willing to act as it required.

34. Postema, "Law's Rule," 25.

35. See Lon L. Fuller, *The Morality of Law,* rev. ed. (New Haven, CT: Yale University Press, 1969).

36. See Waldron, "The Concept and the Rule of Law," 7–8.

37. Waldron, "The Concept and the Rule of Law," 8–9.

38. David Leonhardt and Stuart A. Thompson, "Trump's Lies," *New York Times,* December 14, 2017, https://www.nytimes.com/interactive/2017/06/23/opinion/trumps -lies.html; and Daniel Dale, "The 15 Most Notable Lies of Donald Trump's Presidency," *CNN,* January 16, 2021, https://www.cnn.com/2021/01/16/politics/fact-check-dale-top -15-donald-trump-lies/index.html.

39. Anita Kumar, "How Trump Fused His Business Empire to the Presidency," *Politico,* January 20, 2020, https://www.politico.com/news/2020/01/20/trump-businesses-empire -tied-presidency-100496.

40. Michael D. Shear and Matt Apuzzo, "F.B.I. Director James Comey Is Fired by Trump," *New York Times,* May 9, 2017.

41. See Charlie Savage, "Trump Vows Stonewall of 'All' House Subpoenas, Setting Up Fight over Powers," *New York Times,* April 24, 2019.

42. Michael J. Klarman, "Trump's Ukraine Shakedown," *Boston Globe,* December 2, 2019, https://www.bostonglobe.com/2019/12/02/opinion/trumps-ukraine-shakedown/.

43. Luke Broadwater, "'Trump Was at the Center': Jan. 6 Hearing Lays Out Case in Vivid Detail," *New York Times,* June 9, 2022, https://www.nytimes.com/2022/06/09/us /politics/trump-jan-6-hearings.html.

44. Maggie Astor, "Trump's Call for 'Termination' of Constitution Draws Rebukes," *New York Times,* December 4, 2022, https://www.nytimes.com/2022/12/04/us /politics/trump-constitution-republicans.html.

45. Seana Shiffrin, *Democratic Law* (New York: Oxford University Press, 2021).

46. Joseph Raz, *Ethics in the Public Domain* (Oxford: Oxford University Press, 1994), 218.

47. See Scott J. Shapiro, *Legality* (Cambridge, MA: Harvard University Press, 2011).

48. Here is how Shapiro puts the argument:

> Shared plans must be determined exclusively by social facts *if they are to fulfill their function.* . . . Shared plans are supposed to guide and coordinate behavior by resolving doubts and disagreements about how to act. If a plan with a particular content exists only when certain moral facts obtain, then it could not resolve doubts and disagreements about the right way of proceeding. For in order to apply it, the participants would have to engage in deliberation or bargaining that would recreate the problem that the plan aimed to solve. The logic of planning requires that plans be ascertainable by a method that does not resurrect the very questions that plans are designed to settle. Only social facts, not moral ones, can serve this function.

Shapiro, *Legality,* 177.

49. I discuss Raz's and Shapiro's arguments in more detail in "The Model of Plans and the Prospects for Positivism," *Ethics* 125, no. 1 (October 2014): 152, and "The Authority of Law," in *Routledge Companion to Philosophy of Law,* ed. Andrei Marmor (New York: Routledge, 2012), 65–75.

7. Lawyers and Morality

Epigraphs: Marc Galanter, *Lowering the Bar: Lawyer Jokes and Legal Culture* (Madison: University of Wisconsin Press, 2005), 31 (citing several sources), 36 (citing several sources), 180 (citing several sources), 238 (quoting a Lee Cullum cartoon, *New Yorker,* July 7, 1997, 68).

1. Bernard Williams, *Making Sense of Humanity: And Other Philosophical Papers 1982–1993* (Cambridge: Cambridge University Press, 1995), 205.

2. C. D. Broad, *Ethics and the History of Philosophy* (London: Routledge and Kegan Paul, 1952), 244. For a more recent version of the claim, see David Archard, "Why Moral Philosophers Are Not and Should Not Be Moral Experts," *Bioethics* 25, no. 3 (2011): 119–127.

3. Broad, *Ethics and the History of Philosophy.*

4. Sarah McGrath, "Skepticism about Moral Expertise as a Puzzle for Moral Realism," *Journal of Philosophy* 108, no. 3 (2011): 111.

5. Williams, *Making Sense of Humanity,* 205.

6. David Enoch, "A Defense of Moral Deference," *Journal of Philosophy* 111, no. 5 (2014): 229–258.

7. See Archard, "Why Moral Philosophers," 121–122.

8. Archard canvasses the most common arguments and finds them wanting. He adds his own but admits it has limited scope. See Archard, "Why Moral Philosophers."

9. Peter Singer, "Moral Experts," *Analysis* 32, no. 4 (1972): 116.

10. Singer, "Moral Experts," 116.

11. Singer, "Moral Experts," 116.

12. Singer, "Moral Experts," 116.

13. Singer, "Moral Experts," 116–117.

14. Galanter, *Lowering the Bar,* 3 (citing Max Radin, "The Ancient Grudge: A Study in the Public Relations of the Legal Profession," *Virginia Law Review* 32 (1946): 734–752).

15. Aaron James, *Assholes: A Theory* (New York: Doubleday, 2012), 5.

16. James, *Assholes,* 5.

17. James, *Assholes,* 5.

18. James, *Assholes,* 6.

19. James, *Assholes,* 6.

20. James, *Assholes,* 39–43.

21. James, *Assholes,* 43–44.

22. James, *Assholes,* 37–39.

23. James, *Assholes,* 66–68. This is how James typed Donald Trump, well before he ran for president. Eventually, he wrote a second book, *Assholes: A Theory of Donald Trump* (New York: Doubleday, 2016).

24. James, *Assholes,* 78–87.

25. Most assholes are men, a fact James discusses at length. But women can be assholes too. See James, *Assholes,* 88–118. For discussion of cable news assholes, see James, *Assholes,* 68–74.

26. See Rebecca Dana, "Did Nancy Grace, TV Crimebuster, Muddy Her Myth?," *Observer*, March 6, 2006.

27. David Carr, "TV Justice Thrives on Fear," *New York Times*, May 23, 2011, B1.

28. Carr, "TV Justice Thrives on Fear."

29. See Dana, "Did Nancy Grace, TV Crimebuster, Muddy Her Myth?"

30. Margeaux Sippell, "Nancy Grace Revisits the Murder of Her Friend in Her New Series, 'Injustice': 'Victims Have the Right to Be Heard,'" *Wrap*, July 13, 2019.

31. Jeena Cho, "Stop Training Lawyers to Be Jerks," *HuffPost*, February 3, 2015.

32. Keith Lee, "It's Okay for Lawyers to Be Jerks (Sometimes)," *Above the Law*, February 5, 2015.

33. Lee, "It's Okay for Lawyers to Be Jerks."

34. Model Rules of Professional Conduct (MRPC) Rule 1.1 (2019).

35. MRPC Rule 1.3.

36. MRPC Rules 1.7 and 1.8.

37. MRPC Rule 1.2.

38. MRPC Rule 3.1.

39. MRPC Rule 3.3.

40. MRPC Rule 3.6.

41. MRPC Rule 1.3, comment 1.

42. MRPC Rule 1.3, comment 1.

43. MRPC Rule 1.3, comment 1.

44. James, *Assholes*, chapter 5.

45. See David Luban, *Lawyers and Justice: An Ethical Study* (Princeton, NJ: Princeton University Press, 1988), 75.

46. Liam Murphy, "Better to See Law This Way," *NYU Law Review* 83 (2007): 1095–1098.

Conclusion

1. The facts here are drawn from *Rhode Island Hosp. Tr. Nat. Bank v. Zapata Corp.*, 848 F.2d 291 (1st Cir. 1988).

2. R. I. Gen. Laws Ann. § 6A-4-406 (1985) (quoted in Rhode Island Hosp. Tr. Nat. Bank v. Zapata Corp., 848 F.2d 291, 292–293 (1988)).

3. R. I. Gen. Laws Ann. § 6A-4-406.

4. Rhode Island Hosp. Tr. Nat. Bank v. Zapata Corp., at 294.

5. Rhode Island Hosp. Tr. Nat. Bank v. Zapata Corp., at 294–296.

6. That's not to say that we should be textualists about provisions like § 4-406. The question is always, What rights and responsibilities do people have in light of the enactment of this statute—and the rest of our legal history? Those rights and responsibilities might be the ones expressed in the text, but as we saw in Chapter 2, sometimes they differ.

7. St. Thomas Aquinas, *Summa Theologiae,* ed. Thomas Gilby, vol. 28 (New York: Cambridge University Press, 2006), 103–107 (I-II, Q. 95, a. 2).

8. For an excellent overview of Kant's ideas about law, see Arthur Ripstein, *Force and Freedom: Kant's Legal and Political Philosophy* (Cambridge, MA: Harvard University Press, 2009). For Kant himself, see Immanuel Kant, *Metaphysics of Morals,* ed. Mary Gregor (New York: Cambridge University Press, 1991).

9. See Seana Valentine Shiffrin, *Democratic Law* (New York: Oxford University Press, 2021).

10. Hans Kelsen, "Law, State and Justice in the Pure Theory of Law," *Yale Law Journal* 57 (1948): 383–384 (quoted in Liam Murphy, "Better to See Law This Way," *NYU Law Review* 83 (2007): 1097).

11. The phrase comes from H. L. A. Hart, "Positivism and the Separation of Law and Morals," *Harvard Law Review* 71, no. 4 (1958): 595. Bentham embraced the distinction in Jeremy Bentham, *A Fragment on Government,* ed. F. C. Montague (Oxford: Clarendon Press, 1891).

12. John Austin, *The Province of Jurisprudence Determined,* ed. Wilfrid E. Rumble (London: John Murray, 1995), 157.

13. See, for example, Jules Coleman, "Rules and Social Facts," *Harvard Journal of Law & Public Policy* 14, no. 3 (1991): 724; and Gerald Postema, "Coordination and Convention at the Foundation of Law," *Journal of Legal Studies* 11, no. 1 (1982): 165.

14. See section 4 of John Finnis, "Natural Law Theories," *The Stanford Encyclopedia of Philosophy* (Summer 2020), ed. Edward N. Zalta ("No one has difficulty in understanding locutions such as 'an invalid argument is no argument,' 'a disloyal friend is not a friend,' 'a quack medicine is not medicine,' and so forth.").

15. For further grounds for doubt—and skepticism about this sort of argument more generally—see Murphy, "Better to See," 1098–1101, and Finnis, "Natural Law Theories."

16. And not in the way that so-called inclusive legal positivists propose. Morality does not play a part in legal judgment because there's a social practice of appealing to moral criteria for legal validity. Morality plays a part because legal claims are moral claims; morality determines what rights and obligations are generated by our legal practices.

17. This is the puzzle Ronald Dworkin pressed in the opening chapter of *Law's Empire* (Cambridge, MA: Harvard University Press, 1986). For possible positivist responses, see Scott J. Shapiro, "The 'Hart-Dworkin' Debate: A Short Guide for the Perplexed," in *Ronald Dworkin,* ed. Arthur Ripstein (Cambridge: Cambridge University Press, 2007), 22–55, and Brian Leiter, "Explaining Theoretical Disagreements," *University of Chicago Law Review* 76 (2009): 1215–1250.

18. And neither did Raz: "One popular way of arguing for one's view is to show that all alternatives to it are false. I have little trust in that way of arguing." Joseph Raz, "Normative Powers," in *The Roots of Normativity,* ed. Ulrike Heuer (Oxford: Oxford University Press, 2022), 169.

Appendix

1. Ronald Dworkin, *Justice in Robes* (Cambridge, MA: Harvard University Press, 2008), chapter 8.

2. Dworkin, *Justice in Robes,* 223. The sociological concept (which we use "to describe a particular form of political organization") also has some relevance to this project. I'm employing it when I talk about law as a practice. I agree with Dworkin that this "concept is not sufficiently precise to yield philosophically interesting 'essential features,'" which is why I've resisted supplying any. Dworkin, *Justice in Robes,* 228.

3. Dworkin, *Justice in Robes,* 239.

4. Dworkin, *Justice in Robes,* 238.

5. Dworkin, *Justice in Robes,* 239.

6. For an overview of different ways the term is used, see Kenneth Himma, "Natural Law," *Internet Encyclopedia of Philosophy,* accessed March 22, 2023, https://iep.utm.edu/natlaw/.

7. See Himma, "Natural Law" ("[T]he classical naturalist seems committed to the claim that the law necessarily incorporates all moral principles.").

8. See, for example, John Finnis, "Natural Law Theories," *The Stanford Encyclopedia of Philosophy* (Summer 2020), ed. Edward N. Zalta, https://plato.stanford.edu/entries/natural-law-theories/.

9. Ronald Dworkin, *Taking Rights Seriously* (Cambridge, MA: Harvard University Press, 1978), 46–80 and 81–130, respectively.

10. Scott Hershovitz and Steven Schaus, "Dworkin in His Best Light," forthcoming in *Interpretivism and Its Critics,* ed. Nicos Stavropoulos (manuscript on file with author).

11. For the fullest statement of Greenberg's view, see Mark Greenberg, "The Moral Impact Theory of Law," *Yale Law Journal* 123 (2014): 1288–1342. Other papers that have substantially influenced my thinking include Mark Greenberg, "The Standard Picture and Its Discontents," in *Oxford Studies in Philosophy of Law,* ed. Leslie Green and Brian Leiter, vol. 1 (Oxford: Oxford University Press, 2011), 39–106; Mark Greenberg, "Legislation as Communication? Legal Interpretation and the Study of Linguistic Communication," in *Philosophical Foundations of Language in the Law,* ed. Andrei Marmor and Scott Soames (New York: Oxford University Press, 2011), 217–256; and Mark Greenberg, "How Facts Make Law," *Legal Theory* 10, no. 3 (2004): 157–198.

12. Greenberg, "The Moral Impact Theory," 1323.

13. See Scott Hershovitz, "The End of Jurisprudence," *Yale Law Journal* 124, no. 4 (2015): 1197–1202. For further worries, see Steven Schaus, "How to Think about Law as Morality: A Comment on Greenberg and Hershovitz," *Yale Law Journal Forum* 124 (2015): 224–245. For further elaboration of the idea, see Mark Greenberg, "The Moral Impact Theory, the Dependence View, and Natural Law," in *The Cambridge Companion to Natural Law Jurisprudence,* ed. George Duke and Robert P. George (Cambridge: Cambridge University Press 2017), 281–291.

14. Greenberg, "The Dependence View," 276.

15. See Chapter 1, n. 52.

16. Greenberg, "The Dependence View," 276.

17. Steve Schaus helped me appreciate this point.

18. Greenberg, "The Moral Impact Theory," 1323–1324.

19. Joseph Raz, "Authority, Law, and Morality," in *Ethics in the Public Domain* (Oxford: Oxford University Press, 1995), 215.

20. See Joseph Raz, "Incorporation by Law," *Legal Theory* 10, no. 1 (2004): 2–7.

21. Raz, "Incorporation by Law," 7 ("[W]here the law is normatively valid, it is so in virtue of a moral principle.").

22. Raz, "Incorporation by Law," 6.

23. Raz, "Incorporation by Law," 6.

24. Joseph Raz, "Normative Powers," in *The Roots of Normativity,* ed. Ulrike Heuer (Oxford: Oxford University Press, 2022), 163.

25. Raz, "Normative Powers," 175–177.

26. Raz, "Normative Powers," 165.

27. Raz, "Normative Powers," 176.

28. Raz, "Normative Powers," 176.

29. See Raz, "Incorporation by Law."

30. Scott Hershovitz, "The Authority of Law," in *The Routledge Companion to Legal Philosophy,* ed. Andrei Marmor (New York: Routledge, 2012), 65–75. Dworkin, *Justice in Robes,* chapters 7 and 8.

31. Berman, "Of Law and Other Artificial Normative Systems," in *Dimensions of Normativity,* ed. David Plunkett, Scott Shapiro, and Kevin Toh (New York: Oxford University Press, 2019), 138.

32. Berman, "Of Law," 138.

33. Raz, "Incorporation by Law," 6.

34. Berman, "Of Law," 138.

35. For further discussion of these issues, see Hershovitz, "The End of Jurisprudence," 1181–1186.

36. C. Thi Nguyen, *Games: Agency as Art* (New York: Oxford University Press, 2020), 174, 180.

37. Nguyen, *Games,* 174.

38. Nguyen, *Games,* 176.

39. Nguyen, *Games,* 177.

40. Berman, "Of Law," 154–157.

41. Berman, "Of Law," 155.

42. Berman, "Of Law," 156.

43. Berman, "Of Law," 156.

44. Berman, "Of Law," 156.

45. Berman, "Of Law," 156.

46. Otherwise, it wouldn't remain to discover.

47. Berman suggests that I think it's "superfluous" to talk about rules for playing chess (see Berman, "Of Law," 155). Far from it. I think it's central to the practice to talk about many different sets of rules—the rules printed, the rules enforced, the rules that are authoritative, and so on. What I once said was superfluous was imagining that a new sort of normativity comes into being when, say, FIDE publishes rules for playing chess (see Hershovitz, "The End of Jurisprudence," 1184). Berman actually agrees with that (see Berman, "Of Law," 155n51). He thinks that artificial normative systems merely have what he calls "ostensible normativity"—that they lack real normative force (Berman, "Of Law," 143). The difference is that he thinks that FIDE's rules are part of a normative system, which includes "nonmoral" FIDE obligations (Berman, "Of Law," 155). He can't explain how that system gets its content, except to say that the published rules "may not perfectly fix [it]" (Berman, "Of Law," 155). I think those ideas are also superfluous. We don't need to talk about artificial normative systems or nonmoral obligations in order to make sense of our gaming lives. We do, of course, need to talk about norms—which is why I talk about them, somewhat endlessly.

48. As Nguyen puts it, games "are not simply representations of alternate social arrangements. They actually change how we interact with each other" (Nguyen, *Games*, 172). It's the fact that games bring about changes in the way we interact that makes them, in Nguyen's words, "morally active" (Nguyen, *Games*, 176). Before we start playing a game, we can imagine what it might be like to act in accord with, say, the rules in the rule book. But those rules are inert on their own. It's only once we start playing that they have purchase (if they do). Sometimes, it's other norms that turn out to matter, in addition or instead.

49. Berman suggests that it's too hard to figure out what, morally, we ought to do on every occasion (Berman, "Of Law," 153). Artificial normative systems, he argues, help us economize our cognitive resources. I think that's misleading. We rarely retreat to first principles to solve moral problems—we economize our thought in all kinds of ways. We say things like "promises should be kept" or "lying is wrong." Those phrases conceal an awful lot of complexity, but they are true enough in most cases, so we pass them on to our kids—and rely on them ourselves. Elsewhere, I've explored some of the ways we economize, suggesting that "we often have reasons to be morally obtuse about our moral obligations" (Hershovitz, "The End of Jurisprudence," 1191–1192). But when we have conflicts about what we ought to do, we have to slow down and make our arguments explicit. That's what we do in court. And when games don't go as we expect, we do just the same.

50. See, e.g., Scott J. Shapiro, *Legality* (Cambridge, MA: Harvard University Press, 2011).

51. In jurisprudence, Jules Coleman is the leading proponent of the Baskin-Robbins view. See Jules Coleman, *The Practice of Principle* (Oxford: Oxford University Press, 2001), 143–144: "[L]aw . . . is in principle the sort of thing that is capable of possessing a normative power to confer rights and privileges and to impose genuine duties and responsibilities. It doesn't follow that the duties and rights thereby created are necessarily moral rights." Coleman further explains that legal duties count as "genuine" because they "figure in our

determination of what we ought to do generally and not just in our deliberations about what we ought to do in playing the game 'law.'" In saying that, Coleman implies that games don't create genuine rights and duties, but I suspect others would extend the Baskin-Robbins view to them as well. For what it's worth, I don't read Berman as a proponent of the Baskin-Robbins view, since he says that artificial normative systems are ostensibly normative, not genuinely so (Berman, "Of Law," 143).

52. I said more about them in Hershovitz, "The End of Jurisprudence."

53. Daniel Wodak argues that *obligation* has a generic meaning, rather than a distinctly moral meaning. See Wodak, "What Does 'Legal Obligation' Mean?," *Pacific Philosophical Quarterly* 99, no. 4 (2018): 790–816. The claim can be read in a way that supports the Baskin-Robbins view, but I see it as consistent with the picture I've presented. I've argued that the domain of practical normativity is unified—that rights and obligations are the same sort of relationship wherever we find them. And though I've employed *moral* in a capacious sense, I've allowed that we often use the word more narrowly. When we do, moral obligations will be a subset of our genuine obligations, and possibly distinct (depending on how we draw the boundaries) from our legal obligations (which would also be a subset of our genuine obligations). The fact that *moral* is often used more narrowly may account for the linguistic intuitions that drive Wodak's argument. That said, I'm not sure how much weight we should place on linguistic intuitions anyway, since they may reflect confusions about the underlying subject matter or embed shortcuts that allow us to communicate efficiently. All this is a bit beside the point, however, since my claim isn't about (or dependent on) the way we use words. It's a claim about the nature of practical normativity and law's place within it.

54. Hart once rejected as "extravagant" the possibility that there are "two independent 'worlds' or sets of objective reasons, one legal and the other moral." H. L. A. Hart, *Essays on Bentham: Jurisprudence and Political Theory* (Oxford: Oxford University Press 1982), 267.

55. Hershovitz, "The End of Jurisprudence," 1193.

56. See Hillary Nye, "Does Law 'Exist'? Eliminativism in Legal Philosophy," *Washington University Jurisprudence Review* 15, no. 1 (2022): 29–78; Liam Murphy, *What Makes Law: An Introduction to the Philosophy of Law* (New York: Cambridge University Press, 2014), 88–102, 182–187; Liam Murphy, "Better to See Law This Way," *NYU Law Review* 83 (2007): 1088–1108, 1104–1108; Lewis A. Kornhauser, "Doing without the Concept of Law" (New York University School of Law, Public Law Research Paper No. 15-33, August 3, 2015), https://papers.ssrn.com/sol3/papers.cfm?abstract_id=2640605.

57. See Murphy, *What Makes Law,* 89–99.

58. I take this to be Nye's view as well. See Nye, "Does Law 'Exist'?," 61–62.

Acknowledgments

A series of great teachers shaped my life. This book is for five of them: Billy Jones, who made high school fun; Clark Wolf, who introduced me to philosophy; Joseph Raz, who set high standards; John Gardner, the best friend and mentor one could want; and Jules Coleman, who believed in me enough to help me get a job. This book wouldn't exist without them, and in an important sense, neither would I.

When I arrived at Michigan, Scott Shapiro was writing *Legality*. The ideas in this book were born in conversations about that book. I've lost count of the ways Scott has helped, with this book and with life in general.

Nicos Stavropoulos taught me that it's possible to do philosophy by text message. He's endlessly encouraging and right most of the time.

Chris Essert handwrote comments on the manuscript—and took my calls to discuss them. He pushed in all the right places.

The substantive debt I owe Mark Greenberg and Seana Shiffrin is clear from the book. Less obvious is the fact that two visits to UCLA played an important role in the book's development. Seana and Mark are wonderful friends and mentors.

I've got an all-star set of colleagues at Michigan. The best thing about my job is that I get to hear their ideas and bother them with mine. Special thanks to Liz Anderson, Nico Cornell, Daniel Fryer, Don Herzog, Gabe Mendlow, Sarah Moss, Richard Primus, Don Regan, Steve Schaus, Will Thomas, and Ekow Yankah.

Charles Barzun, Jules Coleman, Chris Essert, Don Herzog, David Plunkett, Scott Shapiro, Steve Schaus, and Nicos Stavropoulos read the entire manuscript (or large chunks of it) and helped me improve it immensely. I appreciate the heavy lift.

A larger set of people read parts of the manuscript and sent me comments— or taught me things along the way: Nick Bagley, Mitch Berman, Chris Blythe, Sarah Buss, Ruth Chang, Samuele Chilovi, Nico Cornell, Conor Crummey, Hasan Dindjer, Timothy Endicott, David Enoch, Daniel Fryer, Kate Greasley, Mark Greenberg, Amanda Greene, Alon Harel, Jeff Helmreich, Aaron James, Nevin Johnson, Tom Kadri, Larissa Katz, Greg Keating, Leslie Kendrick, Dmitrios Kyritsis, Massimo La Torre, George Letsas, Michelle Mealer, Gabe Mendlow, Ezequiel Monti, Sophia Moreau, Len Niehoff, Hillary Nye, Jessica Paduganan, George Pavlakos, John Pottow, Richard Primus, Veronica Rodriguez-Blanco, Blake Rutherford, Angelo Ryu, Fred Schauer, Seana Shiffrin, Will Thomas, Ernie Weinrib, Fred Wilmot-Smith, and several people I'm surely forgetting.

I'm grateful to audiences at the ALPC, Catanzaro, Glasgow, Hebrew University, ITAM, Michigan, Oxford, Queen's, Toronto, UC Irvine, UCL, UGA, USC, and UTDT for sterling conversations about bits of the book and its antecedents. I also appreciate all the students who have helped me work out these ideas over the years and especially those who read chapters in draft form.

Josh Petersen provided excellent research assistance. The book is better for his help. And it was finished months before I could have managed on my own.

I've worked with three editors at Harvard University Press, all of whom have been terrific: James Brandt, Ian Malcolm, and Sam Stark. James gave me detailed comments even after he left HUP, which improved the manuscript a lot. I also appreciate three anonymous reviewers who provided detailed comments.

My agent, Alison MacKeen, is always a source of sound advice and generous support.

But my largest source of support is my family. I've been writing this book for most of Hank's life, and I've got no idea what it would look like absent his inspiration and ingenuity in argument. His older brother, Rex, pulls me away from the computer, provides comic relief, and teaches me a ton. The boys make me smile. And so does Julie, who's been my best friend for thirty years. I couldn't begin to tote up her contributions to this book or my life, but I'm grateful for that more than anything else.

Index